Anne-Marie Ambert, PhD

The Effect of Children on Parents
Second Edition

The Effect of Children on Parents

Second Edition

HAWORTH Marriage and the Family
Terry S. Trepper, PhD
Executive Editor

The Effect of Children on Parents

Second Edition

Anne-Marie Ambert, PhD

The Haworth Press
New York • London • Oxford

Published by

The Haworth Press, Inc., 10 Alice Street, Binghamton, NY 13904-1580.

Cover design by Jennifer M. Gaska.

Library of Congress Cataloging-in-Publication Data

Ambert, Anne-Marie.
    The effect of children on parents / Anne-Marie Ambert.—2nd ed.
       p. cm.
    Includes bibliographical references and index.
    ISBN 0-7890-0854-8 (hard : alk. paper) — ISBN 0-7890-0855-6 (soft : alk. paper)
    1. Parenthood—Psychological aspects. 2. Parent and child. I. Title.

HQ755.8 .A47 2000
306.874—dc21

                                                         00-033536

CONTENTS

ABOUT THE AUTHOR

Anne-Marie Ambert, PhD (Cornell University), is Professor in the Department of Sociology at York University, Toronto, where she has taught for well over three decades. In addition, she is currently a member of the graduate program in Psychology and is also an Associate Fellow at the LaMarsh Centre for Research on Violence and Conflict Resolution. Prior to joining the faculty at York University, she taught at three different American universities.

The author of eight other books and the editor of two volumes, Dr. Ambert has published widely in the areas of the family, child development, and youth in the *Journal of Marriage and the Family, Criminologie,* the *American Journal of Psychiatry,* the *Canadian Review of Sociology and Anthropology,* and *Social Science and Medicine,* among many other journals. She has also just published a textbook, *Families in the New Millennium* (Allyn and Bacon) and is the author of *The Web of Poverty: Psychosocial Perspectives* (1998, The Haworth Press). Dr. Ambert is a member of various sociological, psychological, and child development associations.

Preface

Nine years have elapsed since the first edition of *The Effect of Children on Parents* was published. A great deal of research has since accumulated in various disciplines, particularly sociology and psychology, on topics related to the parent-child relationship. In addition, the books and articles I have since written have allowed me to become acquainted with a broader range of perspectives that can shed some light on the effect of children on parents.

As a result of these developments in the literature and in my research, this second edition actually constitutes a new book. Eight of the thirteen chapters are entirely new, that is, Chapter 1 and Chapters 7 through 13. Chapters 5 and 6 are entirely rewritten and substantially altered while Chapters 2, 3, and 4 have been updated and considerably revised. Consequently, this edition entirely replaces the first one.

The second edition contains new topics on the effect of children on parents. For example, the new chapters discuss the effects of children's peers on parents, professionals' role in the parent-child relationship, the effect of adult children on parents, as well as some aspects of the life conditions of immigrant and adoptive parents. Chapter 12 reminds us to consider the interaction between heredity and environment and discusses some of the results and interpretations of behavior genetics within a sociological perspective.

The framework amalgamates interactional, social constructionist, and social structural theories as well as behavior genetics theories. The effect of children on parents is thus studied within the global social contexts in which families are situated, parental roles defined, and children socially constructed.

I sincerely hope that this second edition will be more useful to instructors, researchers, and especially parents and professionals, such as teachers and clinicians, who provide services to children. I wish to thank Bill Palmer, Vice President, The Haworth Press, as well as those who have contributed to making this edition a better one: Patricia Brown, Yvonne Kester, Dawn Krisko, Peg Marr, Andrew Roy, and Donna Biesecker.

I dedicate this book to all parents and their children. I particularly wish to acknowledge my daughter Stephanie, not only because she did all of the word processing and indexing, but also because of our close bond.

Chapter 1

Child Effect: What *Is* This?
An Introduction

"Child effect *on parents?*" I was once asked by an incredulous clinician. "Surely, you mean how parents treat their children?"

This misunderstanding is by no means unusual, even though researchers and professionals are becoming more aware of the interactional nature of the parent-child relationship. A slow awakening occurs, consequently, to the fact that causality can also flow from children to parents. Nevertheless, as we will see, there is still a widespread tendency to assume that the direction of effect is from parents to children only. This perspective is based on social constructions of parenting and children that are widely accepted in our society. Therefore, the way parents and children are perceived and the erroneous conclusions that may flow from this situation are important topics of this book.

I have chosen to introduce our subject matter with a series of quotes from everyday parents and adult children to illustrate the range of child effect on parents' lives. These comments are abstracted from my research, including my interviews with divorced and remarried couples, my recent fieldwork on the effect of delinquency and adolescent "difficultness" on parents, as well as my research based on over 1,400 student autobiographies. The first is a quote from a male student responding to a specific autobiographical question asking what effect, if any, he had had on his parents while growing up.

What effect I had on my parents' lives? I never thought about this until now. I can see how they affected me and I think I've covered this in the other question. . . . I was always a model child, especially as boys go and I honestly think that when my parents compared me to other children they were always relieved that I was turning out so well, was doing so well in school. I am certain that I messed up their plans once in a while but on the whole they were thrilled with me. I had a positive effect on them. *(Male student, about twenty-one years old)*

What has been the happiest moment since I've turned twenty-five is bound to be the birth of my son. I cannot describe how much joy and how much life he has added to our lives. An added bonus was that he is the first male grandchild my parents have and this has contributed a lot to my parents' respect for me, something that had been lacking in my life up to this point. *(Married male student, about twenty-six years old)*

I'm sorry if I am late in turning in this paper but my daughter had the chicken pox, ran a high fever, and I found it impossible to concentrate on my schoolwork. *(Married female student, in a letter attached to her assignment)*

If I had to do it over again, I wouldn't have children. I guess mine are fine, well sort of. But being a parent is a downgraded occupation in our society, plus the fact that you get no breaks from the system: everything conspires against your attempts to raise children decently. I sincerely feel that this society is against its parents. And then we get blamed. *(Employed, remarried mother of two, age thirty-four, during an interview)*

I hope our sons stay with us as long as they can. I really enjoy their company. They are interesting, they do well, and they have nice friends. What more can parents ask for? *(Married female student, about forty-five to fifty years old)*

For their part, the following two students refer to their birth order and anticipate what are called "child characteristics" in Chapter 2:

At the age of zero to five I feel that I had a great impact on my parents' lives in that I was their first born and they seemed to feel that they had so much to look forward to . . .

I was the first child in the family and I can remember taking care of my sisters quite a bit. I am sure that I influenced my parents positively . . .

Overall, students could talk about the effect they had had on their parents when prompted by a specific question. But otherwise this did not seem to be a topic that came up spontaneously when describing their lives and their relationship with their parents in general. In fact, for quite a few, this question came as a surprise, as illustrated by the first quote on page 1. Many students also pointed out that they would not have been able to answer such a question just a couple of years earlier, during adolescence. One woman wrote:

Such a question would have made me downright hostile at age 14 or even 17. There is no way I ever thought of my affecting my parents then because my whole thinking was oriented to what they were doing to *me*, how *they* affected *me*. . . . When you're in a period of your life that you don't see eye to eye with your parents, you think they're wrong and you're right, you think they just want to be mean to you. . . . Even now, I had to do a lot of thinking and I made an effort to get out of my little universe. . . . I think that when I am older and have children, I will reread this autobiography and I will probably think how awful I was to my parents.

Most of the students who thought they had had a negative impact on their parents pointed to adolescence as the most highly detrimental stage of theirs and their parents' lives in this respect (Ambert, 1992: 134). In fact, only 8 percent felt that the effect they had produced at that age had been entirely positive, despite the fact that fully a third of all students described always having had a great relationship with their parents. Without being prompted, students confirmed what researchers have found: adolescence *is* a difficult period for *parents,* a topic to which we return, particularly in Chapters 5, 6, and 7.

The above quotes are from average situations and express mainly a positive child effect on parents with a normal mixture of mild negative effect. With the next quotes, a few problems emerge in the families but they still fall within the range of normalcy. We begin with a student who, in the course of describing all the sacrifices her parents had made to lift their family out of poverty, concludes:

> I really do not think that they regret the sacrifices they have made because they are very proud of my academic accomplishments as I am the first one of my entire family to have completed high school and am on my way to becoming a university graduate this year.

> From fifteen to eighteen, I think I had again regained their positive feelings towards me as I was no longer rebellious and I [had] matured. I entered university which made them proud because neither of them had been to post-secondary school. I was overall becoming successful.

> Since my mother was divorced at the age of twenty-six, and left to raise three children on her own, I feel I have had a great impact on her life at all stages. . . . I am sure that my mother's opportunity to remarry would have been far greater if she had no children . . . between eleven and fourteen. . . . she would often ask for my opinion concerning someone she was dating . . .

The above student quote is particularly interesting because it highlights an important aspect of child and parent effects that are paramount to the orientation of this book: both effects are interactive phenomena. In other words, not only are the children affected by the mother but, as they age, they play a very definite role in her life. In this case, the daughter becomes a confidante and, as such, helps her mother emotionally; in turn, her own development is affected by these early maturity requirements. Thus, there is an interaction of effect that takes place between parents and children.

Below, we turn to parents who have experienced a great deal of negative child effect and students who are conscious of having been quite detrimental to their parents' lives at some point:

They had to change their views about boys and me going out. It was a long and emotional battle. My father didn't sleep, he always yelled at my mother (because she was always on my side), and my mother was depressed a lot. *(Female student, about her adolescence between the ages of fifteen to eighteen)*

This was a period of experimentation for me, e.g., heavy metal music, different clothing, staying out late and drinking. Being that I was the first child, this must have been new and difficult for them. I was struggling against good behavior, and they would have to learn to handle it.

What was sociologically interesting about this last student is that she was very casual in her autobiography concerning the pains she had inflicted upon her parents. As she reiterated later in her narrative in support of her last sentence, it was part and parcel of her *parents' job* to adjust to the trials and tribulations of her adolescent experimentation. This perception was not an isolated instance: while most students indirectly perceived that they had had a negative impact on their parents at some point during adolescence, a quarter of these felt that this was "normal" and something that their parents *had* to go through—as if they themselves had had little say in the matter. Thus, we continue to see how people, in this case students, define or socially construct what adolescence is and what being the parents of an adolescent entails. In other words, this is a "job description" with many duties. In the next quotes, we progress to more drastic child effect:

Eleven to fourteen [years]. As far as my mother is concerned, I feel I really affected her life in a negative way. I was very rude and rebellious toward her. I made no effort to understand her point of view. I simply blamed her for everything. I know my behavior made it more difficult for her to develop a secure marriage with her new husband. For I did not give him a chance either. I would not let him get to know me, nor I him. I realize that I made their first years together very difficult. *(Woman student)*

I try to reason with myself and think positively. I have one very nice daughter [aged eighteen]. I mean she is easy, happy, she's affectionate and she has never caused us any problems. But while I should think positively I can't erase the fact that her sister is a nightmare. [The girl, aged 15, is regularly absent from school, repeats grades, drinks, uses drugs, has shouting matches with her parents, and is generally out of control.] The first thing I think when I wake up in the morning is where is she and the last thing I think before falling asleep is the same or oh, God, why did this have to happen to us? She fills my entire life and it has reached the point where my husband doesn't even want to talk about her. *(Upper-middle class mother during an interview)*

I am sure that he's [delinquent son] going to outgrow this stage, at least that's what everybody says, but when all is said and done, I have nevertheless wasted years of my life uselessly trying to teach him right from wrong, uselessly worrying about him, putting up with his moods, his threats to leave and whatever, oh yes, the teachers' complaints. For what? Just because he is surrounded by friends who are just like him. At first, I blamed these children; now I see that he likes to be with them. It's all so useless and you can't imagine how lonely it is to have a life like this even though I have a nice husband. We can't even get to enjoy each other. *(Mother during an interview about her sixteen-year-old son)*

This mother's son has been difficult for five years already and she has no guarantee that it will be over any time soon. The last two mothers' reflections begin to illustrate what we will discuss in Chapter 4: many areas of parents' lives are affected by their children, whether positively or negatively. Later in the interview, this mother added that she wondered if she would ever "feel right" and "well-disposed toward my son later on in life even after he has straightened out." She felt that, by then, he would have ruined so many years of her and her husband's life that "something might die in me" and that "I may never feel he has a right to be forgiven." This mother introduces an intriguing research question related to the *life course* of parents who have very problematic children: what happens to them in their later years? Unfortunately, this is a topic that has not yet received much attention by scholars.

As did many other mothers and even a few fathers, the mother quoted above cried several times during the interview. Nevertheless, these parents were grateful for having been given the opportunity to express themselves without feeling that they were blamed or judged negatively. Apparently, this was the first such professional encounter among many negative ones in their lives. The following mother, like the previous one, also unknowingly adopts a life-course perspective during her interview. She sees no end to negative child effect:

> [I] can't stand it anymore. When I retire, I am going to move as far away from here as I can. I am tired of being exploited and if I stay here I'll always have their problems in my face. They can go on welfare if that's what they want [this is a middle-class mother] but I don't want any part of this. I have just wasted ten years of my life. *(Single mother of three difficult but not delinquent girls ages eighteen to twenty-six)*

THE SOCIAL CONSTRUCTION OF PARENTS

I have noticed that, in the late 1990s, many such parents have begun using the word "waste"—the waste in their children's lives as well as in theirs. This term was rarely encountered among similar parents in the 1980s. I think that some parents are becoming conscious of the fact that there are alternatives in child development to difficultness and delinquency. Some are especially becoming aware that, if the social situation was different, if children were not surrounded by so many negative influences, if parents received more support, this "waste" would not occur. If, if, if. In Chapter 3, we refer to this situation as part of the characteristics of the societal response.

As I was writing the first edition of this book in 1990, I often had to explain *what* child effect was when people inquired about my topic. Nine years later, with the exceptions just noted, there has not been a huge evolution in the social constructs that people hold about children and parents. Overall, the lay but educated public continues to see parents as the prime, and often only, influence on children. Even if they perceive that peers can be very important, it is still believed that, if adolescents suffer from the effect of the detrimental influence of their peer group, it is parents' fault: parents should supervise their children better. Although one can certainly agree that parental supervision is a key element in an adolescent's life, not all adolescents accept supervision, especially as they get older. Furthermore, when it is suggested that the media might bear a heavy responsibility, it is still pointed out that parents should monitor what their children watch. Unfortunately, parents have no say as to what comes into their home via the television and the Internet. Yet they are held responsible, no matter what.

At another level, it is also revealing to observe the reactions of students who have taken my honors seminar on the parent-child relationship. These students, mainly women, are sociology, psychology, and education majors in their senior year. They already have acquired quite a substantial background in the fields related to this topic. Yet, for most, it is obviously a difficult enterprise to think in terms of *child effect*. Unavoidably, discussions turn to parental causality and responsibility in child development. Even exam questions focusing specifically on child effect are turned around and answered along the lines of parental causality. Although still young, students have already been programmed to think in terms of what parents do *to* children; it is difficult for them to adapt to this new perspective because they are surrounded by opposite viewpoints or social constructions, many of which are in their textbooks on child development and family studies.

So basically, both for the general public and the specialized student population, the topic of child effect is one that does not belong to the daily ways of speaking and thinking. How children affect their parents, what kinds of children most affect their parents, and what characteristics make parents especially vulnerable to child effect are questions that are not commonly raised, even among professionals. Especially absent is the notion that society's response or support plays an important role in determining how children will affect their parents and whether they will do so negatively or positively. Finally, the circularity of feedback between parent-child and child-parent effects is an even less widely known or accepted phenomenon, although it is a tenet of interactional theories. The topics just enumerated are developed in the next chapters.

The 1992 edition of *The Effect of Children on Parents* has brought two different reactions. First, the most common: countless parents have been in touch, particularly after radio or television programs where I discuss these topics, often just to thank me for having written the book—and then to tell me their problems. As one put it, it is an "incredible experience of self-validation" to read a book that recognizes their experience and is written by a university professor. At a much more minor level in terms of numbers, a few professionals, mainly psychologists, lawyers, and social workers who specialize in children's rights are angered by the title of this book (not about its contents because they do not go so far as reading it!). As other sociologists have pointed out, these professionals make a good income as child advocates, and this book may seem to present a threat by challenging the assumption that children are merely passive receptacles, instead of participants in the parent-child relationship.

This is an understandable, however misguided, reaction: there is no incompatibility between children's rights and the recognition that children affect their parents. There is no incompatibility between our duty to protect children against abusive parents, who are a minority, and our duty to recognize that parents in general are affected by their children and by society's often negative attitude toward them. Furthermore, one also has to start thinking in terms of children's and adolescents' *duties,* not just rights, otherwise youths are squarely relieved of the responsibility for the consequences of their actions. Actually, it is one of my theses that if parents were given *moral* authority over their children, the latter would be less likely to be abused, neglected, and, particularly, less likely to become delinquent.

At the scholarly level, textbooks on child development and the family just recently have begun mentioning, however briefly, child effect or "reverse" causality. Texts on juvenile delinquency generally do not even raise the topic. Yet, at the theoretical level, the topics of child effect, of the interaction between parents and children, and even children as producers of their own development have long ago been recognized, as we see in Chapter 2. Empirical research has failed on the whole—with some exceptions—to follow through with these more recent advances in thinking about parents and children. It is thus not surprising that textbooks generally lag behind theoretical advances in the sociology of the family and in child development. The result is that students as well as many professionals are being educated within an outdated perspective that no longer fits the current social situation.

Basically, whereas the topics of reciprocity of effect and child effect were introduced three decades ago, the general research literature merely pays lip service to them. The paradox is that child effect has yet to be integrated into mainstream research although many theoretically oriented scholars believe it to be a well-accepted notion. This book thus offers a review of what is already "known" but generally ignored in the area of child effect. Above all, it offers additional perspectives in this field. It is also meant to suggest avenues for research, present new ideas, and restate recently advanced ideas that have been accepted only at a very superficial level. The study of child effect as presented herein is designed to complement, not negate, the more traditional perspective of parental causality and responsibility.

ORGANIZATION OF THE BOOK

I shall say just a few words about the organization of this volume. Chapters 2, 3, and 4 pursue some of the discussions herein initiated; they situate child effect historically, theoretically, and in terms of research. They present an overall framework for the topic in general. These chapters are an updated version of the 1992 edition. The subsequent two chapters, on children with difficult behaviors and emotional problems (Chapter 5) and on adolescents who are delinquent (Chapter 6) are new. These topics were included in the 1992 edition but at the theoretical level only: I had not yet conducted actual fieldwork in these domains. These two chapters are now entirely rewritten, contain recent information, and include new research perspectives coming to us from the field of behavior genetics.

All subsequent chapters are entirely original to this edition. Chapter 7, on the effect of children's peers on parents, is a very unusual one, needless to say, because the literature on children's peers tends to focus on two points: (1) how children function with their peers and how they are influenced by them; and (2) what is wrong with parents of children who have bad peers or are rejected by their peers. Obviously, this book's theoretical leanings consider the second question out of line; the rationale for this becomes evident as we progress through the book. Rather, we ask: given that children have "good" or "bad" peers, how does this impact their lives and consequently their parents' lives?

Then, in Chapter 8, the role that professionals play in enhancing positive and exacerbating negative child effect on parents is examined. Questions are raised that are generally not considered—in great part because professionals themselves, not parents, are the ones who decide the types of research questions that are asked. The following three chapters examine three categories of parents. Chapter 9 inquires into adult-child effect toward parents, including elderly parents. This topic is very much "in," but, as the reader will see, it is often examined from the perspective of caring for elderly parents as a burden to adult children. One of the questions we ask within the social construction perspective is this: Why is it a *burden* for adult children to care for their elderly parents when the care that parents give to their young children is never qualified as a "burden"? As the reader can see, a researcher who develops a different perspective can ask different questions.

Chapter 10 focuses on immigrant and minority parents, while Chapter 11 discusses adoptive parents. These groups experience very specific situations in North America; we want to see how they are affected by their children, particularly as a result of the way society socially defines them and treats them. Finally, Chapter 12 is graphically titled, "Let's Not Forget About Genes!" This chapter presents a perspective that is only beginning to be acknowledged in the sociology of the family: the role that the interaction of genes and environment (nature *with* nurture) plays in the development of children's personalities and life outcomes as well as in the parent-child relationship. The research originating from the discipline of behavior genetics and the interactional perspective helps us understand the limitations that are placed on parents' efforts at raising their children. The topic of the roadblocks—cultural as well as genetic—that parents encounter in raising their children and consequently produce so much negative child effect is further pursued in the conclusions forming Chapter 13.

Basically, for want of a better term, this book falls within the vein of critical sociology or even the sociology of sociology. It presents a critique of the traditional literature on parent-child relationships and suggests alternative lines of inquiry. Social constructionism is an equally salient theoretical orientation in this discussion. Social constructionism is a perspective arguing that various phenomena which are taken for granted and seem to be natural are actually culturally defined or socially constructed—as is the case for parenting, adolescence, and child/parent roles. Finally, as has begun to transpire in previous pages, the chapters contain a great deal of material on gender roles, particularly regarding the fact that child effect is more salient in mothers' than fathers' lives.

This is an unusual book—but it should not be. The new research clearly indicates that children have an incredible impact on their parents' lives, generally unwittingly so, but often consciously so. Parents would do a far better job at raising them were this fact accepted, adequately researched, and supported socially. Therefore, *both* parents and children would benefit from the recognition that children, even small ones, affect their parents.

Chapter 2

The Neglected Perspective: Children's Effect on Parents

This book focuses on the effect of children on parents within a multiple-causality perspective—an interactive and transactional theoretical framework (Magnusson, 1995). This framework posits that individuals cocreate their own development and environment while being simultaneously affected by the environment and the interactions in which they participate. Parents and children contribute to the creation of their relationship within the context of their individual personalities and their environment. Thus, children do have an impact on their parents, which is a way of thinking that has been neglected in the vast sociology and psychology literature on parents and children. As far as children and parents are concerned, analyses have been informed by the concepts of socialization, childrearing, and child development, all of which implicate parental causality in parent-child interaction and child outcomes. This perspective has too frequently resulted in a narrow interpretation of family dynamics emphasizing the effect that parents have on their offspring without regard for other, more potent influences on children. Interactive effects between parents and children are usually omitted along with the question of child effect on parents.

FAILURES OF TRADITIONAL PERSPECTIVES

Within the traditional perspective, research questions are generally framed to measure the impact that parents presumably have on the well-being of their children and the development of their abilities and personalities. More specifically, researchers have focused on the background and characteristics of problematic children's parents: What is *wrong* with such children's *parents* that has contributed or even caused these children's problems? A related type of research compares parents of well-adjusted children to parents of children with problems in order to see what parental aberrations, lack of skills, and/or deficits in childrearing practices produce problematic children. This approach totally ignores the larger environment in which children evolve and which could have contributed to their problems. Furthermore, children's genetic constitution is equally overlooked, although this neglect is finally being addressed, as we soon see.

What are the results of the traditional studies? Interestingly enough, most indicate that parenting explains only a *modest* part of children's outcomes—depending on which outcomes are studied. For instance, parents are fairly important in the development of certain behaviors in their offspring, such as school success, alcohol use, and premature sexuality. In contrast, parents are only minutely relevant to the formation of personality traits in general, whether it is agreeableness, extroversion, impulsivity, shyness, or persistence. Socioeconomic variables such as poverty, neighborhood characteristics, types of peers, single-parent families, young maternal age, and low parental education *combined* are far more potent explanatory variables than parenting itself for a wide range of child outcomes. These include outcomes for which parents are still considered "fairly" important: low school achievement, behavior problems, delinquency, premature sexuality, and procreation. In other words, larger sociodemographic variables are more deterministic than parenting behaviors: they present a more forceful combination of influences than parents and they can undermine parents' ability to guide, monitor, and support their children. Were children's genetic inheritance added to the environmental context, the explanatory power of studies pertaining to child outcomes would be even stronger.

All in all, the traditional, unidirectional research focusing on parents represents a *scientific bias:* it misrepresents reality. It particularly negates environmental, genetic, and reciprocal effects between parents and children. The sum of these studies generates the erroneous belief that parents are unavoidably *the* main and, often, *the only* influence on their children's development. Finally, these studies obliterate from our consciousness the matter of the effect that children have on their parents—the focus of this book.

As discussed later on, the blame for the simplistic view of parents and children rests in part on the double concept of socialization and child development which respectively dominate Western sociology and psychology of the family. As construed, these concepts deprive children of their agency (Thorne, 1987). Within the context of this traditional literature, the child is merely a *recipient*, a *future product*, and parents do not receive *from* the child. The psychologization of children as human "becomings" rather than human "actuals" is preventing us from focusing on the fact that children have important sociological attributes and perform key social functions (Corsaro, 1997).

Even in 1980, a review of the 1970s literature on parent-child relationships pointed to a redirection of the thinking in this area to include mutual parent-child effect as well as child effect (Walters and Walters, 1980). The contents of the review, however, clearly indicated that most research still proceeded within a traditional perspective, despite early warnings concerning the influence of children on parents, and despite indications that children were at the very least participants in their own development, and even coproducers in this enterprise (Scarr and McCartney, 1983).

The increased role of children as consumers in technological societies presents a particular dilemma in terms of traditional socialization theory. Children now constitute a substantial market for consumer goods (toys, electronic equipment, fashion) and culture goods (music, books, movies, videos, and concerts). As consumers, children *make decisions* for themselves and, very often, against the desire or preferences of their parents. Not only do parents often pay for their children's choices, but many older children *earn* the money to purchase these items by working part-time.

This double agency of Western children clearly places the role of parents as agents of socialization in an interesting theoretical and practical limbo. Children have already been socialized by the media and by their peers. Children socialize children. Children are members of a culture of their own. Neither parents nor teachers, for better or worse, play a prominent role in this phenomenon. Actually, children have always socialized other children, especially in the context of large families and in agrarian or village societies. But the newness of the phenomenon here resides in that child influence on other children is now one of consumerism rather than familism—thus outside of parental control. The peer culture is no longer part of the familial culture: the peer culture has been defamilialized.

The critique of the traditional (past and current) research and theorizing on the family herein presented in abbreviated form may lead us to wonder whether some adults, as social constructors of theories, may have a vested interest, albeit unconscious, in avoiding the reality and the issue of child effect. Is it not possible that, as feminist Firestone once asked, we are "living out some private dream" on behalf of children when we discuss them so sentimentally (1970:94)? The parallel between the powerless position women have been depicted as holding in past theory in general and the current powerlessness and actorlessness position of children is quite evident.

As mentioned in Chapter 1, many researchers pay lip service to child effect (*"of course* it exists!") and then proceed to ignore it completely in their own research. They are unable or unwilling to include child effect in their research models and instead merely mention it, generally briefly, in their conclusions. Others say, "Well, it's not a new idea, really." But, if it is not, why is it not integrated into mainstream research in fields as diverse as child development, family sociology, and juvenile delinquency? The main answer lies in an antiquated social construction of childhood, around which an entire industry has been built, including a research industry. One of the methods of most of the child-saving industry is to rein in on *parents*. Were children to be recognized as effective social actors (and even planners), this would make this industry less lucrative. It could certainly, if not ruin, at least recycle certain careers! As the British sociologist David Oldman (1994:45) points out, "the growth of child protection work must be explained by changes in the adult labor market," rather than in "any recent change in the condition of childhood itself." Protecting children from parents is a necessary but also lucrative market. However, in light of recent school massacres and the obvious violence and exploitation of the media, investments in child protection should be extended beyond the family, to include peer groups and the media.

As we see later in this chapter, there fortunately exists a healthy trend, at least in some theoretical and empirical quarters, toward counteracting the biased perspectives. But, as we have just learned in the Introduction, the literature has generally failed to follow suit in any substantial manner, particularly pertaining to reciprocity of effect. It is thus important to keep in mind the gap that exists between these enlightened developments and research publications at large. It is consequently relevant that we examine the perspective that still predominates in the area of parent and child interaction in general, as well as in some of its subareas, especially child development.

CHILDHOOD IS ONLY ONE OF THE STAGES IN THE LIFE COURSE

The unidirectional perspective of parental effect on children flows in part from a well-established and popular tradition particularly evident in clinical research. This tradition describes the first five years of life as the decisive years in the molding of personality and, consequently, in determining the life course. This theoretical perspective, or even category of theoretical perspectives, especially of Freudian, psychoanalytical origins, posits that children's first experiences mark them for life. Their personality is set in those few early years and their adult personality will not escape from this original mold. The child will repeat as an adult the initial parent-child interactions and will pursue the character traits imprinted upon him or her by the familial situation of these early years.

This line of inquiry is now generally recognized as far too simplistic. First, it treats the parent-child unit as if it were totally isolated from the rest of the world. Second, the traditional line of inquiry ignores the genetic influences that begin to manifest themselves at birth. Third, this line of inquiry negates the potential for human growth after age five. In fact, longitudinal studies from infancy into adolescence and even adulthood suggest that personality changes to some extent over the years, particularly until early adulthood (Caspi, 2000; Shiner, 2000). Even later in life, people mature and, for instance, many become more conscientious and agreeable as well as receive lower scores on neuroticism, extroversion (or introversion), and openness—which are considered the "big five" personality factors (McCrae et al., 1999). There are also indications that certain personality traits, such as shyness and aggressiveness, may be more enduring in a proportion of children, while other traits may be much less stable from year to year. Moreover, people's attitudes, values, and coping styles evolve as they mature and encounter situations that require new approaches to life. Adults can unlearn detrimental as well as positive patterns of human interaction learned through their parents as preschoolers and through their peers as older children and adolescents.

In other words, childhood is only one of the stages in a person's life; it is not the irreversible mold that earlier causality models have led us to believe. Development is a life-long process (Lerner, 1988). The life course perspective ideally attempts to integrate all stages of a person's life and is becoming more prominent in the literature, including the typical "child development" literature (Arnett, 2000).

This does not negate the fact that early experiences are important in a child's life, particularly in terms of cognitive development. But our perspective suggests that they are so only within the context of that same child's personality, resilience, and vulnerabilities, as well as other opportunities that his or her environment provides. Even traumatic early experiences do not produce an identical result in all children, nor do they necessarily produce a long-lasting effect (Steinberg and Avenevoli, 2000). For example, a majority of children who are abused, whether psychologically, physically, or sexually, never abuse their own offspring. There is agreement with Widom (1990), who has estimated the rate of transmission of family violence to be about 30 percent or lower. Parents who use abusive punishment methods with their children may be more likely to pass on a tendency for violence if they exhibit other antisocial characteristics, that is, if they have an overall antisocial orientation (Simons et al., 1995) that their children could copy later on or might have genetically inherited (Frick et al., 1992). Furthermore, little girls who are sexually abused rarely reproduce this pattern toward their children. However, they often suffer from other problems, such as depression and early sexuality with peers. Thus, overall, even traumatic early experiences are not repeated by most individuals as they become older, although they often produce negative consequences. Put another way, early traumatic experiences do not produce *one* same effect in all children. For some, the effect is painful but brief. For others, it initiates a series of negative life course events that are not equally predictable from child to child and that can often be interrupted with appropriate clinical interventions.

In contrast to children who have been abused by their parents, which is a minority situation (Ambert, 2001), are children who have enjoyed an ideal home relationship, have lived an idyllic childhood, including receiving genuine love. Yet some of these children grow to become maladjusted and deeply unhappy adults. How can this anomaly be explained? It can easily be understood if, once again, we keep in mind that parents are not necessarily the prime causality and that the first few years of life are not unavoidably a blueprint for the future. To begin with, many of these children were born with unfortunate vulnerabilities that blocked the positive effect of their parents' love and efforts. Others experienced severe stressors during adolescence and adulthood that erased the benefits of a happy and well-adjusted early personality and home life. In other words, the life course is strewn with both positive and negative opportunities for development.

This being said, positive childhood experiences do provide the best basis upon which to build as life unfolds. The sooner in life a person learns successful habits, the easier it is thereafter. In contrast, negative experiences at an early age are potentially dangerous: they have to be surmounted and therefore require greater readjustment from individuals who, because of their age, are vulnerable and ill-equipped to cope with them. Early negative experiences form a more stressful basis for life and waste precious mental energies that could be channeled into more positive actions. Moreover, not everyone can recover from a detrimental early life. Thus, early experiences certainly mark *many* individuals for life, but the exceptions are so numerous that this statement becomes vacuous and leaves much room for consideration of complementary explanations.

It seems that early experiences may be the most deterministic in the area of intellectual development, particularly in terms of school readiness. This is a domain in which parents can play an important role and can easily be trained to do so. However, even here, it is generally the parents' social class, education, or poverty level that determine their children's intellectual development. Poverty during the first years of life is a very deterministic variable (Caspi et al., 1998;

Duncan and Brooks-Gunn, 2000; McLoyd, 1998). It is deterministic in itself as well as indirectly, as it often stands in the way of proper parenting: it thus is a double-action social causality.

Then one has to consider that an infant is born with a set of predispositions or characteristics variously called traits, temperament, or personality, depending on the theoretical leanings of each researcher. It is the *interaction* between these predispositions and the treatment received from parents and older siblings at first, and later from other agents of socialization and social forces, that will ultimately shape a child (Collins et al., 2000). These same characteristics also determine how affected a child will be by a negative environment (alcoholic parents, poverty amidst affluence, a delinquent sibling) as well as by a positive environment (loving parents, a good school). For instance, at one extreme, an autistic child reacts less positively to loving parents; this deficit may not be substantially compensated for by an ideal environment. At the other extreme, a child with a jovial, easygoing nature may be less affected by parental mistreatment and family poverty than a fussy and nervous baby.

PARENTING:
ONE IMPORTANT INFLUENCE AMONG OTHERS

The evidence clearly suggests that childhood experiences, whether negative or positive, are not always key markers in a person's life. Above all, it suggests that parents are one among many influences upon a child's life course. Thus, the traditional model has misled entire cohorts of parents into believing that they could control their children's future and shape its contours. Generations of specialists who have made it their profession to serve children and adolescents, that is, teachers, social workers, psychiatrists, and psychologists, have only too willingly swallowed this one-sided perspective; this has made their lives easier because parents are an "obvious" target, easy to reach, easy to blame and control. Once parents are blamed, one does not have to look elsewhere for causes to children's problems. For instance, one does not have to do anything about poverty or media violence or materialism.

Consequently, when the process of child socialization breaks down or fails, the blame is immediately placed on parents. This is especially so when the failure results in unprotected teen sexuality, adolescent pregnancy, substance abuse, school dropout, and delinquency—to mention only some of the problems that have high social visibility and have been widely studied within this traditional perspective. Undoubtedly, some parents are at least partly responsible for their children's misfortunes and misbehavior as well as good behavior, but many are not: other social groups and institutions affect children.

Nevertheless, supportive parental monitoring can compensate to a great extent for and offer protection to children against some of the negative impacts of, for instance, poverty (Hanson, McLanahan, and Thomson, 1997). There are also strong indications that lack of supervision is related to delinquency, drug use, and risky sexual activities (Miller, Forehand, and Kotchick, 1999; Rodgers, 1999). However, one has to consider that many parents fail at supervising their children because they are prevented from doing so due to work schedules, difficult neighborhoods, lack of social support, and their children's rebellious attitudes. Other children who are poorly supervised manage well on their own because they benefit from a good peer group and/or a stable personality: children are not passive and do contribute something to their own development and, especially as they age, to their behavior (Corsaro, 1997). Thus, although on average, parents are the prime influence on a child's *early* development, this is so only through the environment in which the family lives, and only until that child enters the school system, including nursery school and even day care.

It should be pointed out here that we possess little knowledge on the comparative impact of parents, day care, and kindergarten on children. It is possible that even very young children are more affected by day care workers than by parents, at least in certain areas of development. Consequently, as children acquire additional primary caretakers, and do so at an early age, it is only reasonable to postulate that parental effect will be lessened, especially if the values of the other caretakers differ from those of parents. These issues are currently being debated by researchers and the following references are of interest: Scarr, 1998; Singer et al., 1998.

In view of the multiplicity of influences that, in our society, affect children and especially adolescents and often compete with parental influence, it cannot automatically be assumed that parents can remain highly influential in their children's lives, a topic to which we return in Chapter 13. In order for parents to remain influential, a set of converging circumstances has to exist. That is, there must be a conducive mix of parental and child characteristics (in terms of personality, health, and resources), as well as conducive socioeconomic circumstances. In other words, if parents are to remain strongly influential in their adolescents' lives in the United States and Canada, circumstances favorable to the parents and to the child have to be in place. An example would be a child whose peers' values are similar to those of his or her parents, who attends a school where little difference exists between parental and school goals, and who either watches few negative television programs or is untouched by such viewing. Unfortunately, few are the parents today who benefit from such a favorable set of circumstances.

In the all-encompassing and rapidly evolving technological world we live in, it is certainly naive to assume that parents can be totally in control of their children's development. Consequently, it is reasonable to study how other social forces (peers, mass media, advertising, popular culture, politics, religion) affect children and, in turn, how these forces lead children to affect their parents. This multicausality model is certainly more complex to analyze than the basic parent-child model. But it is a causality path that avoids the pitfalls of simplistic theories that are scientifically erroneous and even immoral considering the human costs they exact when people, especially professionals, follow them to the letter. This model also allows us to study the effect that children have on their parents' lives.

THE EMERGENCE
OF INTERACTIONAL THEORIES

Over two decades ago, Bell and Harper prefaced their 1977 book, *Child Effects on Adults,* by underlining the extent to which children's influence on their parents as well as on other caretakers was overlooked in the literature. Peterson and Rollins (1987) and Maccoby and Martin (1983) looked at socialization from the perspective of parent-child reciprocity. Siegal (1985) discussed the importance of the perceptions children have of their parents in the quality of parent-child relations. Clarke-Stewart (1973) found that child and mother took turns in "causing" one to be attached to the other and that, when the father was involved, the direction of influence became even more intricate. Elder, Liker, and Cross (1984) allowed "for the possibility that children can be important influences in the lives of their parents" and, consequently, that the "developmental trajectory of children and parents" should be viewed within a joint context.

Belsky, Robins, and Gamble (1984) and Lerner and Busch-Rossnagel (1981) added to the discussion by presenting children as producers of their own development; they directed our attention to the circular interactions between child effect and parental effect. For example, a colicky and moody infant who persistently fails to be comforted or to respond when her father holds her unwittingly discourages him from further attempts at soothing her. The father may even refrain from interacting with the baby and avoid her. In turn, the father's response to the child's stimuli (frowns, cries) may inadvertently reinforce the child's tendency toward an adverse pattern of interaction or, at the very least, of avoidance and social withdrawal.

Thus, in this way, even an infant can lead a parent toward a pattern of response that in time will contribute positively or negatively to her own development. Korner (1971) found that neonates initiated four out of five of the mother-infant interactions observed. Although these authors were predominantly interested in the effect that a child has on its own development, their perspective can be used as a stepping stone to the focus of this book. Indeed, if children are seen as social actors contributing to their own development, it is only one logical step to see these children as actors *upon their parents*.

Thomas and Chess (1980) posited that negative interactions with parents can result from a child's difficult temperament. One of the results of a study by Rutter (1978) on families with a mentally ill parent was that children with more adverse temperaments were twice as likely to receive criticism from their parents compared to more easily adaptable children. For their part, Tyler and Kogan (1977) have shown how mothers whose disabled children respond negatively to them often suffer from "affect turn-off." In other words, these mothers become discouraged and refrain from initiating contact with their children; or they become less responsive to them because they feel rejected and come to believe that they are inconsequential in their children's lives.

In 1978, an article in *Psychology Today* heralded for the general public the new era in child effect. Unfortunately, the article did not produce the impetus it should have; perhaps it was too early and the public was not ready for it. In "Bringing up Mother," Segal and Yahraes summarized whatever little literature existed on the topic and discussed the fact that "parents are the product of the children born to them." They questioned whether it is valid to conclude that children who exhibit an overly dependent personality do so because their parents treat them restrictively. Might it not be plausible, they asked, that parents treat them restrictively *because* the children are dependent? Such questions will be raised again in this book, especially in the chapters on delinquency, on behavioral and emotional problems, as well as on genes.

Until now, the limited but burgeoning literature on child effect has dealt almost exclusively with infants and preschoolers, as well as with disabled children (McKeever, 1992), rather than older children or anti-social children. This is because it is easier to do research with young children and their mothers than to study older children and adolescents. Fathers are still rarely included in this research—another result of bias. After children are six years old, they may be more difficult to study within a restricted mother-child model because of all the other external influences competing for their time and attention.

A relatively limited but important literature focusing on the child as socialization agent for parents also developed (Brim, 1968; Peters, 1985). For instance, in Peters's studies, a great proportion of university students' parents admitted to having been influenced or socialized by their offspring in terms of attitudes and behaviors. The areas discussed ranged from politics to sports to personal appearance and grooming. The first edition of this book (Ambert, 1992) actually contained a chapter in which students explained their own effect on their parents, and we have read a sample of such quotes in Chapter 1.

In the 1980s, research of feminist inspiration initiated a critique of the clinical literature that focused on parents as the causative agent in their children's emotional problems. In this vein, Caplan and Hall-McCorquodale (1985) have analyzed mother-blaming in clinical journals and criticized the predominant maternal causality model. For their part, Chodorow and Contratto (1982) have critiqued the works of such women authors as Friday (*My Mother/My Self,* 1977) and Dinnerstein

(*The Mermaid and the Minotaur,* 1976), which implied that mothers are all powerful in determining their children's destinies and that these children suffer for the rest of their lives because of the most minute lapses committed by mothers. Similarly, Saraceno (1984) pointed out that social policies which concern women always assign them responsibility for the children. For instance, child care is associated with working *mothers,* not working fathers. Thorne (1987:98) has mentioned one additional pitfall of the mother-blaming ideology: "it distorts children's experience of the world, denying their intentionality and capacity for action within circumstances that extend beyond ties with mothers."

Another bias in the research denounced by those who alerted us to mother-blaming or "mommism" is that the role of the father is completely overlooked, although the disciplines of psychology and sociology are finally beginning to address this issue (Cabrera et al., 2000; Hawkins and Dollahite, 1997; Lamb, 1997; LaRossa, 1997). The accompanying problem is that child effect, if studied at all, is studied mainly on mothers (on mothers of children with disabilities, for instance), and rarely on fathers—although, as we see later, there is a basis in reality: fathers are far less affected by their children than are mothers. Similarly, fathers are always studied as part of the social support of mothers in their parenting role. Recent research, however, has determined that fathering is even more affected by the father's relationship with the mother than is mothering by the same relationship (Doherty, Kouneski, and Erickson, 1998; McBride and Rane, 1998).

CHILDREN AND PARENTS
IN HISTORICAL PERSPECTIVE

It is quite possible that it is only during recent decades that the effects of children on parents could be studied for the simple reason that, in the past, children were probably less negatively influential on their parents' lives than they can currently be, with the exception of birthing for mothers. I use the term less "negatively influential" here to mean that children were then more *useful* to their parents, were less costly, and contributed to reinforce parents' lifestyle rather than alter it, as has since become the case. In the past, children were essential *resources* to their parents, whether as baby-sitters for younger siblings, or as co-workers at home, and later on as wage earners (Coontz, 2000). Thus, although children were then powerful actors within the family context, they were generally acting to *reinforce* or support family life and to affect parents positively in terms of the requirements of earlier times. Working-class children, often heavily immersed in factory and street activities, grew up quickly and became independent from their parents earlier, thus decreasing the potential for individual child effect (Nasow, 1985). Children affected their parents *collectively* rather than individually because families were still quite large at the turn of the twentieth century.

Studies of Canadian, American, and European material from the nineteenth century and early on in the twentieth century clearly indicate that children's earnings constituted a substantial proportion of a family's income (Nett, 1981). Working-class parents counted on the wages earned by their older children while the younger ones helped with household chores. Gillis (1981) found that, as late as 1914, 10 percent of English families in many communities had no other source of income but their children's wages. Moreover, farm children were always heavily involved in farm labor and many are to this day. The family was a unit of production and, under these circumstances, it was a more complete, organized, and total institution than it is today (Thornton and Lin, 1994). Children were largely educated within the home context and external influences were filtered through a rather homogeneous community with a great deal of value consensus. Parents could use their children for the survival of the family and for their own benefit, although this situation certainly varied by social class and urbanization level (Graff, 1995).

As is well illustrated by the LeVines (1985:31), a prominent value in agrarian societies is a lifelong loyalty of children to their parents: ". . . agrarian parents feel entitled to expect obedience from their offspring when they are children, loyalty from them when they are young adults, and increasing respect and support as they grow older." In many of these societies, by the time children are six, they work side by side with their parents. Because these societies are kinship dominated, children are a source of security, help, and prestige. Consequently, large numbers of children are desired. Boocock (1976: 422) has pointed out that a society organized around family productivity is particularly well suited for the care of small children at home on a full-time basis. Moreover, agrarian societies provide greater kin involvement in childrearing, as is often still the case among Native Americans, for instance (Machamer and Gruber, 1998:358; Mintz and Kellogg, 1988).

In North America, formal education of children as opposed to their economic contribution to the family took precedence among the middle-classes by the mid-nineteenth century. Zelizer refers to this phenomenon as the "construction of the economically worthless child" (1985:5). Children had, until then, been "objects of utility." On the other hand, as the Danish sociologist Qvortrup (1995) points out, children have remained useful through school labor that prepares them to assume adult roles later on in society and to become taxpayers supporting the older generations. Today, especially in urbanized areas, children need their parents' resources to survive and constitute a financial liability. Thus, the new ideology as well as the new economic realities have shifted younger family members' economic contribution and have oriented it toward the society at large rather than toward their parents.

In this sense, children's impact has been altered toward a cost factor for parents. As children became less useful financially and more expensive to raise, fertility rates declined. Consequently, each individual child became vested with greater parental affection, devotion, and resources. In smaller families, each child came to mean more to his or her parents emotionally. Children, says Zelizer, became sacred (the "sacralization" of children): they were transformed into objects of sentimental value. This, in turn, opened the door for parental emotional dependency on children and for increased individual child effect. Philippe Ariès (1962) and Lawrence Stone (1977), among other social historians, have discussed at great length the shifts that have occurred in the definition and meaning of childhood.

As children's role and status were evolving, so were their rights. Children became objects of state protection and regulation. Not only was child labor regulated and even proscribed, but parental obligations were encoded in the legal system so that parental duties became more subject to public scrutiny. Thus, an imbalance was created that increased the effect of children on parents, both directly and indirectly. Zelizer concludes her book with a realistic note: "But, perhaps, within the household, with proper guidance, new attitudes, and safeguards to prevent their exploitation, children may well become invaluably useful participants in a cooperative family unit" (1985:228).

THE CULMINATION
OF HISTORICAL CHANGES

In 1974, Marvin Koller wrote that most parents today are proud to say that their children's well-being takes precedence over their own. He was not referring to infants but to adolescents. These families are called *filiocentric* rather than patricentric or even matricentric. He pointed out that, in many ways, the "United States can be singled out as the prototype of a society that, for the first time in human history, is essentially and forthrightly youth-oriented or youth-dominated" (1974:13). But this situation is, at the societal level, an ambiguous one. On the one hand, children have acquired rights over the century and many institutions have been created to enhance their well-being and education. Society largely forces parents to subsidize their children's education and access to other institutions. On the other hand, the market economy exploits children and youth as sources of profit and offers them "mediatic" products that often endanger the development of their human qualities. In other words, the youth-orientation of society is not one that necessarily benefits youth and this is reflected in the higher rates of all kinds of problems afflicting children and adolescents.

This societal failure results in greater negative child effect on parents as the latter have to invest more of themselves in their children at a time when the economy is also demanding more of them (Hays, 1996). The self-denial required of parents goes counter to the individualism they learn from their culture and the increasing individualism of their personal lives. Therefore, a hiatus has been created between parental duties that have become more onerous and adults' tendency to indulge their own self-gratification. In addition, children and adolescents have been relieved of responsibility in terms of familial duties.

The values that the media portray are often antithetical to those of many parents, thus potentially diminishing parental influence, or, at the very least, diluting it. Allan Bloom, a prominent critic of our education system, even contended that rock music, universally listened to in North America by children, has resulted in "nothing less than parents' loss of control over their children's moral education at a time when no one else is seriously concerned with it" (1987:76). Neil Postman, in *The Disappearance of Childhood* (1982), cogently described television as a medium that not only "aldultifies" children but "childifies" adults. In short, parents no longer are in a position to exert as much moral influence on their children as before, once again leaving the door open wider for child effect.

Another historical element that has contributed to enhancing child effect is the invention of adolescence as a distinct social category, bringing in its wake the influence of the peer group. We have become so conditioned to the notion that adolescence is a necessary, and often unavoidably rebellious stage in human development, that we often forget that it is not a universal phenomenon but a particular cultural construction of the past century. The status of adolescence began to shift from the mid-seventeenth century in England, where, according to Musgrove (1964), adolescence was "invented." Kett (1977) sees the period between 1890 and 1920 as the crucial time when, as economic conditions changed, youth between fourteen and eighteen years old were labeled adolescents. (See also Demos, 1974.) Preteen and teenage consumerist subcultures are certainly a new phenomenon that arose after World War II in North America. As peer groups became more autonomous and salient, they also exerted more influence on children's lives. There are also indications that children become peer oriented at an earlier age than was the case even two decades ago. All of these indicators point to an increased influence of the peer group on children with a consequent reduction of parental influence and a concurrent increase of child effect.

CONCLUSIONS

The sum of the sociohistorical developments reviewed in this chapter points to heightened moral and social child independence from parents. Parents have become less influential. In turn, these developments allow for the possibility of greater child effect than in the past. As society evolves, different cohorts of parents are more or less affected by different cohorts of children. Put otherwise, even within one society, as each generation of children succeeds another, parents are affected differently. The "nature" of children and of parents as well as of parenting is not static but is subject to the socio-historical context in which it is embedded: parents and children are social constructs that change over time.

Chapter 3

Determinants of Child Effect
on Parents

This chapter addresses three questions. First, what types of children affect their parents negatively or positively? In other words, what child characteristics or variables are linked to effect on parents? Then, we inquire into the types of parents who might be most susceptible to being affected by their children. Finally, since parent-child interactions take place within a particular environment, we need to explore the social situations allowing for child effect, contributing to it, alleviating it, or exacerbating it when it is negative, or even causing it. In summary, three sets of characteristics determine or influence child effect as well as its quality: the characteristics of the child, of the parents, and of the societal support for parents and their children.

These three sets of characteristics are the focus of this chapter. Hypotheses covering the direction (negative versus positive) and the intensity of child effect are presented based on these characteristics and their combinations. When parents' and children's characteristics are considered, they are often examined jointly in light of the reciprocity of effect perspective (Lerner, 1995). Children and parents influence one another so that the characteristics of each set of actors become a very important element in this circulation of effect. The theoretical perspective is largely interactional rather than unicausal and involves transactions between children, parents, and the environment (Magnusson, 1995). Although this book focuses on child effect, this model is equally valid in the study of parental and societal effect on children. It has rarely been used in its entirety and few scholars have integrated all three sets of variables in the original *design* of their research. One exception by Crouter and colleagues (1999) looks at the conditions affecting parents' knowledge of their children's daily lives. They include a few child and parental characteristics, the interaction between the two levels, as well as one extra-familial variable.

CHILD CHARACTERISTICS

Infants enter the world as tiny personalities, with specific needs, to which their parents respond. Parents continue responding to their offspring as they grow, acquire different needs, expand their behavioral repertoire, and enlarge their contact with society. Children possess individual characteristics that place more or fewer demands on parents and provide gratification or cause frustration. Put somewhat differently, some children require a great deal of *parental investment* (time, effort, teachings, personal sacrifices) because of their characteristics or their special needs. Other children are more "average" and parental investment does not have to be extraordinary or sustained over the life course.

Child characteristics are divided into demographic and personal ones. The demographic characteristics pertain to children who are eighteen years and younger. In addition, some of the child's demographic characteristics are the same as those of parents. Socioeconomic status is a prime example and is therefore not considered: children generally belong to their parents' social class, religion, and ethnicity. Thus, the demographic characteristics are less numerous than they would be were we to study adult children who might belong to a different social class, for instance. Adult children are discussed in Chapter 9.

Children's Demographic Characteristics

1. Age
2. Sex
3. Birth order
4. Single or multiple birth
5. From a first marriage or a remarriage
6. Quality and composition of sib group
7. Quality and composition of peer group

Children's Personal Characteristics

8. Physical health, including birth weight
9. Physical appearance/disabilities
10. IQ and other abilities
11. Personality traits, attitudes, mental health, affectivity level, attachment to parents
12. School performance and achievement
13. Performance and achievement in other activities (e.g., sports or music)
14. Behavior (at home, school, with peers, and in neighborhood)
15. Relationships with other significant persons (siblings, peers, relatives, teachers)

In terms of demographic characteristics, there is a vast literature illustrating how a child's sex affects the expectations that parents will have, their plans, their dreams for the child's future, the way in which they handle him or her, even the color scheme of the child's room. This is where gender roles come into play. Moreover, some parents who have a daughter when they expected a son may be momentarily disappointed. Couples with daughters or one daughter only are more likely to have another child in the hope of having a son than are couples with sons only. Males are preferred over females. Thus, even the sex of the child affects parents' family planning (Yamaguchi and Ferguson, 1995).

Throughout the chapters, the age of the child will come into focus as a potent determinant of child effect. For instance, following up on the analysis of the students' autobiographies presented in Chapter 1, many studies point to the period of adolescence as particularly stressful for parents. Indeed, adolescence is socially defined as a period of difficulties and, as a result, a variety of parent-child conflicts emerge, especially in terms of daily life activities (Gecas and Seff, 1990).

Another demographic variable that has been studied extensively is the child's birth order. Research has shown not only that later-born children receive less attention than first-born, but also that their arrival signals a change in maternal behavior toward the older sibling (Teti et al., 1996). Thus, a newborn restructures parental investment. In turn, we should be interested in studying how later-born children affect their parents in comparison to first-born children. The least that can be said is that the first-born presents the framework within which most adults learn firsthand their parental roles. Thus, the first-born child unwittingly occupies the role of socialization agent for his or her parents (Ambert, 2001).

Twinship or multiple births is a child characteristic that has become more prevalent as a result of a remarkable increase in such births following fertility treatment (Ventura et al., 1999). Additional stresses are incurred in having twins. Twins tend to be born smaller, have more medical complications, and their arrival causes added emotional and financial strains on parents. Mothers of twins spend much more time in infant-caretaking activities, and fathers of twins are also more likely to contribute to their care than parents of single children. Although parents spend more time caring for twins, they interact with each twin individually less than parents of single children.

Lytton (1980) called twinship an ecological factor that has great impact not only on the babies' development but on parenting conditions as well. Parents of twins often receive a great deal of positive attention and may harbor feelings of pride not experienced by other parents. Unfortunately, the effect on parents of having twins has not been adequately studied after the early childhood period. It would be especially important to learn how teenage twins affect their parents in comparison to a single teenager. This question is particularly relevant in view of peer group effect. Are such children less or more likely to be peer oriented, school oriented, parent oriented? Are they less or more likely to be cooperative with their parents? Are they less or more likely to be "rewarding" adolescents for their parents?

As for personal child characteristics, this chapter studies them globally within the framework of hypotheses. Subsequent chapters focus on some of these characteristics individually, particularly Chapters 5 and 6.

> It is herein hypothesized that *the more a child deviates from the socially accepted average in child characteristics 8 through 15, the greater the child effect on parents.*

This hypothesis is further refined along a continuum from a highly positive deviation from the average to a highly negative deviation from the average:

(A) The more a child deviates *negatively* from the socially accepted average in characteristics 8 through 15, the more negative the child effect on parents.

The negative effect may be temporary, sporadic, or lifelong. It would be interesting to pursue hypotheses on a longitudinal basis, but our knowledge is yet too fragmented to allow us to do so in a constructive way. To complicate matters further, many parents also experience positive effects, in spite of the negative deviation, as they draw on their own personal strengths to cope with the situation. Above all, the negative child effect could be largely mitigated by a favorable social response.

It is also hypothesized that a child's negative deviation from the norm will impact more negatively on parents when the deviation is perceived to be *child driven* rather than externally driven or the result of an accident of nature or of the environment. For instance, juvenile delinquency and difficult child behaviors are relatively child driven as well as peer driven in terms of causality. In contrast, cerebral palsy, pneumonia, or an injury caused by a drunk driver are not the child's "doing": the causality is external. In the latter instances, parents close ranks with their afflicted children while in cases of child-driven problems, parents often have to "fight" with their children in order to socialize them according to the norms of their society.

Each society has explicit and implicit expectations concerning what a normal child should look like, should be, and how he or she should behave. Thus, parents develop broad expectations even before their child is born. When the child arrives, their initial visual encounter with the infant presents the first test of how their expectations have been met. The healthy newborn elates parents while a low-birth-weight infant arouses concern. As the child ages, culturally driven maturational milestones enter into play, in terms of walking, language development, and expressions of attachment. The child who deviates from normal expectations affects parents differently than the child who meets or even exceeds these expectations. Varying child effects on parents ensue (as well as feedback parental effect on the child) depending on the nature of the discrepancy between norms and child. Parents of children who deviate negatively from the socially accepted average have to reeducate themselves regarding what to expect. A great deal of adaptation on their part is necessary and the discrepancy between expectations and reality may produce stress. Parental adaptation is studied at great length in Chapters 5, 6, and 7.

> (B) The more a child deviates *positively* from the socially accepted average in traits 8 through 15, the greater the positive child effect on parents.

For example, parents who have a musically gifted child—a positive deviation from the average—may enjoy their child's performance; they may bask in the praise bestowed upon them by friends and teachers; they may compare themselves favorably to other parents; they may have fewer worries about the child's future.

Hypothesis B can be refined as follows: the effect on parents will be positive in *some domains* and perhaps even negative in others. The direction of the effect will depend on parental characteristics and the quality of the societal response. For example, an insecure parent may feel threatened psychologically by a child with a high IQ while at the same time benefiting from social praise. If the child comes from a background in which the parents are less educated, the parents may feel inferior because the child overtakes them intellectually and role reversal occurs at some levels of functioning. These parents may feel helpless, especially when the child performs well in school and they are unable to help him or her.

In contrast, more educated parents may not be negatively vulnerable to this child characteristic—quite the contrary: the "fit" between parents and child will be better. In a majority of the cases, parents may feel particularly close to the gifted child. Educated parents may identify more with these children. On the negative side, they may also feel overwhelmed by the attention and the special lessons that these children require. The child may, in turn, make direct demands on parents for special attention and favors. Parental investment in terms of time and money may be very high. Thus, the child's needs may be in competition with the parents' need for personal time.

Child characteristics are a key determinant of child effect on parents. We return to this topic at greater length in subsequent chapters, in which we study the effect on parents of child characteristics that deviate negatively from the average. Children with emotional and behavioral problems as well as those who are juvenile delinquents will be discussed in this respect.* A chapter is also devoted to the effect of peer group on children as well as on parents.

PARENTAL CHARACTERISTICS

We now focus more specifically on the interaction between parents' and children's characteristics; parental characteristics in great part magnify, mitigate, or prevent child effect: *certain parents are more vulnerable to child effect than others because of their own characteristics.* The term *vulnerable* is not used within a necessarily negative connotation. It means that certain parents are more open to receiving enjoyment from their children, while other parents are more likely to be casualties. It also means that, given certain of their child's characteristics, some parents are more likely to suffer from a negative effect than other parents with similar children.

Unavoidably, a few of the following parental characteristics overlap with areas of parental lives that can be affected and are discussed in the following chapter. This is particularly evident for health. Moreover, several parental characteristics can be the direct result of child effect: an example here is variable 18 of parents' personal characteristics or commitment to parenting. One frequently encounters parents of difficult or rejecting children who *become* less committed to parenting as a direct result of the type of children they have. Put otherwise, the parental characteristic is actually caused by the child. Thus, as we see, situations feedback on each other or interact so that it is important, when studying parental variables, to keep in mind the child and societal characteristics that could affect them.

Parents' Demographic Characteristics

1. Parent's age (at birth of child and currently)
2. Sex
3. Socioeconomic status (SES): education, income, occupation

---

*No chapter is devoted to children who deviate positively from the average for the simple reason that I could not find sufficient research that would have helped prepare a synthesis of this topic. It seems that our society notices problem children more than "good" or even gifted children.

4. Marital status
5. Adoptive versus biological
6. Ethnicity and minority group status
7. Immigration status
8. Religion and religiosity
9. Parents' other children; these children's characteristics; their
    number and spacing

Parents' Personal Characteristics

10. IQ and other abilities
11. Personality, affectivity, responsiveness
12. Quality of parenting they themselves received as children
13. Gender role ideology and implementation (including division
     of labor)
14. Coping patterns
15. Parenting skills
16. Parenting expectations
17. Perceptions of child (attributions)
18. Commitment to parenting
19. Health: mental and physical
20. Physical appearance/disabilities
21. Material resources
22. Social resources (such as friends, often referred to in the
     literature as "social support")
23. Quality of marital relationship
24. Quality of relationship with other family members, particularly
     own parents.

Beginning with the demographic characteristics, children affect
mothers more than fathers, largely because mothers are the primary
caretakers (Larson and Richards, 1994). In this role, they interact
with their children more than fathers do and interactions range over a
wider variety of patterns. For instance, children are both closer to and
more often in conflict with their mothers than with fathers (Noller,
1994; Patterson, Reid, and Dishion, 1992). Furthermore, the numbers
of single mothers are high and this family type places most of the
parenting duties squarely on mothers' shoulders. When divorce occurs,
children are generally in the care of their mothers, while the father

role vanishes in many cases or is drastically altered in others. Thus, much of what children *do* and of what children *are* (child characteristics) is likely to affect mothers much more than fathers. Moreover, as Arlie Hochschild (1983) has so well illustrated in *The Managed Heart,* society expects more of women than of men in terms of nurture, support, and feelings. Children certainly do not escape this rule of expectations, and, as a consequence, place more nurturing demands on their mothers than on their fathers.

To move on to other parents' demographic characteristics, single parents may be more affected by their children's behavior than married parents, if only because no other parent is present to mediate or aggravate the relationship or to support the parent. In our society, single parents are often poorer than other parents, and this situation may exacerbate the parent-child relationship and contribute to negative effect from and for both parties. Furthermore, the financial burden on single mothers is heavy. Studies also indicate that children may have a positive effect on the well-being of widowed parents (Umberson and Gove, 1989) and that divorced fathers who remain in touch with their children are positively affected (Umberson, 1989), while fathers with custody experience a mixture of negative and positive effects (Shapiro and Lambert, 1999).

Parents' age is another important characteristic creating effect both on children and on parents. Very young parent age is related to poverty and single status (Coley and Chase-Lansdale, 1998). In turn, both are related to negative child outcomes. As a result, the baby, and later the child, will influence its young mother's life differently than if the mother had been older at the time of the child's birth. Such children may present the young mother with more problems and will be a greater financial burden than if she were older and well established on the labor market. On the other hand, as they grow older, children who have a narrower age gap with their mother may be more rewarding companions to her as young adults than are children of older and more educated mothers. Because of the economic disadvantages early in their lives, these children may not reach a much higher educational level than that of their own mother, so that the cultural gap between mother and child may not be wide and may be advantageous to her as she ages. There are no studies using a life course perspective that would shed light on the quality of the mother-child bond across the life span, comparing mothers who were very young at their children's birth with mothers who were older.

But a few studies indicate that first-time parents who are older experience fewer childrearing difficulties (Garrison et al., 1997), and that older fathers are more likely to become involved in the care of a first child than young fathers (Heath, 1995). It would be interesting to know if the older father is then more or less at risk of being negatively affected by a variety of adverse child characteristics: his closer involvement makes him more similar to a mother in terms of role structure.

Parents' employment may be an important variable. For instance, mothers of children with disabilities find relief in their work. It provides a "break" in their demanding routine and, as such, may contribute to lower negative child effect:

> It's marvelous because when I get to work I forget all about, you know . . . you're with women who haven't got mentally handicapped children. . . . You're in a more normal environment. (Mother of a 4-year-old girl with epilepsy and cerebral palsy, quoted in Baldwin and Glendinning, 1983:66)

On the other hand, parents whose employment situation is stressful may be particularly vulnerable to child effect—both positively (the children may act as a compensation) or negatively (the children may be an added stressor).

Parents who have several children may be affected differently than parents who have a small family: parents' resources in terms of time and money are diluted by the addition of each new baby. (This is called the *dilution of parental resources* theory.) With more children, parents spend less time and material resources on each child individually but more time and money on them collectively. Large families in turn produce a differential impact depending on how *closely spaced* the children are. Parents often cope with a large family by adopting more managerial and less flexible childrearing techniques (Richardson et al., 1986). Overall, the dilution of parents' resources, particularly in closely spaced families, may be one of the reasons why, on average, children from large families do less well in school than children from smaller families (Downey, 1995). Maternal health is particularly vulnerable to large family size. Overall, parents' socioeconomic conditions would be a very important intervening variable in terms of child effect in large families.

As we will see in Chapter 7, large sib groups may be better able to form coalitions against parents who are then less able to socialize their children as they see fit. Children in closely spaced families are more influenced by their siblings and less by their parents than children from more widely spaced families. We can also hypothesize that parents who have several children may feel less in control of their family life, and may feel that they cannot contribute as much as they would like to their children's future. This may result in lower self-esteem as well as health problems, especially for mothers. (The opposite occurs in agrarian societies, in which children contribute to the economy of the family and are a source of pride as they grow numerically.)

We now look briefly at some examples of the role that parents' personal characteristics play in child effect. In terms of the quality of parents' marriage, the research is unanimous: a good marriage is correlated with positive child outcomes and a more affectionate parent-child relationship (Amato and Booth, 1997). A happy couple is supportive and companionable, thus more likely to be positive toward the children and be affected by them in a more rewarding manner. Similarly, if such a couple has a problematic child, the spouses will find in each other a compensatory outlet. In contrast, an embattled couple will not benefit from this advantage. Thus, the former parents should be less likely than the latter to suffer from negative child effect.

Furthermore, the quality of the parents' relationship impacts indirectly on child effect in the sense that *parental conflict* has been causally related to negative child outcomes, particularly difficult behaviors (Buehler et al., 1998; Seltzer, 1994). In turn, these child behaviors affect parents negatively—although this is certainly not a topic that is much researched. These same parents will be particularly vulnerable to negative child effect because they are already overwhelmed by a conflictual marriage.

In the realm of the extended family system, if parents have maintained a warm relationship with their own parents, they can together share in the joys of parenting and grandparenting. However, in situations where parents and grandparents do not get along, where grandparents meddle or disagree with their own children's socialization practices, or where grandparents do not help out when they actually could, the intergenerational situation exacerbates negative child effect.

I have, in this section, proposed research topics and hypotheses stemming from parental characteristics. The goal is to identify parents who might be more vulnerable to negative child effect compared to parents who are the most likely to reap positive child effect. The reader probably knows that the family and child development literatures focus on identifying parents who are at risk of maltreating their children, or in other words, of producing a negative effect on their children, often their infants—who are often called "children at risk." For instance, young, single, or cohabiting mothers who are disadvantaged and live in a poor neighborhood are more likely than others to abuse and neglect their small children (Bell and Jenkins, 1993; McLoyd, 1995; Pelton, 1991).

It is difficult to know at this stage if there is an overlap between the types of parents who are at risk of mistreating their children and those who are at risk of being negatively affected by them. It is possible that parents who are easily frustrated, irritable, and are burdened by problems they cannot cope with will be more negatively affected by infants and small children, and, as a result will either lash out at them or will neglect them. But, as children grow, such parents may actually be less affected by their children because of a high level of preoccupation with matters of survival and self-preservation. In contrast, prosocial and tolerant parents may be very negatively affected by a difficult small child but simply suffer and try to cope.

Parental characteristics and child characteristics interact with each other to produce effect in a transactional model—effects on children and on parents feeding back on each other. Certain parental and child characteristics may be active only at given stages in the family life cycle—whether to promote negative or positive child effect. For instance, it is possible that parental commitment to their role fluctuates over time, so that a parent is very committed while the children are small and becomes much less so during adolescence. Such fluctuations in commitment might make parents more or less vulnerable to child effect over time. Thus, the characteristics discussed herein are meant to be looked at within a dynamic and developmental or life course perspective.

CHARACTERISTICS OF THE SOCIETAL RESPONSE

Parents' and children's interactions do take place within a social and cultural context. Thus, a society's characteristics act as a catalyst to or a buffer against child effect on parents (Horowitz, 2000). Each society offers a set of structural constraints and opportunities as well as a cultural content that guides child and parental behavior. Furthermore, the level of support extended to parents and children will in great part determine parents' reaction as well as the direction of child effect on parents. What is important to parents is the help and moral support they receive from society at large, as well as the resources that society offers their children to maximize their development and enhance positive parent-child interaction. The opportunities a child has in terms of development are in great part related to the extent to which the parents' social situation helps or hinders them. Generally, the social support extended to parents benefits children. It is at this juncture that the study of child effect overlaps with the search for factors that enhance children's development and well-being.

Societal support refers to the *resources* that a society places at the disposal of parents in order to facilitate the fulfillment of their role. When a society has few resources available or chooses, out of socioeconomic and political considerations, not to invest in families, parents are effectively deprived of societal support. The use of the word "societal" instead of the more commonly utilized term "social support" is intentional. Indeed, social support has generally been defined in research as the support one receives from *individuals*, and more specifically, from individuals whom one should be close to, such as family and friends. While relatives and friends may indeed be sources of support, they represent only a minute portion of what is here called "societal" support or response. In this chapter, we refer to aspects of the *society* rather than of individuals; we refer to the way the society is organized to meet parental needs and children's needs.

Characteristics of the Societal Response

1. Adequate housing
2. Quality and existence of early child care systems
3. Quality of schools

4. Quality and existence of after-school programs
5. Income supplements for impoverished families
6. Adequate dental, medical, and psychiatric resources
7. Availability of parenting education programs
8. Quality of the contents of mass media (two adverse qualities are media violence and gender-role stereotyping)
9. Safety of neighborhoods
10. Appropriate recreational facilities for youngsters and families
11. Home and community support for parents who have special-needs children and for special-needs parents
12. Society's open acknowledgment of parental contribution
13. Fostering of a positive peer group culture among children and adolescents
14. Society's acceptance of minority parents and children (as opposed to discrimination)
15. Society's acceptance and fostering of a gender-egalitarian ideology
16. Society's acceptance of diverse types of families, for instance, same-sex-parent families

These societal characteristics are resources that contribute to foster healthy child outcomes and prevent the development of negative child attributes and behaviors (Lerner, Fisher, and Weinberg, 2000). In turn, any one of these social assets can lessen or even prevent the potentially detrimental impact that children could have on their parents, who in turn are differentially vulnerable or resilient. Moreover, these societal characteristics can also increase the potential for positive child effect in general. Obviously, a combination of effective societal characteristics will have an even greater positive potential than just one or two considered in isolation. Absence of societal support can increase the negative effect of children on parents as well as the reverse: parents living in situations of low societal support can have a negative impact on their children. It is obvious that the adequacy of the societal response helps parents cope and, in turn, respond more appropriately to their children's needs. Parents who are socially supported can invest in their children more adequately. In turn, they are less likely to be negatively affected by their young ones.

In the 1980s, several studies relevant to our topic were carried out. For instance, Crnic et al. (1983) found that high-stress mothers who received adequate support were better equipped to foster healthy emotional growth in their babies than similar mothers with low levels of support. Seitz, Rosenbaum, and Apfel (1985) reported that societal support extended to impoverished mothers had a long-term positive impact when these mothers were compared to a control group who had not received the same support. In this case, mothers had been provided with medical as well as social services, including day care. A study by Crockenberg (1981) showed that mothers of irritable babies who had received support were more securely attached than mothers and babies who had received inadequate support. Societal support did not, however, have much of an impact when mothers had nonirritable babies. These results could indicate that *the adequacy of the societal response is of greater consequence to parents of children with problems.* Thus, parents who have disabled, difficult, or disturbed children should receive more support than parents of average children. The opposite generally occurs as such parents are often marginalized by professionals whose job it is to help children. In addition, blame often follows, a factor that contributes to an increase in negative child effect on parents (see Chapter 8).

Particularly important for parents of problematic children are special classes and after-school programs, which could give such parents a respite from responsibilities. Such services reduce the negative impact that these children can have and increase parental enjoyment. This should be especially evident for parents who are poor, isolated, in ill health, or are going through difficult times, such as separation, death in the family, or unemployment. For instance, several studies indicate that single parents do not have as many contacts, such as Parent-Teachers Night or Open School Night, with schools as other parents, and that, at the same time, there is a correlation between parental involvement in school activities and children's grades (Trusty, 1998). Single parents may be unable to attend such functions because the schools fail to provide child care during these hours, or because teachers are prejudiced and do not treat such parents with dignity. The societal response, through the school system, does not meet the needs of single parents and their children.

The societal response has the potential to compensate for negative child characteristics as well as negative parental characteristics that make parents particularly vulnerable to child effect. Such a statement has widespread application because there are very few parents who do not have at least one or two negative characteristics that place them at risk for child effect. Neither should we assume that negative child characteristics cannot affect "perfect" parents. Thus, appropriate societal responses and the provision of resources are key determinants in parents', as well as children's, welfare.

Another important element that contributes heavily to either negative or positive child effect is neighborhood quality, particularly safety. While studies abound concerning the negative influence that impoverished and crime-ridden districts have on children (Miller, Forehand, and Kotchick, 1999), much less is said about the heavy cost that these children's parents pay. Parents may not be able to allow their children to play outside, not only because they may fear the criminal influence but because they may be afraid that the child will be attacked, robbed, raped, or caught in the cross fire of gang warfare. Such parents suffer doubly because their small apartment may already be overcrowded and the cooped-up children may become difficult to manage. Often, parents have to walk their children to school. They become captive, not only to avoid neighborhood dangers, but as their children's constant keepers. We can surmise that these "supermotivated" parents (Furstenberg et al., 1994) might suffer from premature burnout, high levels of stress, and a multitude of physical and psychosomatic ailments as a consequence. Thus, lack of societal resources in the guise of safe neighborhoods for the poor exacerbates child effect to highly undesirable negative levels.

Finally, one aspect of the societal response that has to be taken into consideration is its timing. Crnic and Greenberg (1987) suggested that there may be periods in parents' and children's lives when social support is more necessary and more effective. Their study of the first year in a child's life led them to conclude that parents benefit more from individual social support during the immediate transition to parenthood than later on in that first year. However, for certain types of parents (very young or ill) and/or certain types of children (special challenges), the societal response may be needed even more as the child ages, and particularly so during adolescence.

CONCLUSIONS

Parent and child characteristics interact to produce child outcomes and effect on parents within the context of the characteristics of the social environment. Which set of characteristics has primacy depends on where there is imbalance or deviation, the degree of imbalance, as well as the stage of the child's and parents' lives. Although I hypothesize a primacy of the societal response in fostering or preventing negative and positive child effect, one also has to consider that certain parental or even child characteristics may be so extreme that no amount of societal support could prevent them or compensate for them. As well, certain parental characteristics, such as severe mental illness, drug addiction, and hard-core criminality, prevent parents from utilizing existing societal resources. Parents and even older children may actually resist efforts at reaching them.

Parental characteristics become less important than child characteristics as the child enters adolescence. At that point, both child and societal characteristics may supersede parental ones in producing child effect on parents—as well as child outcomes. As parents and children age, different characteristics from each, as well as resources from society, assume a greater or lesser importance in this equation of child effect. Similarly, the areas of parental lives that are affected differ over time.

It is interesting that Roskies long ago recognized the importance of this triumvirate of conditions, which we call here characteristics. She used this model, consisting for her of child/mother/society, to discuss the impact of the birth of a thalidomide child. She pointed out, in 1972, that this birth upset "the delicate network of interlocking needs and obligations—child's, mother's, and society's—on which the successful rearing of a child depends" and, within our own analytical model, from which child effect on parents flows. She further explained that "what makes this event so disruptive . . . is that the failure does not occur on one level, or in one partner. Instead, there is a chain reaction in which the needs of mother, child, and society, rather than working in harmony, become embroiled in a complex conflict of interests" (1972:289). Unfortunately, Roskies' words have too frequently been ignored in the literature.

Finally, let me add that the theoretical synthesis herein advanced is informed by a sociohistorical perspective of family life. Each society constructs its definition, not only of childhood, adolescence, and what a family is, but also of what good parenting is. These constructs are buttressed by the ideologies and institutions prevailing at any given point in the history of a society. Thus, one of the tenets of the transactional theory herein described is that the contents of the three sets of characteristics evolve over time, and so does their interaction. The relationship between parents and children is largely a cultural phenomenon or a social construct.

Chapter 4

Areas of Parents' Lives

This chapter delineates the domains of parents' lives that can be affected, whether by the mere presence of children or by specific children's behaviors, characteristics, and attitudes. Although an unavoidable overlap exists between some of these areas, I have divided parental lives into eleven major domains, from which vantage point child effect can be studied with greater specificity. As each area is described, examples of results from studies are presented. Above all, as the chief task of this book is to generate ideas, research questions that could be studied are offered at each level. The areas presented are those of maternal health, parental place/space/activities, employment, economic situation, marital and familial relations, human interaction, parents' relations with their community, their personality, attitude/values/beliefs, life plans, and feelings of control over one's life. To this list could be added the effect that the child has on parental behavior toward the child. This is discussed at greater length in subsequent chapters.

MATERNAL HEALTH

Chronologically, the first child effect occurs in pregnancy and childbirth. A pregnant woman experiences many bodily changes and may even suffer from morning sickness, fluid retention, and, in some cases, diabetes. She may need to adjust her diet and if she is a smoker and drinker, she should abstain from both to protect the health of her baby. Currently, because of sociomedical trends, often to ease the physician's schedule and insurance risk-taking, up to one-fifth of births are by caesarian section, in itself major surgery. Moreover, women hospitalized for childbirth are also subject to hospital-acquired infections. These afflict approximately 10 percent of any hospital-ized population. They also are prey to iatrogenic illnesses caused by medical errors, such as medication wrongly prescribed, which may affect as many as 20 percent of patients. Thus, the birth of a child becomes as much a medical event as a familial one.

Women who nurse benefit from an enjoyable experience but also have to adjust to certain standards of hygiene. It is interesting to note a very direct child effect on nursing mothers: babies who nurse more avidly stimulate milk production in their mothers' breasts. Parents, especially mothers, report fatigue during infancy because of night duty and infant illness. About 13 percent of mothers suffer from post-partum depression, which is to be distinguished from "baby blues," a much milder and more common affliction (Deater-Deckard et al., 1998). In addition, small children are more susceptible to colds than adults. They may have, on average, five to nine episodes of flus and colds yearly, and even more than that in their first years in child care centers. Parents of young children, especially mothers, who have to monitor the contagious little ones, often become ill themselves.

Impoverished mothers frequently skip meals in order to provide the basic necessities to their children. Mothers who have large families are less healthy than those with smaller ones. Not only is this difference caused by repeated childbearing and birthing, but it is due to a heavy workload, sleep deprivation, lack of leisure, and concerns over chil-dren's health and behavior. In large families, mothers may have to put the needs of husbands and children before their own. Single mothers who shoulder most childrearing responsibilities alone are especially vul-nerable and are consequently a major consumer of medical resources.

Caring for disabled children has been shown to affect mothers' mental health (McKeever, 1992). Cook (1988) has well described the stress suffered by mothers of mentally ill adults; added risks involved physical violence from these same children. It is obvious from gen-eral surveys and from the research on violent delinquents that assaults against parents are not an isolated phenomenon (Mirrlees-Black, Mayhew, and Percy, 1996; U.S. Department of Justice, 1994). Unfor-tunately, I have not been able to locate a single study focusing specifically on the effect of such violence on various areas of parents' lives. This is partly because parents go to great lengths to hide the abuse. Moreover, there exists a researcher's bias against addressing the issue: even researchers want to preserve the myth that "all children love and respect their parents" (Agnew and Huguley, 1989:699). The few studies mentioned above suggest that the mental and physical health of parents should be carefully mapped, depending on the characteristics of their children.

PLACE/SPACE/ACTIVITIES

This area focuses on the *place* and *space* parents occupy in society as well as the *structure* of their daily lives. Generally, this area is considered "natural," and is therefore taken for granted and not studied. To begin with, parents may have to move after a child is born or may have to do so when the child begins school, whether because of space considerations or to relocate to a neighborhood considered more appropriate for raising children. Moving carries economic consequences for the family in the form of higher rents, a mortgage, and the acquisition of furniture. In addition, this move may restrain or increase parents' community and leisure activities, depending on the type of neighborhood in which they resettle. For instance, parents who move to a distant suburb may miss out on the social and recreational activities provided by the strictly urban environment. Furthermore, they may have to face a long commute to and from work on a daily basis.

Thus, basically, the mere presence of children influences where parents live, the space they require, and how the space is organized (for instance, the necessity to "child-proof " a house to prevent accidents), as well as the feelings parents develop concerning their space. For example, parents who cannot afford to move to a "better" neighborhood, either because of financial or racial restrictions, may find that the arrival and the growth of the child is particularly stressful. They may not have enough space and the lack of neighborhood safety may have long-term effects both on them and on their children, particularly when the children witness violence (Aneshesel and Sucoff, 1996).

Parents' *schedules* change. In order to meet their children's survival needs, especially during infancy, parents often have little control as to when they sleep, eat, or visit with friends and relatives. As the child ages, additional changes occur in the parental schedule in order to facilitate a variety of requirements from the school system as well as extracurricular activities. One research question that immediately surfaces in this respect is whether middle-class parents' schedules are more (or less) altered by their children's requisites than are the schedules of working-class parents. Indeed, middle-class children are frequently involved in a vast array of organized extracurricular activities such as lessons, sports, and competitions (Adler and Adler, 1998). It would seem that these requirements would have a particularly strong effect on the schedule of parents responsible for the chauffeuring of children. On the other hand, in some inner-city neighborhoods, parents are so concerned about their children's safety that many accompany them to school and return to pick them up—walking all the way.

Parents' *activities* are also altered. For instance, lovemaking becomes less frequent and more inhibited (Call, Sprecher, and Schwartz, 1995). Parents' freedom of movement is curtailed after the arrival of a first child: they can no longer simply leave the house whenever they so desire. Loss of freedom is indeed the disadvantage that both parents and adults in general mention the most frequently. Moreover, after the birth of a first or a second child, the mother may have to take a maternity leave that sets her back in her work. Others abandon their job, or find one that is less demanding, or is closer to home. Overall, *mothers'* activities are even more affected than fathers'.

Parents experience varied degrees of restrictiveness in terms of activities in which they might have previously engaged. But, at the same time, other activities related to their role broaden their horizons. For instance, parents meet with teachers, get to know other parents, consult with pediatricians, play children's games, read children's books, and engage in a wide range of extracurricular tasks at schools. In contrast, nonparents do not benefit from these contacts. When children suffer from behavioral, emotional, or even academic problems, parents have to consult with a variety of professionals, not all of whom are competent. Thus, adults' activities as they become parents can be both a source of limitations and frustrations as well as a source of personal growth and new social contacts.

Because so much time has to be devoted to child care, especially during infancy, parents' *workloads* consequently grow. Mothers acquire a more substantial load than fathers. One of the most basic domestic chores, cooking, can be greatly affected in frequency and complexity by a child's medical problems, weight, or even fussiness. As the workload increases, additional effects are added to the list of changes in adults' lives, whether in terms of quality of the marital relationship, availability of free time, general well-being, time to socialize, or, as we have seen earlier, health (Hochschild, 1997). In our society, parents' time has to be managed more carefully if they are to avoid stress and role overload.

PARENTAL EMPLOYMENT

We have already mentioned that, upon the arrival of a baby, if a woman is employed, she is likely to take maternity leave. She may also abandon paid employment altogether, at least until the children are older. For example, women physicians with children practice fewer hours than men and than childless women physicians (Grant et al., 1990). Although a great deal of media attention focuses on paternal leave and on fathers who become their children's primary caretakers because of maternal employment, these cases are still too few to alter significantly the general profile. Most of the fathers who become primary caretakers do so because they and the mothers work shifts; father care is utilized as a means to save money (Casper and O'Connell, 1998). Maternal employment can be stressful for certain women who have to juggle two roles. This may explain why many mothers prefer to take some time off for the care of young children, particularly women who have less education and low-paying jobs (Volling and Belsky, 1993).

It is generally mothers who are responsible for children when they are ill. Thus, the health characteristics of a child has a great impact on a woman's occupational development during the child's infancy. Galambos and Lerner (1987) have found that certain child characteristics, such as "being difficult," are important factors in determining whether a mother returns to work. Carr (1988) has shown that mothers of children with Down's syndrome are less likely to be employed, at all of the children's age levels, than a control group of mothers. Furthermore, the characteristics of the societal response, such as the availability of quality child care, are more likely to affect maternal than paternal employment directly and to alleviate negative child effect on maternal employment.

Men are less likely to switch jobs after the birth of a first child. In other words, new fathers feel a need for greater employment stability because of the added financial responsibility presented by the baby. But when they do switch jobs, it is generally for a better-paying one (Gorman, 1999). Men's hours of work also often increase after they become fathers (Kaufman and Uhlenberg, 2000). When the addition of a child requires a move to a larger and more expensive dwelling, both parents may be obligated to seek higher-paying occupations.

FINANCIAL/ECONOMIC ASPECTS

This section is brief because the economic and financial domains are very closely interrelated to other areas, such as employment, life plans, activities, and even the health of parents. Current estimates indicate that it costs over $180,000 to raise a middle-class child to age eighteen. Granted that this estimate varies by region, having a child obviously represents a substantial investment for adults. At the same time, having a child may force one of the two parents to stay home, thus doubly lowering the family's resources. Moreover, in part because of inflation, but also because of the increasing consumerism surrounding children, this cost has been steadily increasing: it had been estimated at only $85,000 in 1980.

The period of adolescence can be a very expensive one for parents because of consumer demands fostered by media advertising. Furthermore, children stay home longer than in the past, often up to age thirty, both because of higher educational requirements and because starter jobs pay only minimum wages, not enough to allow for independent living (Boyd and Norris, 1995). Other children return home because of unemployment, divorce, or mental illness. The economic effect of children is especially acute in situations of unplanned single parenthood among young women and in situations of separation and divorce. Divorced women with child custody are heavily penalized in this respect: their household income drops by about 40 percent (Smock, 1994). Many have no other alternative than welfare.

Chapter 1 summarized the historical development of the financially expensive child phenomenon. Suffice it to say that this situation stems from the necessity to keep children dependent for educational purposes and thus to delay their economic contribution. Moreover, as we have seen, children in other types of societies still constitute an economic asset to their parents.

MARITAL AND FAMILIAL RELATIONS

When the first baby arrives, this diminutive human addition transforms the couple into a family. Or, alternatively, when a woman has a child on her own, she and her baby form a small family system. The first segment of this section focuses on married couples and the second on remarried couples.

Longitudinal studies that have followed couples through the transition to parenthood find that 50 percent of the partners experience stress and many experience some disenchantment with their marriage (Cowan and Cowan, 1992). In a society where companionship, intimacy, and romantic love are so highly prized, the infant unavoidably places a certain strain on these aspects, at least temporarily. Joint activities decline sharply and the situation persists throughout early childhood (Kurdek, 1993). The level of adaptation required of parents is generally underestimated. Even couples who were well aware of potential stressors ahead are caught unprepared. Obviously, the simple shift from being a couple to becoming a family with a tiny infant is not without its inherent problems:

> Right now, it is difficult for me to concentrate on anything with the baby. I think I had not expected to be so tired. I thought it would be a cinch because I am young but I just wasn't prepared for all that is involved in the care of a baby even though I had read books before. My husband was even less well prepared than me so you can imagine that the house is one big mess right now and I am very discouraged. When she starts crying I could lie down and cry with her. I just don't have any energy left. I

can't imagine how we had this idea of having a second one soon
after. *(Female student in her autobiography)*

New mothers often wish that their husband participated more in
child care. In a longitudinal study of couples who were interviewed
two months after their wedding and then two years later, preferences
about the division of child care tasks were evaluated and compared
over time. Johnson and Huston (1998) found that, when wives' love
was strong, their preferences changed in the direction of their husbands' far more often than the reverse. Husbands' love for their
wives did not translate into similar accommodating changes. Thus,
the traditional social constructions of motherhood and fatherhood are
maintained throughout the transition to parenting by the love work
that mothers provide. This adaptation is even more radical when multiple births occur or when a special-needs child arrives with particular frailties and even life-threatening conditions.

The transition to parenthood is smoother for couples who were well-
adjusted before and for those who had planned the timing of their family. Nevertheless, in over half of the cases, communication between the
spouses declines. In the Cowan and Cowan study (1997: 24), ". . . the
couples who stayed together but remained childless showed remarkable stability over the 7 years of the study in all five aspects of life that
we assessed. By contrast, the couples who became parents described
significant and often unexpected or disturbing shifts in every domain."
By the time the children had reached age five, 20 percent of the couples
had separated or divorced. These divorces cannot, however, be attributed to the transition to parenthood alone. In fact, becoming parents
was related to a lower divorce rate: 50 percent of the couples who had
remained childless during the seven years of the study had divorced.
Either being parents reduces the risk of divorcing or couples who
decide to have children often have a more stable relationship to begin
with. Evidence actually supports both explanations, but perhaps for
different couples. In fact, some couples wait to divorce until the children are older.

All in all, children continue to alter their parents' marital relationship
as they age, whether positively or negatively, as in the following quote:

For my parents, the years 14-16 [of her life] were certainly the
worst ones. I was difficult to be with to say the least. I was very

sneaky and manipulative and I would play one parent against the other in order to achieve my goals which were boys, boys, boys. My parents were upset at me most of the time and used to take it out on each other because I think they were basically afraid that I would run away which I used to threaten to do all the time. They were also afraid I'd get pregnant although they never said as much. Looking back, I am surprised that my parents didn't divorce because of me. I am even ashamed as I write this. *(Twenty-year-old female student)*

It is also important to look at the effect of children in remarriages. Each year, close to half of all marriages are remarriages for at least one of the spouses. When neither spouse has children, adjustment to remarriage is no different than in a first marriage. It becomes somewhat more complex when stepchildren live in or visit and the complexity increases when there are both live-in and visiting stepchildren (Ambert, 2001). Being a stepparent is not a role one expects to occupy or for which one is prepared: it is not a normative one. It is also a vilified role when one thinks of our cultural inheritance of the "wicked stepmother" in fairy tales. There are no norms or rules guiding the behavior of a "good" stepparent as is the case for a good parent. Each stepparent more or less has to reinvent the role and the relationship, which can be both an advantage and a disadvantage.

When children, visiting or resident, are present, the newlyweds must adapt to two key roles simultaneously—parent and spouse—while these two roles are generally initiated separately in first marriages. The complexity of the adjustment requirements may contribute to making remarriages more unstable than first marriages. When children are involved, adjustment to remarriage is in part eased or complicated by the relationship with the children's other parent. There is a wide spectrum in the quality of the parents' relationship and in the frequency of face-to-face and over-the-phone contact. We then ask: What happens in terms of the relationship between a person's ex-spouse (the children's other parent) and his or her new spouse (the stepparent)? Relatively little research exists on this interesting and complex topic, so I have borrowed qualitative data from my files, beginning with a married mother:

We don't socialize. It's strictly business for the children's sake. I didn't marry my husband to acquire his ex-wife or her new husband, and my husband certainly does not want to be saddled with my ex-husband and his girlfriend. No. These relationships are nice on a TV screen but not in real life.

Noncustodial fathers frequently express serious concerns about their ex-spouse's new partner, who has become their children's stepparent. They are worried about the way the new stepfather treats the children, the example he provides, as well as the potential for sexual abuse:

My ex-wife's husband is a burden to me in a way [he is an alcoholic]. I told my wife, my ex-wife, that she's got to be very careful never to let the girls alone with him. She was offended but she got the point. I just don't trust him . . .

For their part, adolescents frequently resent the intrusion of additional authority figures in their lives at a time when they may be seeking autonomy from their family. In the autobiographies, I encountered students who wrote about having "hated" their stepparent and who had decided to break up their father's or mother's remarriage and succeeded. They made the stepparent's life so unpleasant that the newly married spouses were soon embroiled in conflict with each other as the adolescent played one against the other. One girl pointed out that she was now very ashamed of her role in the break-up of her mother's remarriage

because it had been my mother's only chance to rebuild her life and I ruined it. Today my mother feels very vulnerable after two failed marriages and is quite lonely. I feel quite guilty and go out of my way to make her happy.

If we pass from the marital to the broader area of kin relations, the mere presence of children may contribute to the better integration of a couple within the web of family relations (Munch, McPherson, and Smith-Lovin, 1997). When the adult or the adolescent becomes a single parent, the effect may be quite different, depending on the age, class, and ethnic status of the families involved. Single parenthood may place a great deal of strain on parents if they are morally opposed to such a state of affairs. They may not benefit as much from their status as grandparents, and may in fact merely inherit another child in the person of their grandchild.

While many children probably bind their parents more closely to their kin, certain children may unwittingly be a divisive force. For example, grandparents may meddle or disagree with their adult offsprings' childrearing practices; these adult children may consequently resent their parents and harbor conflicting feelings, as they do not want to deprive their children of a relationship with grandparents. Or some grandparents indulge the children so much that parents may find themselves in a difficult position. These intergenerational conflicts and bonds beg to be researched, not only in themselves (as they have to some extent in the gerontology literature), but also from the point of view of child effect.

HUMAN INTERACTION

Children contribute to the expansion of adults' interactional repertoire because the parent-child relation, especially when children are very small, is unique. Adults who are nonparents do not generally benefit from this educational experience. As parents and children interact, they do so on a wide range of levels, whether in terms of body language, facial expressions, behavior, or verbal communication. In a unique study, parents reported that children widened their emotional repertoire, from intense rage to joy (Purrington, 1980). For better or worse, parents compared to nonparents partake of a very special mode of human interaction.

Children directly affect their parents' speech pattern: parents use a simpler vocabulary and more repetitions when explaining something to children who are younger or mentally delayed. As children age, parents' verbalizations become more complex because they know that children can understand better. Thus, parents alter their speech patterns as a direct result of changes in the child.

In addition, children may impel their parents to adopt new patterns of interaction. This phenomenon is more evident among immigrant families, particularly when parents do not speak English, as we see in

Chapter 10. In contrast, their children, who are fluent in the language, can explain North American attitudes and habits, as well as patterns of interaction to their parents.

Children may be excellent companions. This might be especially so for younger parents and parents who are relatively isolated socially, or are disabled. Bolton (1983) reported that working-class mothers in England derived more companionable benefits by being with their children than was the case for women who were more educated. The latter found their children's conversations more boring. To the companionable aspect, we can add the close emotional and physical bond generally existing between parents and child, especially between mother and child. Many mothers spontaneously comment on how surprised they were to find breast feeding such a source of emotional gratification. Others mention the pleasurable physiological aspect.

Moreover, children often nurture their parents. They may help them through bad times, may encourage them, may simply comfort them by offering to share a toy with them when small. They may give them physical affection. For instance, in a study meant to test for something else, children between the ages of two and five offered verbal comfort to their mother who, in the course of an experiment, was being angrily confronted by a researcher (Cummings et al., 1989). Even the proximity of a small child may have a soothing effect on parents. It would be interesting to learn more about the effect on parents of receiving physical affection from their children. Physical affection on the part of parents promotes well-being in children. We can assume that the reverse may be equally important.

COMMUNITY

In order to meet their children's needs and to function as a family unit, parents have to reach out to the community more than childless adults. For instance, parents attend church services more than childless adults (Nock, 1998). They have recourse to physicians, schools, special classes, such as ballet or karate, to teams, such as hockey, and to babysitters, to name only a few community contacts. These social interactions can be positive or negative depending on the various contexts. For example, as mentioned earlier, parents who have special-needs children who deviate negatively from the average may have to consult with a vast array of professionals and may even become advocates or activists dedicated to protecting the rights of people with disabilities. But, generally, it is women who serve as mediators of outside services in matters of health. As such, their community life expands with the arrival of children.

Mothers are more likely to be on welfare than childless women. As a result, they must conform to the demands of welfare agencies and personnel who basically control their lives. Social workers and clerks scrutinize mothers' personal lives and mothers, in turn, have to accept the fact that "their family's boundaries will need to become highly permeable" (Rubin and Quinn-Curan, 1983:89). In other words, as the double result of being poor and having children, these women's family lives suffer the intrusion of nonrelated persons. Single mothers also learn coping mechanisms that allow them a measure of freedom and the ability to earn money from employment they do not report and to receive informal support from their child's father without letting social workers know (Edin and Lein, 1997).

It also seems that children increase parents' contact with and help from kin and friends, although small children may reduce their mother's leisure social contacts. But later on, children act as a resource in terms of augmenting the number of friends the family, as a sum of persons, has. Parents may become acquainted with peers' parents. As adults, children cohabit or marry: thus, two families become indirectly related to each other. It would also be important to know whether parents' social networks are more or less positive and supportive than those of childless persons. For instance, do the requisites of parenting lead adults to find their social interaction less fulfilling? Or more so?

As we will see in Chapter 6, parents of delinquents often experience problems with neighbors, friends, and even relatives as a result of their children's behaviors or, yet, are blamed by them, which leads to a distancing. Others place their relationships on hold because they feel that they cannot confide in anyone. Children with disabilities or serious illnesses may also interfere with their parents' opportunities to form and maintain leisure activities that are social in nature. The care required by such children places time and space constraints on parents. We have also mentioned earlier the fact that parents have to reach out to teachers and other professionals. Such official interactions have the potential of being either rewarding or detrimental. The latter outcome may be more likely when the child is deviant. Unfortunately, we possess relatively little information on these research questions.

PARENTAL PERSONALITY

What effect do children have on their parents' adult development? How children impact on their parents' personalities certainly depends, in great part, not only on the child's age and sex, but on parents' stage in the life cycle. Young parents whose personalities may not be as stabilized as would be the case were they much older might be significantly more changed by having children and might be particularly responsive to certain types of children. The entire field of adult development would be a rich laboratory for the study of child effect.

For instance, earlier studies in the 1960s and 1970s by Cummings (1976) and Cummings et al. (1966) found that having a child with an abnormal development was a psychologically stressful situation that resulted in somewhat different personality profiles for the parents involved. Furthermore, mothers and fathers seemed to be affected differently. Thus, the question of the effect that different types of children exert on their parents' own psychological life is a valid one and certainly needs further exploration. For instance, worry and anxiety over their children is, after financial matters, the cost that people mention most often about having children. This being the case, one can only ask what the consequences are in terms of personality development among parents.

The responsibilities of parenting frequently exert a tremendous "pull" toward maturation among young people. Having to take care of a helpless child and being faced with added financial constraints may force parents to mature earlier in *some* aspects of their personalities than nonparents. At the same time, particularly for women, becoming a parent at a very young age may foreclose personality development, especially perhaps when parents are cut off from educational avenues and face employment barriers as a result.

Child effect on parental personality is a theme that recurs, directly or indirectly, in subsequent chapters. Indeed, having children whose behavior deviates from the expected average can be presumed to exert a strong impact on parents' adult development. However, one should not err in the direction of a simplistic causality model. As seen in Chapter 2, child effect on parents' personality will certainly depend on these adults' own personal resilience or vulnerabilities. Parents with strong personalities (this may involve negative as well as positive aspects) may be totally unaffected by child effect in this domain, particularly when they have a highly developed sense of self. Furthermore, what may appear as child effect may actually be a result of genes shared by both parents and children, a topic further discussed in Chapter 12.

ATTITUDES, VALUES, AND BELIEFS

Parents transmit their attitudes and beliefs to their children by the example of their own behavior, by direct teaching, and by acceptance or rejection of their children's behavior (Grusec, Goodnow, and Kuczynski, 2000). But while parents thus fulfill their socialization role, their offspring will have, at the very least, an indirect influence on their parents' values. Parents frequently point out that the arrival of their first child gave them an entirely new perspective on life:

- "I became more responsible. I now have a family to support and it is no longer me on my own."
- "Before, I used to not mind what went on the television set but now I do mind. I have become much more conservative because I know that these programs can affect my children."
- "I have always been in favor of free sex but now that my daughters are growing up it's a different matter. I simply don't see it the same way."
- "When I was younger I never cared much for money or material possessions but now that I have children I need these for them. I have become much more materialistic."
- "As a student, I did drugs but as a parent I am strictly against them. I no longer see anything positive in them."

These few comments made by adults during casual conversations point to an evolution in their value system as a result of their parental role and as a result of the age or even the sex of their children. The simple fact of having become a parent has an impact because a new perspective on life emerges. Parenting is a role that places demands on adults' performance. Some of these changes might have occurred because of age rather than being a parent. But it is reasonable to assume that being a parent is responsible at least in part for these changes. Although there is some literature comparing childless couples with parent couples, the issue of value change/stability as related to parental role (and child characteristics) has not been addressed.

Longitudinal studies of a group of new parents with a group of nonparents of the same age would be a first step in order to see which values change over time for both groups and which values change only for one of the two types of couples. It is quite possible that parents as opposed to childless adults of the same age held different values to begin with. Thus, we need to control for the possibility that people who choose to become parents have at the outset different values than people who prefer to postpone parenting and than those who remain childless.

The presence of maturing adolescents and young adults who hold different values may be a catalytic factor: parents may become more conservative or more liberal. For instance, they may be presented with the more environmentally conscious views of their youngsters and their values may evolve in this direction. During adolescent and adult years, a great deal of give-and-take occurs between parents and children. And, of course, the children's influence may be even greater if they become highly educated, successful, or, in the case of immigrant parents, integrated into the new society.

One important area is parental gender-role orientation. Here as well, the entire literature has focused on the development of children's gender-typing and gender-role orientation via the process of socialization, especially within the context of the family. It is possible that simply becoming a parent affects one's gender-role ideology. For instance, we know that the household division of labor becomes less egalitarian and more gender typed after the arrival of a first child. We would need to know if this change is accompanied by one at the value level. The cause and effect is not clear: it is possible that people who decide not to have children are less gender typed. But the possibility still exists that becoming a parent renders one more traditional in terms of gender roles.

Ganong and Coleman (1987) compared parents with sons only, daughters only, and families with an equal number of sons and daughters. They found that parents of sons were more gender typed than parents of daughters. Specifically, fathers with sons were significantly more masculine in attitudes than those who had only daughters, while mothers with sons were more feminine than those with daughters only. The authors propose that, since sons are more highly valued than daughters in our society, "then it is logical that parents would invest more in socializing them into" appropriate gender roles. "Sons have more to lose than daughters if sex role socialization is incomplete or inadequate, and parents, similarly, have more at stake" (Ganong and Coleman, 1987:280). Consequently, parents of sons may try harder at providing an appropriate example in their own behavior and may, as a result, become more gender typed themselves.

LIFE PLANS

Another aspect of parents' lives affected by the presence of children is their plans for the future. These plans may refer to material resources, such as the desire of young couples who start a family to own a house. They can refer to their own career development, as when a woman decides against pursuing a doctorate upon learning that she is pregnant. Or when a parent consciously decides to build his or her career in a certain geographic area to provide children with residential stability.

It would be interesting to know whether childless couples plan their future less carefully and less ahead of time than do parents. Childless persons can perhaps better afford not to plan ahead too carefully as they have more discretionary income and opportunities. Their time is more free and so are their movements. They may wish to leave certain things to chance and be more receptive to opportunities. Yet one can also assume that they can plan ahead, say for an early retirement, more precisely than couples with children. It is possible that childless couples are better able to predict their future and to plan for the outcome accordingly. They have fewer "hazards" to encounter in the form of childhood illnesses, disabilities, educational expenses, and young adults who remain home longer than antici- pated. Children, in the long term, represent unpredictable factors. They do not always leave home when desired, do not complete their education "on time," do not find a job as expected, or fail to marry and even to produce grandchildren! Thus, children can delay adults' plans and even wipe them out entirely.

Although the possibilities raised in the three preceding paragraphs seem logical, it is surprising that they are not tested empirically. What expectations for the future do childless couples compared to parents have? Moreover, if there are differences, how do important sociological variables such as social class and ethnicity intervene to create additional differences or simply attenuate potential ones?

FEELINGS OF CONTROL OVER ONE'S LIFE

It could be argued that, in the old days, when offspring constituted an important economic resource and fecundity was a source of pride, children added to adults' sense of control over their lives—and per- haps of control over life and others in general. The same argument could apply in societies that are still largely agrarian. However, today, the unpredictability of a postmodern child's life may represent an element of instability and of insecurity for parents. Parents are at the mercy of an array of professionals—from pediatricians, ortho- dontists, child care workers, teachers—not to omit the demands made on them by their children, as well as by their children's friends. (Sub- sequent chapters are devoted to these issues.)

Thus, parents have to structure their schedule and have to restruc- ture their own needs (or become burdened by guilt feelings if they do not do so) for the very survival of their infants and, later on, to meet the requisites of a child's development in an educationally demand- ing society. What effect do these requirements have in terms of feel- ings of control over one's life? Studies of chronically ill children, for instance, have well illustrated how such requisites can place parents in a straitjacket (McKeever, 1992). Yet, in our society, one does not need to have a chronically ill child to feel squeezed by the demands of the experts and semi-experts who care and serve our children. An example will illustrate the point:

> A dentist requests that his young patients be checked and re-ceive a fluoride treatment four times a year. The mother has two sons, one of whom already has to see an orthodontist several times yearly; both sons are driven to hockey and football prac-tices weekly. In addition, the mother visits an assortment of dentists and doctors. She feels harassed by all these health re-quirements. She explains that her sons do not have cavities, have good oral hygiene, and two visits a year would suffice. The dentist becomes agitated and points out to her that "you are jeopardizing your sons' dental care." The mother leaves, "not knowing whether I should laugh or cry. If I listened to all of my sons' dentists and physicians and then mine, I would be in the taxi-driving industry. On top of it all, I am supposed to feel guilty. They all seem to think that *their* own little narrow spe-cialty deserves my unswerving priority. They're so myopic. At least, if I were neglecting my children, they might have a right to complain!" At that point, her voice has reached a high pitch: she definitely feels externally controlled.

CONCLUSIONS

Children can affect their parents in a wide spectrum of situations. Some of this effect is indirect, as is well illustrated in the vignettes mentioned in this chapter. We have always taken for granted that chil-dren, by the very nature of infant helplessness, do bring necessary changes to parents' lives. Yet, because of the "naturalness" of this situ-ation, we have failed to study it adequately. In the case of older chil-dren, we have failed to study it at all. When something is taken for granted, or is considered normal, it is often obliterated from our con-sciousness. What is socially constructed as obvious rarely becomes a topic for research.

Moreover, the foregoing sections clearly illustrate that parents can be affected by their children in many more areas or ways than previ-ously presented in the scientific literature and in the mass media.

Again, this oversight may stem from the apparent naturalness of the situation. In addition, the entire realm of possibilities in these respects has not been fully exhausted, and more could be added to this subject by other researchers.

It is taken for granted that *parents* affect their children rather than vice versa; it is also taken for granted that parents have to take care of their children. Past research and discussions have omitted the distinction between effects that are positive and negative for parents in various areas of their lives. In fact, as well illustrated in Chapter 5, it is not generally considered socially proper for parents to admit that they have problems with their children or that their children are affecting them negatively. Many parents, because of this ideology, do not even dare to admit this negative effect to themselves.

This chapter has not generally offered a life span approach. An absence of longitudinal research in this field indicates that we have been unable to look at all areas of parental lives to see how child effect can vary over time. In other words, the *development* or evolution of child effect as both parents and children age could not be presented. Thus, future researchers might want to explore the effect of children on parental health as children age and compare a group of initially very young parents with a group of late-timing parents. This technique would allow for the simultaneous control of the respective aging processes of parents and children. Similarly, one might be interested in discovering how children affect their parents' self-esteem and feelings of control over their lives as both children and parents age. These are only two examples of questions that could be studied from a life span perspective.

It is important to specify the areas of parental lives that can be subject to child effect (positive or negative) because it is logical to assume that the "goodness of fit" between having children and being an adult in this society differs from area to area of life. For instance, there may be a better contextual fit between parents' lifestyle and children's needs than between parents' employment, sexual life, health, and children's needs. Or, to be even more specific, the goodness of fit may be more deficient for some of the areas of parental lives depending on the type of child involved, the type of parents, and the adequacy of the social response.

Chapter 5

Children with Behavioral
and Emotional Problems

Research has shown that conflictual interactions between parents and young children occur 1.5 to 3.5 times an hour (Dix, 1991). Over thirty years ago, Minton, Kagan, and Levine (1971) found that mothers of two- to three-year-olds issued a command or disapproved every third minute. These studies indicate that even normal children in our society exhibit difficult behaviors, at least occasionally. Therefore, at times, only a thin line separates the average child from the difficult one, and we truly do not know how many children with behavioral problems exist. Hence, although the focus of this chapter is on children with true behavioral and emotional problems, professionals and parents alike who come into contact with average children can still benefit from the discussion.

WHAT ARE BEHAVIORAL PROBLEMS?

The definition of what constitutes behavioral problems, at times called conduct disorders, is complex (Earls, 1994). In a nutshell, these children are very difficult. They engage in some or many aversive acts regularly and persistently, as a way of life, so to speak. Often, but not always, the pattern begins at an early age and, for many children, is chronic thereafter. Aggressiveness is a good example of a problem that is fairly persistent, unless an intervention occurs at the outset.

The first category of behavioral problems falls under the rubric of aggressiveness. Those problems consist of overtly hostile acts such as fighting, hitting, bullying, name calling, and taunting. The second category includes disobedience, refusal to comply, and resistance to requests. A new term has been recently coined for openly defiant behavior: the oppositional-defiant disorder. The third category encompasses other aversive acts such as unwarranted crying, interruptions, sharp and immediate demands that are impossible to meet, and repeated temper tantrums. Fourth, the attention deficit and hyperactivity disorder (ADHD) is a related entity and is characterized by high physical activity and fidgeting, a short attention span, impulsivity, and a low level of self-control. Hyperactivity is often encountered with other conduct disorders; for instance, more than 65 percent of hyperactive children are also aggressive (Barkley, 1997).

Fifth, attention-seeking behaviors fall in any one of the above categories: some of these children can be oppositional or have temper tantrums to get attention. What they seek is *any* kind of attention, whether positive or negative. This means that a reprimand or a punishment is often self-defeating because it simply gives the child what he or she wanted, namely attention. For instance, one ten-year-old girl explains to her mother her bad behavior at school: "When I act like the other children, the teacher doesn't pay attention to me." Such children simply cannot tolerate going unnoticed. A last category to be mentioned is more covert and involves dishonesty: lying, cheating, and stealing. The child generally engages in these acts behind everyone's back. Some children shoplift as a "stage," for instance, while others steal and lie as a way of life, often from an early age. In order to remain focused, we will not expand this discussion to include behaviors that are pathological, such as firesetting, cruelty to animals, sexual deviances, and children/adolescents who are psychopathic and have absolutely no conscience.

WHAT CAUSES BEHAVIORAL PROBLEMS?

There certainly are genetic influences in a good proportion of the cases, but they have yet to be determined (Eley, Lichtenstein, and Stevenson, 1999). More important, conduct disorders are specific to the culture in which they appear (Braungart-Rieker et al., 1995): different types of societies produce different sets of behavior problems. In some societies, conduct disorders are absent or extremely rare.

Environmental Causes in Behavioral Problems

The most succinct way of explaining the etiology of behavioral problems is to say that children are born with certain predispositions for negative behaviors. Most of these predispositions are fairly mild in the sense that a positive home and school environment generally "erases" them (O'Connor et al., 1998). Other children have stronger predispositions and, once again, the environment may be able to counteract them, particularly so in societies where few opportunities are given to children to follow bad examples or to learn antisocial behaviors. However, with exceptional children who have very strong negative predispositions, a good environment does not always "win."

For instance, it is difficult for a child predisposed to aggressiveness and sensation seeking to activate related behaviors in a well-regulated and monitoring family (Bates et al., 1998) or in a society devoid of violent television programs and similar video games. Such a child receives a good start in life. But if the child's predispositions are strong, as he or she ages and becomes more independent, the child can choose an environment that suits his or her temperament better— that is, if he or she lives in a society such as ours that provides a range of environments, from positive to negative. The early family environmental influences then diminish (Kendler, 1995). However, if the advantages the child has gained within the family persist, he or she may select a prosocial environment (Collins et al., 2000). In turn, this environment, like the family, guides him or her toward functional behaviors (Simons et al., 1998). The person then retains the advantages of the earlier family environment.

Longitudinal research in New Zealand indicates that most adolescents who exhibit *several* behavioral problems (early onset of sexual activity, substance use and abuse, police contact, mood disorders) come from seriously disadvantaged and dysfunctional families, even though 13 percent of all children from such backgrounds are problem free (Fergusson, Horwood, and Lynskey, 1994). For children reared in advantaged homes (economically and emotionally), only one out of 400 to 500 becomes a multiproblem adolescent, and 80 percent are totally problem free. Such studies seem to point to a certain level of genetic inheritance between parents and children that is then aggravated or entirely ameliorated by the environment provided by the parents, neighborhood, and schools. Thus, whatever genetic inheritance exists in behavioral problems is facilitated by the environment (Bohman, 1996).

Conduct disorders find a wide range of possibilities for actualization in large and heterogeneous societies such as ours, where social change is rapid, values differ, temptations are numerous, and social control is weak. Older persons are correct when they point out that, in their days, children were far easier to raise than they now are because children's social and cultural environment has changed. Several elements currently combine to prevent children who may be genetically at risk from getting the dosage of *structure,* supervision, stability, and calm that they need to mature normally. These same elements also prevent the actualization of positive tendencies that other children have inherited. In other words, *in our type of society, even children who have no dysfunctional predispositions are provided with opportunities to learn to be difficult.*

First, mass media products and programming of dubious value that contain foul language, violence, too much sex, materialistic goals, and questionable behaviors constitute an important role model for children. So do violent video games: they may serve as a training ground for antisocial behavior and, at the extreme, killing. In addition, there is less parental or adult presence at home to structure children's lives: parents work long hours and many are single. Parents now spend ten fewer hours a week with their children than just two decades ago (Hofferth et al., 1998). Neighborhoods are no longer effective communities, hence there is *inadequate collective adult supervision.* No one ensures that children and adolescents behave properly in public places. Religion has become less important as a life-structuring element and agency of social control. Fewer family rituals anchor children and youth to a regulating calendar of life events. Classrooms are not sufficiently structured, are replete with distractions, and are not effective, whether for learning or for discipline. All in all, today's children lead a hectic life, individually receive less adult attention, and are more easily influenced by the media and equally unsupervised peers than in the past.

Considering all these elements, it may not be surprising that the incidence of various forms of conduct disorders has by all accounts increased (Garbarino, 1999). *Our society, especially for some groups, may present too many opportunities for the emergence of behavioral problems and too few opportunities for the optimal development of children's abilities and prosocial traits.* Conduct disorders, as well as depression and anxiety, may well be the price parents and children pay for rapid and unplanned social change, and a consequent lack of what James Coleman has called a functional community (Coleman and Hoffer, 1987).

Faulty Information Processing

> My only brother is 16 and there is no relationship between us. In fact, I wish he didn't exist. From the time he was very, very small he had temper tantrums, was destructive, got into fights, you name it. My mom would ask him gently (my parents were ever so patient) to do something and he would turn around and do the contrary. Same at school. He can be charming once in a while if he wants something. He is simply a predator. . . . He has ruined my parents' lives and he just doesn't see it this way. He always complains that they don't give him enough. . . . He simply does not think normally. He twists around everything my parents say to prove that he is right and they're wrong. It really makes you sick. He'd need to be trained to think like a person but that's too much to ask of him. Therapists have tried but given up and dash[ed] my parents' hopes. . . . I do my utmost so that my parents have at least one child to hold on to so that they feel that it is worth it being a parent. . . . I worry about having children: suppose one would be like my brother? I know that I couldn't be as kind as my parents have been because I have seen how destructive another young human being can be. I would never accept being so hurt or mistreated.

This student's observations illustrate what researchers have found: aggressive children are often biased in the way they process information. This deficit can be observed in children as young as four to seven years of age (Webster-Stratton and Lindsay, 1999). Difficult children are difficult in part because their perceptions and cognitions are faulty, including the ones they maintain concerning their parents and other authority figures. In other words, these children's thinking processes are often quite different from those of average children. They develop rationales or excuses for their misbehaviors and tend to judge normative children as abnormal, stupid, and "losers."

In turn, their problematic behaviors and the consequences that flow from them reinforce and heighten the level of misconceptions in the youngsters' mentality. Indeed, they are faced with negative social reactions from adults and peers in the form of staring, punishment, reasonings, and even banishment. But they cannot appreciate, accept, or even learn anything from these reactions because they interpret them as a sign that *they* are being unfairly treated and that the world is against them (see Baumeister, 1999; Straub, 1999). It is akin to a case of paranoia. In contrast, prosocial adolescents are more likely to endorse values and motives consistent with conformity to interactional rules and are far less likely to attribute hostile intent (Nelson and Crick, 1999).

On the basis of such results, Bates (1987:1132) has reasoned that infants and children who are difficult may learn less about their parents' attitudes and feelings than average children. They may have a selective attention that orients them to ignore their parents and to focus on other areas of interest to them, such as delinquent peers and activities. Similar attention biases have been observed in adults who suffer from emotional problems (MacLeod, Mathews, and Tata, 1986). Difficult children may be less able or willing than others to learn social cues and to "read" other people, perhaps due to high levels of impulsivity and disagreeableness. This deficit in turn contributes to friction between child and parents, further reinforcing the negative child behaviors (Pepler and Slaby, 1994:35). Moreover, being less prosocial, difficult children may identify less with their prosocial parents and reject them as role models. Such children are far more difficult to raise because they develop a mentality that sustains their negative behaviors.

Disruption of Parenting: The Interactional Perspective

In some families, conduct disorders emerge because parents' problems, lack of skills, or even childrearing philosophies prevent them from adopting suitable socialization practices. Then, as children's conduct disorders become more established, the severity and the rate of such behaviors increase. (Patterson already reported in 1982 that difficult boys engage in aversive-coercive behaviors with their mothers at the rate of 0.75 time per minute, compared to 0.31 for average boys.) Attempts to control these behaviors often result in an escalation of parent-child adversity: the more parents try to reason out or yet coerce the child into behaving, the more the child misbehaves. It can be "total war." In extreme forms of parenting breakdown, the child controls the house. Thus, while adults' inappropriate parenting skills contribute to a child's conduct disorder in some families, as the child gains the upper hand, he or she causes a further disruption of parenting practices, and perhaps even of the marital relationship: "The child facilitates the disruption of its own environment by eliciting maladaptive parental behavior, or increasing the strain on a marginally good marriage" (Earls, 1994:316).

Patterson, Bank, and Stoolmiller (1990) show that, when a child has an extreme antisocial score on personality tests in grade four, parenting practices are much more disrupted when the same child is assessed again in grade six, compared to a child who had been more prosocial in grade four. They suggest that, in any environment, the person who is the most coercive has control of the situation: in these families, it is the children who are the most coercive and therefore control the house. Families with disruptive children are marked by conflictual mutuality between mother and child (Johnston and Pelham, 1990). Although the mother usually prevails with normative children, with difficult boys in particular, it is the child who wins. Hence a role reversal occurs and the parent-child relationship becomes dysfunctional: child socialization fails.

In the long run, many mothers of difficult children get used to the situation: *they become desensitized to misbehavior* and accept it as normal. They are often less able than mothers of nonproblematic children to distinguish misbehavior from regular behavior. This also means that they will not be able to regulate their child's bad behavior because they no longer see it as such. For instance, when visiting relatives, they may let their children "run wild." Not only are they very tired but they no longer have any idea how a well-behaved child should act. Thus, although poor parenting practices have been influenced by difficult child behaviors, these parents' actions and failures to act will contribute to children's subsequent negative behaviors (Collins et al., 2000).

Children who are hostile, conflictual, and even aggressive impair a family's ability to solve problems that are relevant to its good functioning (Forgatch, 1989). Parents often become so distraught by their children's difficult, demanding, and manipulative behaviors that they "can't think straight." At any rate, any attempt to solve a problem is shot down by the child. In turn, this type of interactional deficit contributes to reinforcing adolescent maladjustment. "Some children ultimately 'win' when they perform in such a way as to stop virtually all parental behaviors aimed at changing the misbehavior" (Loeber and Stouthamer-Loeber, 1986:110). It is quite understandable, therefore, if studies find that children with behavior problems occasion far more stress for their parents than do children with physical disabilities (Floyd and Gallagher, 1997). Disabled children are far more predictable and often well intentioned. Single mothers are easy victims of children's lack of compliance and misbehavior (Olson and Banyard, 1993): they are isolated numerically and the children's aversive temperament may be far stronger than theirs.

THE EFFECT ON MOTHERS

Mothers have been studied more extensively than fathers in their interactions with children, in part because they are more available at home to be studied, as well as more interested in such projects. The main reason, however, is that ideologies posit that mothers are a more important causative agent in child development. However, in 1980, Gerald Patterson had already perspicaciously remarked that, "The role of mother is structured in such a manner as to almost guarantee higher rates of aversive events than does the role of the father" (Patterson, 1980:10). Coercive boys actually target their mothers rather than their fathers as victims of conflict, perhaps because mothers "are more likely to reinforce coercive attacks" (Patterson, Reid, and Dishion, 1992:49). That is, mothers tend to respond to their children and often attempt to soothe them or calm them. This provides an opening for a coercive child to intensify his or her bad behavior.

Another likely effect of difficult child behavior, at least on some mothers, is an increasing tendency on their part to issue directives, commands, and threats in a desperate effort to reduce negative behavior (Patterson, 1980). But this is usually to no avail because, although reprimands do lower negative child behavior in normative children, they do not generally affect the behavior of problem children. Quite the opposite often occurs, and children may simply increase the frequency and severity of their coercive and oppositional episodes. Not surprisingly, maternal satisfaction correlates with child compliance: the mother-child interaction is less conflictual when a child is cooperative. A cooperative child is more easily socialized and provides mothers with greater interpersonal and parental rewards.

Fathers engage more in play interactions with their children; consequently, they attract less negative behavior from their difficult offspring than the mother, who may be solely responsible for enforcing rules. One of the results is that fathers may not sympathize with the child's mother when she complains about the misbehavior. This increases the mother's isolation and encourages children to keep targeting her. Unlike mothers, fathers of difficult children are not significantly more stressed than fathers of average children. In other words, mothers of difficult children are more stressed but fathers are not. As Patterson (1982:24) dryly notes, "this leads to the conclusion that the role label most appropriate for fathers might be that of 'guest!' " Overall, fathers are less affected by the quality of their relationship with their children (Umberson et al., 1996).

Many people believe that mothers of difficult children provoke them by "hovering" over them, ready to "pounce" at the slightest misbehavior. This "theory" continues, stating that children then react to their mother's "overbearing" or yet "overprotective" behavior by acting up. It's as if "the mother had asked for it." Undoubtedly, this happens occasionally, but, overall, this maternal portrayal could not be farther from the truth. Mothers of difficult children actually become afraid of disciplining or even contradicting the child. They know that if they scold, *they* will suffer, not the child: "Mothers tend not to provide an aversive antecedent for these chains of behaviors and desperately try to avoid conflict with a 'practiced aggressor' " (Patterson, 1982:32-33). Often mothers try to avoid their difficult children completely, which, of course, leaves them open to the opposite criticism: they are not involved enough or do not "care." In fact, a mother's positive behavior toward a usually disruptive boy may even encourage the latter to take advantage of her (Lavigueur, Tremblay, and Saucier, 1995). Because of their biased thinking, a nice maternal gesture is often interpreted to mean that the mother is weak and is to be taken advantage of. As we can see, these research results, combined with results presented later concerning emotional problems, certainly fly in the face of many professional constructions of how most mothers behave and allegedly cause their children's negative actions and reactions.

CHILDREN WITH EMOTIONAL PROBLEMS

Children who suffer from emotional problems essentially fall into two categories. First, the serious lifelong disorders, such as autism, schizophrenia, and severe depression affect few small children. Except for autism, mental illnesses such as bipolar depression and schizophrenia tend to appear after childhood. Schizophrenia often begins in mid-adolescence or early adulthood. It actually manifests itself earlier among males than females. Bipolar disorder, formerly called manic depression, rarely strikes before a person reaches young adulthood (APA, 1994). However, even young children can suffer from depression. Depression may also occur for the first time late in the life course, even in old age.

Second, we have the category of young children and adolescents who suffer from emotional problems other than those just mentioned. They may suffer from some form of depression, anxiety, irrational fears, or they may be extremely shy and withdrawn, while others are hyperactive. Some are more or less paralyzed by a low self-concept. Most of these problems, except for hyperactivity, which we have covered under behavioral problems, are called "internalizing," and are difficult to diagnose. These children's external behavior is generally prosocial; but they internalize their own fears, anxieties, and sadness. They generally, although not always, direct their problems against themselves rather than against others. They are very unhappy and troubled but they do not, as a rule, disturb those around them.

Most of these children fall through the cracks because neither parents nor teachers notice them, at least not until adolescence. They are generally not very demanding and their good behavior does not attract attention. Their parents are often concerned that they do not laugh and play enough or do not have friends. Most parents try to compensate by spending more time with the child or trying to provide activities to help socialize him or her. Many other parents, particularly those who are less aware of the existence of emotional problems among children, simply accept the child and think that he or she is going through a phase or is simply "quiet." Most children who suffer from mild to moderate emotional problems outgrow these problems, while for others they are the precursors of more serious emotional and even behavioral problems that appear late in adolescence and early adulthood.

Solid research on parents of emotionally disturbed children exists only for severe problems and tends to focus on *older children* and their parents. Thus, the emphasis in this chapter is on schizophrenia and depression. Strong evidence supports that psychotic emotional problems, such as bipolar disorder and schizophrenia, run in families, not necessarily due to cultural transmission or childrearing practices, but mainly due to genetic factors. However, a cautionary note is necessary here: the majority of people suffering from either schizophrenia or bipolar disorder (or autism, for that matter) come from families where neither parent is afflicted with the disease. Such an observation indicates that most mental illnesses are polygenic, that is, they require the presence of several genes together, a configuration that is not easily transmitted in its entirety. The more genetically predisposed a person is for an emotional problem, "the less environmental stress is required to produce developmental deviations" (Wachs, 1992:119). In other words, the stronger the abnormal genetic predisposition, the more likely it is that people develop an illness spontaneously, "whereas other patients in whom there is a smaller and unspecific constitutional predisposition develop their illness as a result of obvious stress" (McGuffin and Katz, 1993:187). It follows that, even in a normal family with loving parents, a person with a strong genetic predisposition will develop schizophrenia or bipolar disorder. Others who have a lesser predisposition may need very detrimental living conditions or high levels of stress to become so severely disturbed.

The next sections explain how schizophrenia and severe depression originate as well as how they are transmitted from parents to children, if at all. These sections are clinical but they are relevant to our focus: they clearly indicate that parents are generally not responsible, as is too often believed, for the development of their children's serious emotional problems.

Schizophrenia

Psychotic problems are often difficult to diagnose in childhood because they contribute to delayed cognitive development, and this makes it a complex task to differentiate psychoses from cognitive disabilities. Schizophrenia in preadolescents is rare. When it does occur, it resembles the adult description. Schizophrenia is now accepted as a disease of the brain that causes dysfunctional behaviors and is characterized by various degrees of distancing or withdrawal from reality. Interpersonal difficulties are also present. The more severe forms involve hallucinations (hearing voices and seeing things), loss of contact with one's bodily needs and external reality, inability to care for oneself, delusions, and rigid bodily mannerisms. Untreated adults with chronic schizophrenia stand out in a crowd. They constitute a proportion of the older street people, wandering about because they have no place to go to which they can adapt. They are true social isolates, shrouded in their delusions, clothed in malodorous rags, and shunned by all.

Because schizophrenia is such a serious illness, one would expect that parents with schizophrenia would "produce" severe disorders in their children. Yet this is not necessarily the case. In order to ground this discussion, we first must refer to other etiological facts. As mentioned, schizophrenia and its precursors tend to appear quite early in life, particularly in males (Burke et al., 1990). Because it is such a debilitating illness, males with schizophrenia seldom marry and have children (Saugstad, 1989). This selection process contributes to reducing the prevalence of the disease in the population. However, a majority of women with schizophrenia still marry, although at a lower rate than other women. Currently, women who suffer from one of the serious mental illnesses are as likely to have children as other women (Apfel and Handel, 1993), and as many as 60 percent of their pregnancies may be unplanned (Forcier, 1990).

Two main reasons emerge for this difference in the marriage and reproductive rates between men and women with schizophrenia. First, the disorder appears a few years later in the lives of females than males, and this allows women to marry and/or to bear children before noticeable symptoms appear. Second, a woman who suffers from a mild case of schizophrenia may still be considered functional enough to marry, especially if she is attractive, because her social role as a woman and homemaker may shelter her from becoming dysfunctional in other spheres of life where she would be noticed as such. In contrast, a man may not be able to escape attention so easily because he is less likely to be sheltered from scrutiny by his gender role as a chief breadwinner. Third, the prognosis is generally more favorable for women than men: women with schizophrenia respond better to treatment and are more likely to be able to lead a normal life—including having children.

The *lifetime* risk for schizophrenia in the general population is 1 percent, but it increases markedly when close relatives are afflicted by the illness. For instance, the siblings of a person with schizophrenia have a 2 to 9 percent chance of also becoming schizophrenic. Identical twins have a 17 to 60 percent concordance or similarity in this respect. Children with either one or two parents with schizophrenia respectively have a 7 to 13 percent risk and a 40 to 50 percent risk (Gottesman, 1991). Schizophrenia that begins in childhood is probably more genetically determined than when the illness originates later in life (Asarnow, 1994). For instance, preliminary analyses indicate a high rate of schizophrenia among family members of children with early-onset schizophrenia (Pulver et al., 1990). Studies of twins with an early onset find concordance rates of up to 88 percent for identical twins and 23 percent for fraternal twins (Kallman and Roth, 1986).

Heston had already shown in 1966 that children of mothers with schizophrenia who are adopted away from their biological family still retained a 13 percent risk of developing schizophrenia as adults, even though their adoptive family environment was normal. If genes played no role, such children would have a 1 percent rate of affliction. Gottesman (1991) has summarized the results of four studies of children whose parents had both been schizophrenic: about 50 percent of the offspring developed schizophrenia, 25 percent had other psychiatric problems, and another 25 percent were unaffected. These statistics are startling if we consider that, despite a very high familial loading and the environmental risks associated with living in a household burdened by double schizophrenia, one fourth of the children were unscathed. Other studies also support the fact that life with a parent who has schizophrenia does not unavoidably lead to the same outcome among children. However, the more severe the parental illness and the more numerous the psychosocial disadvantages the child encounters, the greater the possibility that the child will develop a negative outcome.

When children are already vulnerable because of a genetic predisposition, living with a disturbed parent increases risk above and beyond their initial predisposition. However, one can presume that, when the other parent is stable and has a supportive relationship with them, the children will be far less vulnerable. Offspring with no immediate observable familial loading who are adopted by parents who later develop schizophrenia also suffer from an increased rate of schizophrenia, but not of a great magnitude. In conclusion, while a poor familial environment by itself rarely results in a serious emotional problem of a psychotic nature, a strong genetic predisposition often does. Moreover, the two combined increase the chances of mental illness (Steinberg and Avenevoli, 2000).

The family environment plays an important role in the guise of stressors caused by poverty, a disadvantaged neighborhood, or dysfunctional parents who lack good parenting skills, and are mentally ill or antisocial. Parents with schizophrenia, or other emotionally disturbed parents for that matter, *present an environmental risk:* the parents' symptoms may interfere with proper parenting, impair the quality of the parent-child relationship, and result in stressful life course transitions such as unemployment, poverty, serious marital discord, divorce, and institutionalization (Rutter and Quinton, 1987).

Depression

The lifetime risk for depression in general, including bipolar disorder, may be as high as 10 to 30 percent, depending on the symptoms included in the definition (Kendler et al., 1992). Serious depression usually occurs later in life and does not generally prevent people from marrying, as is the case for schizophrenia and autism. Thus, depression is genetically reproduced on a larger scale than schizophrenia is. For its part, general depression is more dependent upon environmental stressors than is schizophrenia or manic depression so that, during difficult social and cultural transitions, its lifetime prevalence may rise accordingly, even though the gene pool remains constant (Nigg and Goldsmith, 1994:349).

Bipolar disorder is the serious type and is partly hereditary (Harrington et al., 1993), but the varying definitions of what constitutes this disorder or the number of symptoms included change estimates of heritability. The concordance rate for this illness among adult identical twins is about 65 percent compared with 13 to 20 percent for fraternal twins. It seems that relatives of people with bipolar disorder are themselves at a greater risk *both* for bipolar disorder and simple depression. As with schizophrenia, an early age of onset for depression is related to a higher familial or genetic loading: when parents' depression began early in life, their children are at a higher risk than those of parents whose illness started later (Weissman et al., 1987). Conversely, when depression occurs *without* obvious precipitants, there is a greater chance that other relatives are also affected or will be affected by the disease—not because it is contagious but because the absence of observable, causal stressors implies that the problem is largely genetic.

Simple depression is not considered a psychosis. The genetic influence is more modest and leaves "greater room for working environmental effects" (McGuffin and Katz, 1993:219). Symptoms of simple depression in children include sadness, irritability, poor concentration, loss of interest in usual activities, fatigue, self-pity, as well as thoughts of death or suicide. Contrary to bipolar disorder, simple depression is common among children. It may be infrequently diagnosed because of comorbidity with other problems and because these children are generally cooperative (Angold, 1993).

Depression increases during adolescence (McGee et al., 1992), particularly among girls and women who tend to be overrepresented among depressed persons. However, for younger children, boys are overrepresented in some studies, while the rates are equal in others. Follow-up studies into young adulthood indicate that around 75 percent of those who had schizophrenia during adolescence still have related problems, while about 40 percent of those who suffered from bipolar depression continue to have related difficulties (Cawthron et al., 1994).

For *any* psychiatric disorder, unless a high genetic loading is present, cumulative disadvantage or multiple stressors seem to contribute substantially to the development of mental illness, especially for nonpsychotic illnesses such as reactive depression (Sameroff and Seifer, 1995). Several studies indicate that the *number* of risk factors increases the chance that a child will suffer negative psychological outcomes. Within the family, marital discord, poverty, and poor parenting are some of the main stressors that, if they occur jointly, place children at great risk, both for psychiatric problems and conduct disorders (Garmezy and Masten, 1994). But some of these environmental difficulties, particularly parental conflict, that have been related to children's emotional problems, may in part be explained by a genetic link in two ways. First, parents may contribute to the creation of the familial stressors because of their own negative traits. Second, conflictual parents who are also antisocial may beget genetically at-risk children for whom parents' marital malfunctioning triggers and exacerbates negative predispositions.

Other perhaps equally important environmental adversities are child specific rather than family specific. One can think here of a transition to a new school, the loss of a familiar peer group, peer rejection or abuse, a violent peer culture, poor school performance, and a teacher's maltreatment. Peer abuse, as we see in a subsequent chapter, may be of paramount importance. Often, these adversities are specific to one child in a family and do not affect the other siblings (Beardsall and Dunn, 1992). Children who experience stressors in several domains of their lives, that is, in their family, peer group, and school situation, are at an elevated risk for emotional problems such as depression and anxiety even with little genetic predisposition.

EFFECTS ON THE PARENT-CHILD RELATIONSHIP

Little research has been done on the effect on parents of having a small child or an adolescent who suffers from an emotional problem. Rather, the focus of the literature is on how parents contribute to their children's problems. However, there is a sound but still small body of research describing the deleterious effects on parents of having *adult* children who are psychiatrically ill, especially when the child coresides with the parents, or there is a great deal of contact (Heller, Hsieh, and Rowitz, 1997). Adult children with emotional problems can exert a negative influence on their parents all the way into the parents' senior years (Greenberg, Seltzer, and Greenlay, 1993), as explained by a student in her autobiography:

> My older sister is manic-depressive [bipolar disorder] and it seems to be getting worse. She is ten years older than I am and my parents are constantly worried about her even though she gets excellent medical attention. She still lives at home and rarely holds a job for long and her presence is distressing for all of us. When she's down, which occurs less and less, we fear suicide and when she's up and this seems to be a pattern, she gets herself into all kinds of dangerous situations. She's gone through her bank account, she's hitch-hiked and got raped, she's bought stuff we had to return, she's shoplifted and was arrested, she's had several cases of STDs, she walked down the street one night screaming at the top of her lungs, she's tried all kinds of drugs and freaked out for weeks. . . . My parents are worried to death, worried for now and worried for her future because they know that even if the two of us [she and her brother] keep an eye on her we will never be able to do for her as much as they have done and it has never prevented her from relapsing or getting herself into dangerous situations.

It is normal for parents to supervise their children less as they grow older. One can therefore ask what kinds of strains on the relationship result from continued supervision, especially when it is not accepted by the disturbed adult children. Cook (1988) well illustrated the high level of stress that parents of young adults with schizophrenia experience—feelings of hopelessness and despair. There is still a widely-held assumption, especially in private practice, that parents' handling of the child cause all emotional disorders. Consequently, parents may feel needlessly guilty and frustrated, while adult children may turn against a parent whom they erroneously believe to be the source of their problems—a parent who could otherwise be most helpful.

Cook and colleagues (1990) report that mothers of children with schizophrenia try to deescalate negative interactions, as is often the case with mothers of children with conduct disorders. It is relevant here to mention that mothers of hyperactive children whose symptoms diminish after taking methylphenidate (Ritalin) show corresponding behavioral changes: they became far less controlling as there is a lesser need to be so (Schachar et al., 1987). The same maternal changes have occurred in experiments in which children were trained to behave in a compliant or in an oppositional manner (Brunk and Henggeler, 1984). Adults interacted more with a child who had been trained to be responsive. Researchers have established that the presence of a child with schizophrenia in an experimental situation hinders parents' ability to perform cognitive tasks. Goldstein and colleagues (1992) do not report any communication disturbance among parents of adults with schizophrenia. Finally, Liem (1974) noted that parents of average children and parents of children with schizophrenia do not differ in their behavior when, in an experiment, they are paired with either a normative child or one with schizophrenia. These studies taken together indicate that the emotionally disturbed do influence others' responses to them and contribute to the disruption of relationships and childrearing activities within the family, as is the case for behavioral problems. Another effect of children's emotional problems may be that, when difficulties persist and demands on parents mount, parents may become less interested, less affectionate, and less communicative. As Loeber and Stouthamer-Loeber (1986:54) point out, it is "difficult to love children who make one's life miserable," even though the ill children are not responsible for their actions.

As is also the case for behavior disorders, the impact of a child's emotional problems is more serious for the mother than the father (Cook, 1988). Similarly, the effect of a mentally or physically disabled child is greater on the mother, especially in terms of workload. We would therefore expect that the mother-child relationship will be far more affected than the father-child relationship. Mothers and fathers may adopt different styles of communication and of parenting practices with their emotionally disturbed children. These differences may become more obvious as the child passes into adolescence and young adulthood. These gender-related hypotheses remain to be tested.

CONCLUSIONS

Very little literature exists on how parents are affected when their child suffers from behavioral or emotional problems. The emphasis of the research has typically been on the role that parents play in the development of these problems. We have seen in this chapter that parents may play no role whatsoever, particularly in the development of *serious* disturbances. When parents constitute one of the causes, this is generally because of their own problems, lack of resources, as well as parenting skills. Such parents can only be related to the development of minor, not major, emotional problems and in the reinforcement of behavioral problems. Whatever the etiology, the fact remains that parents, particularly mothers, are very negatively affected by their children's problems. Furthermore, such parents receive little support and, particularly, no sympathy from society, a factor that contributes to increasing negative child effect on them. The social construction of parents as responsible and children as victims precludes sympathy for parents. General ignorance about the role of genes in the etiology of problems further adds to society's aversion toward parents of young and adolescent children who suffer from a variety of problems.

In reality, children would be better served were their parents less blamed for their problems. If parents were helped and supported, they would become more effective in the treatment of their children. At the very least, family life would be less miserable: children who are encouraged to believe that their parents are at fault are simply given loopholes through which to escape and thus avoid facing their own problems and taking responsibility for their actions. The consequences of parent blaming become even more obvious in Chapter 6, on juvenile delinquency.

Chapter 6

Adolescents, Parents,
and Delinquency

This chapter is closely related to the previous one because behavioral problems generally precede serious delinquency. Furthermore, this chapter continues to highlight the failure of the research establishment to study the impact on parents of child behaviors that are detrimental. Delinquency has a tremendous impact on the economy, society in general, on families, and on the parent-child relationship, especially after a youngster has been arrested. Moreover, when the delinquency degenerates into adult criminality, there must be sad repercussions for aging parents. Unfortunately, these topics are not studied. Few ask: What is the effect on parents of having a delinquent child? Instead, the universal question is: What kinds of parents do juvenile delinquents have? The assumption is that they are "bad." What childrearing practices correlate with delinquency? In other words, where do *parents* go wrong? This is a strange question when you think of it because, after all, it is the *youngsters* who are "going wrong." The research on juvenile delinquency could benefit from a reconstruction of children as social actors, with agency, as well as from interactional and behavior genetics theories (Ambert, 1997).

OVERVIEW

Official delinquency involves an arrest and therefore an awareness on the part of authorities that a minor has committed a crime. Researchers have access to police statistics for arrests, and these come closer to estimating actual levels of delinquency than court statistics for convictions: relatively few delinquents actually come to court and fewer still are convicted. In fact, only a minority of delinquent acts ever come to the attention of the police, a situation revealed through self-reported delinquency which involves researchers giving questionnaires to adolescents in schools, for instance. They are asked to place check marks alongside a list of infractions to indicate which they have committed and if they have ever been arrested for any infraction. This method is also used in research with delinquents who have been arrested to determine what other infractions they have committed in addition to the known crimes.

Delinquency increased spectacularly between 1970 and 1990; it has since decreased in the late 1990s. However, violent crimes committed by children below the age of twelve have become more frequent, or, at the very least, more frequently reported. Thus, violent juvenile delinquency begins at younger ages than in previous decades. Lethal or deadly child and adolescent criminality too often makes the headlines. Therefore, juvenile delinquency has become more lethal through the decades, attracts more media attention, and spreads feelings of fear and insecurity in the population at large, and especially among law-abiding children who frequently worry about their own safety at school or in their neighborhood (Sheley and Wright, 1995).

The phenomenon of violent youth gangs is especially destructive in inner cities and has victims beyond those who are directly violated. Another recent development is that girls are becoming more involved in attacks on other children and are participating in gang activities more than in the past. Although repeat and serious offenders constitute only a minority of all delinquents, they commit over 60 percent of all recorded offenses (Farrington, 1995). Most juvenile delinquents are arrested only once. Common delinquency has no class boundaries (Wright et al., 1999); in contrast, serious repeat delinquency leading to incarceration occurs far more frequently among disadvantaged youth. In this chapter, the focus is on general delinquency, although we occasionally touch on the topic of repeat offenders.

Developmental Pathways

There are at least two developmental pathways to delinquency. Delinquents who start very young and graduate to more serious crimes are, on average, different from delinquents who start in mid to late ado-

lescence. This is referred to as early-onset versus late-onset delinquency (Simons et al., 1994). Early-onset delinquents exhibit more
behavioral problems, are diagnosed more frequently with personality
disorders, and often come from a dysfunctional or pathological family,
or at the very least from a disadvantaged family. They resemble the
children with serious conduct disorders discussed in the previous
chapter. Early-onset delinquency is usually accompanied and pre-
ceded by conduct disorders that began early in life (Caspi and Moffitt,
1991). This dysfunctional behavior has had a long period to build up
and interferes with normal coping (Garbarino, 1999). As a result, it frequently leads to adult criminality and other problems if no intervention
occurs, especially when the neighborhood is criminogenic.

Late-onset delinquents are more varied and some are similar to
those previously described, but they tend to function better in many
respects. They often come from an adequate family and do not as a
rule become recidivists or adult criminals. Their experience with
delinquency is short lived. Among girls, delinquency rarely develops
until adolescence. Girls who become seriously delinquent follow a
pattern similar to boys, with early behavioral problems, but not necessarily early onset of delinquency itself (Silverthorn and Frick,
1999). Girls are more sheltered and supervised; thus, it makes sense
that opportunities for delinquency present themselves at a later age.

Nagin and Land (1993) divide offenders into three categories:
those who do not commit crimes beyond late adolescence, those who
are "high-level chronic" offenders, and those labeled "low-level
chronic" offenders. The "adolescence-limited" offenders begin their
delinquency two years later, on average, and commit far fewer illegal
acts than the other two categories. Nagin, Farrington, and Moffitt
(1995) found that, by adulthood, high-level chronic offenders also
reported having committed more criminal acts that had not come to
the attention of the authorities between the ages fourteen through
thirty-two than the other groups of offenders. By age thirty-two, the
two types of chronic offenders, high and low levels, lived in poorer
areas and conditions, and were "social failures." In contrast, "adolescence-limited" offenders had, by definition, no convictions after
twenty-one, and, by age thirty-two, their employment pattern was
undistinguishable from that of nondelinquents.

Causes of Delinquency

The etiological models not only differentiate the life course development of delinquency, as seen above, but they implicate a multitude of causal variables. The familial environment continues to be emphasized: parents' background, mental states, personality, disciplinary practices, and criminality are scrutinized. Delinquents who commit *serious* crimes and are arrested seem to originate predominantly from a background that combines multiple risk factors: poverty, questionable peers, deprived neighborhood, unstable parenting, low supervision, and even abuse (Farrington, 1995). A disproportionate number of delinquents come from single-parent families, and this finding holds for both black and white, Canadian and American, or even British delinquents. Moreover, serious delinquency disproportionately originates from disadvantaged families, and this finding has also been replicated in several countries (Fergusson, Horwood, and Lynskey, 1994).

One familial factor that researchers emphasize is parental monitoring. Consensus suggests that poorly supervised youngsters are at a greater risk for juvenile delinquency, as well as for other problems such as illicit drug use, early sexual involvement, and school underachievement (Patterson, Reid, and Dishion, 1992). Patterson and Stouthamer-Loeber (1984) found that 21 percent of the nondelinquents in their sample were poorly supervised by their parents, compared to 50 percent of the one-time offenders and 73 percent of the repeat offenders.

Inadequate supervision occurs more frequently in homes where there is marital conflict, or only one parent, and where one or even both parents are emotionally disturbed, use drugs, or have committed crimes. In such households, family processes, including parental example, may be immediate causes of delinquency. However, inadequate supervision may also occur because well-intentioned parents are too busy at work, trust their children too much, or have been discouraged by their children from supervising them (Jang and Smith, 1997). Proper monitoring may be particularly important in inner-city areas with a high rate of criminality. But a lack of supervision can also be quite detrimental in affluent neighborhoods populated by parents who may be too preoccupied with financial and career success and too trusting about their "good" neighborhood.

Although supervision is emphasized, *other* salutary processes may be going on in families that monitor their children properly. These families are probably better organized, may have more stable and perhaps less individualistic parents, and may be more religious. The children may have easier temperaments, and more time is spent on prosocial parent-child interaction than in other families, whether single- or two-parent families, whether rich or poor. The previous two sentences are speculative but they are derived from other aspects of the literature on child development and, as such, seem plausible. Research to test these assumptions is needed.

In neighborhoods with a high level of criminality, concentration of poverty, and gang supremacy, children do not need a dysfunctional family to become aggressive and delinquent (Sampson, 1993). In contrast, communities that are able to control teenage groups, especially gangs, have less delinquency. The classroom and school is included here as part of this community environment. One could perhaps suggest that it is the *street/classroom/neighborhood/media context combined* that often makes children difficult at an early age, thus at high risk for early-onset delinquency. In turn, their behavior is sufficient to disrupt the functioning of their family, including parenting skills. Such children may constantly escape from family influence and control by "hanging around" with their older siblings, cousins, and peers in gangs that take on the role of socialization agents early on in their lives (Hogan and Kitagawa, 1985). Children with vulnerable predispositions such as low self-control may succumb more easily in these environments. The family may play no role whatsoever, whether positive or negative, because the external environment is too powerful.

In many areas, it is adult supervision in general, in the sense of community supervision, that is lacking. The sociologist Robert Sampson (1993) suggests that social disorganization follows when a community is no longer able to maintain *social control* and to supervise teenage peer groups. In Coleman's term (Coleman and Hoffer, 1987), there is no *functional community* of neighbors or relatives who look after the well-being of all the children. Brooks-Gunn and colleagues (1995) suggest that *collective socialization* exists in areas where parents know one another, supervise all their children, and are effective or authoritative parents. In other words, whatever the concept used, child developmentalists' and sociologists' research is currently converging to indicate the importance of a more general form of adult or group supervision as an important element in the prevention of social ills such as precocious sexuality, teen pregnancy, and juvenile delinquency. Parents often can no longer suffice all alone: they need the support of a like-minded community.

Personality Factors

The relationship between family and delinquency also is affected by genetically influenced characteristics (Bohman, 1996). If a parent and a child share genes that lead to low impulse control and a difficult temperament, a long chain of events results: irritable and erratic parenting practices, a conflictual parent-child relationship, poor supervision, the likelihood that the youngster does not do well in school, that he or she is attracted to peers who are in similar circumstances, and is rejected by peers who are more prosocial. Patterson, Reid, and Dishion (1992) have reviewed five areas of research that point to a certain genetic or innate component to antisocial behavior, and therefore *repeated* delinquency (Krueger et al., 1994).

First, many antisocial children do not respond to punishment, while prosocial children generally do: they alter their behavior to avoid it. Second, there seems to be an element of hyperresponsiveness to stimuli, such as seeking excitement and thrills, even dangerous ones. This may also explain why antisocial children have more accidents than other youngsters. The fear of being caught, for instance, adds stimulation and therefore may be an *incentive* rather than an impediment to engaging in delinquent acts. Such persons like living on the edge. A third factor is what is called hyperresponsiveness to exchanges with authority figures, particularly parents: as seen in the previous chapter, such youngsters immediately respond to requests by becoming more difficult, noncompliant, and aggressive. In other words, they seem to derive gratification from *negative* attention. A last factor reviewed by Patterson, Reed, and Dishion (1992) is slow electrodermal activity. That is, reactions on the surface of the skin, such as perspiration, are not as easily produced by antisocial persons as by prosocial persons when they are experimentally subjected to stimuli designed to create excitement or fear. The reason for this is that fear and excitement do not stress but instead stimulate them.

Therefore, while the role of the environment certainly predominates, the data indicate that early-onset and persistent delinquents, as well as adult criminals, may be more genetically predisposed than casual offenders or those who are arrested for delinquency only once or twice. Of course, *genetic predispositions will more readily be actualized in environments that offer criminal opportunities and that block access to legitimate achievement.* Some schools and neighborhoods present few temptations for delinquent behavior and may protect their vulnerable children. When children have no access to drugs, they cannot become addicts; when guns are unavailable, they cannot kill.

Moreover, parents who have a warm, supportive and monitoring relationship with their youngsters act as deterrents to externalizing behaviors, including juvenile delinquency (Bates et al., 1998). Unfortunately, not all parents who are warm and supportive also monitor their children adequately. As soon as the element of supervision is eliminated from the equation, children are at risk, especially if they have low self-control or other negative traits that would benefit from supervision. In contrast, children who naturally possess self-control, are reasonably intelligent, and have a well-balanced personality may not need parental supervision beyond a certain age. If the parent-child relationship is warm, these youngsters are multiply protected against delinquency: by their own characteristics, their attachment to their parents, and by a parent-child relationship that suits their parents' temperament as well as their own.

However, as seen in the previous chapter, not all parents who want to *can* monitor their children. They may try but their youngsters react aversively so that parents may back off in order to maintain a semblance of peace on the home front. Maccoby (1992:235) points out the possibility that "the failure of parents to guide adolescents effectively may stem largely from the adolescents' resistance to being socialized rather than from parental incompetence. . . ." Simons and colleagues (1994:359) add that "rebellious, antisocial children often punish parental efforts to monitor and discipline while reinforcing parental withdrawal and lenience." As mentioned earlier, Patterson (1982) has discussed the possibility that some children may be genetically predisposed to be less responsive to social reinforcers; this pre-disposition would impair parental efforts to socialize and supervise them, especially in low-quality neighborhoods. This predisposition can also prevent parental sanctions or punishments from having any effect at all.

Delinquency and Teen Births

The teen birthrate is very high although it has been declining steadily in the United States, particularly among blacks, in the late 1990s (Ventura et al., 1999); it is still increasing in Canada, however, but the Canadian rates are far lower than the American ones. This topic is brought up here because a proportion of teen mothers and their babies' fathers are actually delinquent or, at the very least, difficult adolescents. For instance, Elster, Ketterlinus, and Lamb (1990) have found that, before having a baby, adolescent mothers had accumu-lated more instances of suspensions, truancy, drug use, and fighting in school than other adolescent girls. More recently, Serbin and col-leagues (1998) reported from Canada that early pregnancy was related to childhood aggressiveness. In other words, a greater proportion of young mothers were very aggressive as children than had been the case for other adolescent girls. It may not be surprising, therefore, to find that their small children are more frequently brought to hospi-tals' emergency rooms because of injuries that suggest both neglect and abuse (Serbin, Peters, and Schwartzman, 1996). One would expect that this type of "delinquent" motherhood is more related to poverty and to familial dysfunction.

For their part, the sociologists Entwisle, Alexander, and Olson (1997:108) are concerned about the potential for the intergenerational transmission of these patterns, including school failure, because "teen parents have had more problems in school than other teenag-ers," and their children could experience adjustment problems. "Par-ents who had school problems themselves may be unable to coach children about how to behave in school," or may be confrontational with teachers—thus giving their own children a poor example. It can be concluded from the totality of the research that teen motherhood is part of a nonnormative syndrome or package for at least a *subgroup* of adolescents who were problematic children long before their pregnancy.

This pattern is actually replicated among the young fathers. Many have a history of childhood aggressiveness and other behavioral difficulties (Capaldi, Crosby, and Stoolmiller, 1996). More have deviant peers than same-age youths who do not become early fathers (Fagot et al., 1998). It is possible that teenage mothers who are delinquent have boyfriends similar to them. One can immediately sense the problems that arise for their hapless babies who are then at risk of abuse, of spending some of their lives in foster care, and of becoming delinquent themselves later on.

The small children are often placed in foster care with the adolescent parents' own mothers so that these new grandmothers inherit an additional burden. Not only are their children drug addicted, criminal, and/or violent, but now they have to care for the babies. In a U.S. national survey, 11 percent of grandparents reported that they had raised a grandchild for at least six months in their lifetime (Pearson et al., 1997). Research on foster grandparents actually represents one of very few opportunities we have to study the long-term consequences of a certain type of "delinquency" on parents. Many of the parents who foster their grandchildren themselves have a life history of negative events including difficult marriages, poverty, and health problems (Strawbridge et al., 1997). Their new caregiving burdens add on to the difficulties already caused by these old burdens. This topic is further discussed in Chapter 8, on the effect of adult children on parents.

EFFECTS OF DELINQUENCY ON PARENTS

In the remainder of this chapter, I rely on my research, carried out in the 1990s, on the effects of delinquency on parents and on family processes (Ambert, 1999). This research, with the exception of that by Jang and Smith (1997) as well as Stewart, Simons, and Conger (2000), presents a reversal of previous research trends. It includes in-depth interviews with middle-class and upper-middle-class parents who had conduct-disordered or delinquent adolescents, a survey of parents of 116 delinquents arrested by the police, observations of par-

through her bedroom window to meet her older boyfriend, who was on probation for credit card fraud and possession of stolen property.

A second study was undertaken with the help of a colleague who was a criminologist at a Young Offenders' Court in Montreal. In brief, her job and that of her colleagues consists of interviewing delinquents and their parents—although often only the mother shows up—to assess the situation before making clinical and legal decisions. With the court's permission, she and her colleagues distributed 132 questionnaires to parents after conducting the official intake interviews; 88 percent of the questionnaires were returned (Ambert and Gagnon, 1995).

The main statistical findings indicated that a majority of the parents were more stressed, more tired, and less happy since learning of their child's delinquency. Nearly half of them also mentioned a decline in health. Moreover, a majority reported having been ashamed because of their adolescent's behavior, and having been blamed for it by others. A good proportion had had to seek help from police, teachers, or professionals in order to control their youngster's difficult temperament or disobedience. Most parents reported that the adolescent had additional problems, such as school difficulties for boys, association with delinquent peers, disobedience, problematic temperament, being easily influenced by peers, arriving home after curfews, and so on. Multiple problems were more common among boys than girls.

Fathers and Mothers

Another key finding of this research, similar to the preceding chapter, is that mothers are usually more affected by a child's delinquency than fathers (Ambert, 1999). This result emerged in both the qualitative and quantitative studies mentioned previously as well as in a third study described later. In the interviews, fathers even spontaneously offered comments such as the following:

- "This is much harder on my wife."
- "Let me add here [turning to his wife] that she finds our daughter's problems much more difficult to live with than I do because she is with her more."

- "If you interviewed my wife, I know you'd find her much more upset than I am because we've had some serious disagreements on account of this."

Mothers had become more stressed, tired, unhappy, and had more health problems than fathers, although the differences were not large. But there were substantial and statistically significant differences in the number of times mothers compared to fathers had felt ashamed about their adolescent's behavior, had been blamed, and had experienced problems with people because of the youngster's behavior or attitude. They had sought help far more frequently than had fathers. Moreover, mothers mentioned more problems that afflicted their child than did fathers—another reminder of some of the findings concerning the effect of children's behavioral problems on mothers presented in the previous chapter. Thus, the *gendered effect of children* toward mothers versus fathers is an important consideration.

A third study involved observing parents' self-help groups. The weekly meetings included thirty-five to fifty-five parents of conduct-disordered as well as delinquent adolescents. Again, far more mothers participated than fathers. A few couples that had endured quite nicely until then became conflictual, and the conflict was observable during group sessions. In both the United States and Canada, there are networks of such parents' groups and their existence reflects the fact that parents do not find help or sympathy from their regular support network, that is, their relatives, friends, or co-workers. Talking about one's child's problems is taboo in this society: it creates embarrassment in the listeners (Fox, 1999). Parents reported having lost friends in whom they confided because they were perceived to be "losers," or bad parents. One mother explained that mentioning one's child's delinquency is tantamount to "a death sentence socially. People avoid you after that because they think there's something wrong with you."

General Child Effect on Parents

What all three studies in this multimethod research highlight is that the relationship between parents and difficult adolescents is usually unpleasant, to put it mildly. It is conflictual and tense; parents feel as if they are "walking on eggshells"; they often try to avoid the youngster because their mere presence is likely to trigger a conflagration. These children are often manipulative, lie, frequently blame their parents, and take no responsibility for their actions. They may talk back, swear, run away, and some assault their parents. They deny doing anything wrong, even when they are caught with stolen goods in their school bag or throwing them out of the bathroom window:

> The middle-class mother of a fourteen-year-old girl who had elected to live on the streets to avoid home rules recounted the following sequence of events. Her daughter came to visit her occasionally in order to take a shower ("she was so filthy, you can't imagine") and get a decent meal. The mother had the impression that, after each of her daughter's visits, things were missing in the house. But she was not 100 percent certain; she was suffering from depression as a result of her daughter's vagaries and did not trust her memory. However, her older son, a totally well-behaved and successful young man, had no such doubts. He searched his sister's bag a few minutes before she was to leave but could find nothing. On a hunch, he walked around the house and found that the girl had thrown expensive bath towels, a clock radio, and a box of chocolates out of the bathroom window onto the grass. This is how she was stealing from her home and pawning objects for survival on the streets.

Parent-delinquent adolescent relationships are not unavoidably strained, however. Although parents in the studies just described were very distressed, delinquents who had no school-related problems generally maintained reasonable family relationships. In our sample, these less problematic youths usually were girls, given that delinquent boys are more likely to experience school difficulties and drop out. Moreover, when the crime committed was a minor one, such as shoplifting, *and* the youngster was otherwise nonproblematic, not only were parents less distressed, but the parent-adolescent relationship was only temporarily disturbed. In a few cases when adolescents owned up to their responsibilities and welcomed the increased parental supervision as a safety valve to ensure that they would not recidivate, the parent-child relationship actually became closer. But these cases did not constitute the majority.

The overall impression I gained, but which needs to be substantiated with more diverse and larger samples, is that delinquency may not be overly traumatic for parents under the following conditions: when it is not too public, does not lead to contact with the legal system, is not accompanied by other problems that require parent-teacher interviews, counseling, or other forms of external intervention, or yet, when the parents are irresponsible (Stewart, Simons, and Conger, 2000). Two key variables in parental distress are the social stigma attached to the delinquency and concurrent problems created by the youngster, either at home or at school.

The Case of Problematic Parents

In a few instances, parents had merely shrugged off the delinquency as inconsequential and were actually annoyed at being interviewed or responding to the questionnaires.

> One mother, a university professor, wrote in the margins: "This is normal at this age; all children shoplift." The girl had been arrested because she was "known to the police," which means that she had previously been caught but let go. This was not her first offense. Perhaps, then, the mother should have been more concerned. A father whose son had been arrested for attempted rape wrote the following in the space provided for additional comments: "My son can't be blamed: the girl asked for it. She invited him over. So maybe she has learned her lesson."

Such responses were not typical, but they did occur. They represent instances where parents actually support their children's delinquency, either because of their own ways of thinking or because they need to reconcile their lack of supervision with its consequences—they then downplay the consequences. In psychology, this phenomenon is referred to as a way to reduce cognitive dissonance.

Other parents silently reinforce delinquency when they do not inquire about the source of their children's acquisitions. A few examples taken from my students' autobiographies follow.

A boy stole coffee jars and candy bars at the grocery store and gave the coffee to his mother who simply accepted it. A girl who returns home with designer clothes after shoplifting sprees and parents accept her explanation that "Judy [her friend] lent them to me"—even though the clothes are never returned. A high schooler is selling drugs out of her expensive suburban home. Ten to twenty "friends" drop by each Friday, go to her room for a few minutes, and then leave. Her parents never ask anything even though their house has become Grand Central Station. Another student reports that, when he was in high school, his professional parents became so "tired of my escapades that they told me to let them know only if the police were to be involved. They even gave me a car to make their lives easier. To this day, I am still asking myself how it came to be that I am a regular guy."

None of the three studies described earlier in this chapter involved many parents who were experiencing multiple problems of their own, apart from divorce and, at times, poverty. Therefore, it would be important to study how parents who are dysfunctional in many areas of life or are too permissive or rejecting react to delinquency. Are they less affected or more so than average parents? Such parents are already highly stressed from other problems, some self-created (Kendler, Karkowski, and Prescott, 1999). It could be expected that parents who are themselves criminals, who abuse drugs, or are disorganized by severe emotional problems may be less affected than others; they may be detached from their environment and less responsive to negative social reinforcers.

It is also expected, both because of environmental and genetic reasons, that such parents will "produce" a disproportionate number of early-onset, multiple-problem offenders—recidivists who will become adult criminals. In fact, parents who themselves are or have been in jail tend to have children who become delinquent. This finding applies both to jailed fathers and mothers. Currently, 40 percent of the over 1.8 million incarcerated Americans have a parent or a sibling behind bars. Butterfield (1999) reports that a California study of 1,000 girls in detention indicated that 54 percent had a mother who had been locked up and probably an even higher percentage had such a father.

CONCLUSIONS

One of the many questions left unanswered in terms of delinquent child effect on parents is this: What happens to these parents when their children grow up to become adult criminals or commit terrible acts when minors and have to be released early because of their youthful status? How do parents cope with a returning youth who has set fires, raped a younger child, robbed a bank, or killed a person? What happens to them at work, in their neighborhoods, with their friends and relatives? There are no follow-up studies of these parents. Yet one can only presume that they must be terribly burdened, feel guilty, and may perhaps be ostracized socially. The same question applies to parents of adult criminals who may be in and out of jail or have committed a terrible crime of violence. We do not know at all how these parents are affected. We know that perhaps half of them may themselves be criminals. But what about the many others who were simply regular citizens? This lack of research is morally reprehensible in the sense that it is likely that these parents who are "invisible" are terribly isolated and in need of social support.

If we return to Chapter 3, delinquency is a child characteristic that seriously deviates from what is socially acceptable in this society. Therefore, it is a child characteristic that is expected to produce a great deal of negative effect on parents, and the results presented in this chapter amply support this hypothesis. Chapters 5 and 6 complement each other within this theoretical perspective. They also support each other in highlighting researchers' relative indifference to the study of child effect on parents or *parental burden*. The following chapter on peers contributes an additional dimension to the theme of the effect of children on parents, particularly when peers are not desirable from a parental point of view.

Chapter 7

The Effect of Children's Peers on Parents

Peers are one of the key agents of socialization in a child's life. For children and particularly adolescents, peers often constitute their main reference group. In other words, children and adolescents generally compare themselves, what they have, and how they behave to their age mates. In fact, adolescents often guide their own behavior and make decisions based on what their peers say and on their perceptions of what their peers think. This process of orientation toward peers grows in importance with age. It peaks in early and middle adolescence, which is one of the reasons why this period in a youth's life is often difficult, and also why delinquency rates are higher during that time. Then, toward the late teens and for others in young adulthood, age mates recede in importance as the young person is placed in social situations that cut across age groups. Furthermore, by that time, individuals' self-concept is more stable and peer influence becomes less salient as new adult roles are assumed.

In our society, the peer group constitutes a particularly potent form of influence on children because it is embedded in a materialistic culture based on consumerism, immediate gratification, and media-driven activities. From a macrosociological perspective, children and youth are manipulated on many fronts by larger social forces that are individualistic rather than familistic and communal. Youths are situated in an acquisitive nexus of *consumer-driven forces*. Thus, because peers are an adolescent's reference group, this reference group is itself impacted by larger social forces that become symbolic or even virtual points of reference for children.

In the past, children's peer groups were less separated from the adult world and less age graded in terms of values, goals, and even activities. No virtual or "mediatic" voices and persons sold them an ever-changing lifestyle that separated them from the adult world. Children played together and even worked together but they were more likely to encounter adult authority figures who would provide them with a structure that maintained them within the basic realities of their families and their communities. Adults were then far more effective agents of collective socialization; functional communities contributed to integrate children and youth (Coleman and Hoffer, 1987).

As the peer group separated from the adult world and became more influential, parents' influence diminished. In fact, unless children are part of an effective community, peer influence may clash with parental influence several times daily. As adult influence in the form of teachers, clergy, and older kin became more distant, parents remained children's main source of *adult* influence in their lives. Therefore, in terms of socialization, parents were isolated, no longer surrounded by adult support, and, as such, their influence waned. Similarly, as peers became more important in a child's life, they became so in parents' lives. Children are now more affected by their peers and this effect spills over into family dynamics, hence the importance of studying the effect of children's peers on parents.

PEER PRESSURE AND SUPPORT

There is a general adult perception that children and youth engage in unacceptable behavior as a direct result of their peers "pressuring" them. By this definition, direct pressure involves an element of coercion, such as when a small child is told by an older bully to hand over his lunch money "or else I'll beat the shit out of you." Or when a domineering teen gives another one a cigarette and orders him to smoke it. Or when, at a party, a group of boys forces another to engage in sexual activities. Of course, all of these events do occur occasionally, particularly in deviant areas or peer groups, and when children are poorly supervised. Researchers, however, define these instances as forms of bullying rather than peer pressure—and we discuss bullying later on. In terms of peer pressure, these occurrences represent the exception rather than the norm.

Peer pressure is more subtle than bullying. It resides in the fact that most of a child's friends and contemporaries engage or are thought to engage in an activity and not in the fact that they will force him or her to do it as well. Children whose friends are studious receive an indirect message that perhaps they should also do their homework, especially if they value their peers' opinion. This is what we will call a "studious" peer environment. Thus, children feel peer pressure even though no one has asked them to do anything. In terms of symbolic interactionism, friends are an important reference group that contribute not only to how children see themselves but how they choose to behave. But some peer pressure also arises out of a child's erroneous perception that "everyone else has one or is doing it," while, in reality, this is not the case. For instance, adolescents often brag about fabulous weekends or parties when they return to school on Mondays, yet they were simply at home with their parents. But these "stories" lead others who had also been home to think of themselves as deprived. In turn, they feel pressured to "get a life" or "live my life."

A teenager whose friends all smoke cigarettes or marijuana may not be asked to share in their activities, but will feel left out if he or she does not. If things are not going too well at home and the child has weak self-esteem, he or she may feel compelled to join in for fear that friends think he or she is "uncool" or a "loser." Slowly, a message forms in the child's mind and this is where the pressure exists: it is psychological, although its source is environmental. Peer pressure resides in the cultural climate of the peer group and permeates activities as well as ways of thinking. At times, a particularly popular and influential peer engages in certain activities and has a strong impact on slightly younger peers, as seen in the following student's autobiography.

> This twosome of Pete and I became a threesome when we met Alan who was a saxophone player in the band. The three of us got along very well. . . . It wasn't until the end of grade eight that we started to feel Alan's influence over us when he introduced us to cigarettes. This influence was brought about by the fact that Alan had an older brother who was involved in a group of

friends which was made up of what I considered "tough" people. Alan had tried smoking and one day he brought a cigarette with him to school. The three of us went out back at recess and Alan sparked it up. I remember the taste in my mouth after that first puff; it was awful but it was exciting at the same time. . . . Our parents didn't suspect a thing as we would do everything we could to mask the smell. One day as we sat and smoked together behind the school, Alan told us of how his brother had tried smoking pot. The three of us were very interested and arranged for Alan's brother to get us some to try. A few weeks later it happened. It was Saturday and the three of us went to the forest by Pete's house. Alan pulled out a bag of what looked like a few hand-rolled cigarettes. We smoked them and nothing happened. We were disappointed but Alan assured us that one was not supposed to get high the first time. While making the transition from cigarettes to pot, my home life, appearance, and extracurricular activities changed. No longer did I communicate with my family, do homework, or play sports. Instead I started to listen to heavy rock music, hang out at an arcade, grow my hair long, and wear ragged clothes. . . . I had perfected the art of deception, which kept my family in the dark the whole time. I found this quite amusing and keeping my parents ignorant was an exciting game.

The above quote illustrates how negative peer influence may work, particularly within a small friendship group, and leads from one slightly deviant activity to a more serious break with acceptable behavior. The quote also quite vividly describes how these peer activities actually affect the quality of the youth's interaction with his family and how they affect his parents. The direction of causality flows from peer group to adolescent to parents. This quote also illustrates how deviant activities shared with friends can distance an adolescent from prosocial activities such as schoolwork and team sports. In turn, this distancing will have a further negative impact on parents who are concerned about their child's sudden loss of interest in developing his human capital.

Peers who are friends and, even more so, close friends, naturally influence or can influence one another more forcefully. In fact, a child who is surrounded by a negative peer group may well be able to resist this influence if he or she happens to have one or two *close* friends who have similar expectations in life, particularly when these two friends have supportive parents. This combined little group of friends and adults then has a degree of closure from the rest of the world and protects its children. But the characteristics of a *neighborhood* and its schools largely determine the effect of peer support on children.

For instance, Dubow, Edwards, and Ippolito (1997) found that children in inner-city neighborhoods who have recently suffered stressful situations exhibit higher levels of antisocial behavior when they report receiving peer support. In contrast, family support has a positive effect and is related to reduced antisocial behaviors. These researchers point out that "the choice of peers may depend, in great part, on the characteristics of the neighborhoods in which the children reside" (Dubow, Edwards, and Ippolito, 1997:141). In other words, areas with many social problems may have fewer prosocial peers available to a child so that in times of stress, he or she receives "support" from peers who may be antisocial. This factor increases the child's vulnerability both to additional stressors and to misbehaving. In contrast, in a low-risk neighborhood, Gonzales and colleagues (1996) found that peer support predicted higher grade point averages among African-American children. Therefore, where a family lives has a great deal of impact on its children's access to a potentially prosocial, supportive peer network.

Having high-achieving peers can influence children's and adolescents' enjoyment of school as well as contribute to raising their own test scores and expectations (Mounts and Steinberg, 1995). Peers seem to be a relatively more potent source of influence than parents in terms of school performance among African- and Asian-American youngsters than among white adolescents (Steinberg et al., 1995). This stems in part from racial segregation, if not necessarily always at the residential level, at least in schools. Asian Americans have "no choice but to belong to a peer group that encourages and rewards academic excellence—for better or for worse, it is extremely difficult for an Asian youngster to become a 'jock,' or a 'druggie,' or a 'preppie' " (Steinberg et al., 1995:449). The dilemma faced by African-American students is more or less the reverse; for them, belonging to a school crowd of "nerds" is difficult. In fact, Steinberg and colleagues were often told by successful black students that peer support for academic achievement was so limited that they often opted to affiliate primarily with students from other ethnic groups. Black students are far more likely than others "to be caught in a bind between performing well in school and being popular with their peers" (Steinberg et al., 1995:449).

The neighborhood approach to peer support and influence is more sociological and has the advantage of avoiding the psychological reductionism whereby peers and children are described strictly through their personality characteristics or those of their parents. Indeed, it will not surprise the reader to learn that a substantial proportion of the research literature on children's affiliation with peers focuses on *parents* and how they treat their children. Basically, the line of reasoning of this research is as follows: Children who are not popular with their school crowd or are rejected by their peers have certain social incompetencies that originate in their relationship with their parents or the ways in which they were treated at home. Children who experience difficulties at home are less likely to be popular at school. And, indeed, the research finds *modest* correlations supporting this line of reasoning.

But the size of these correlations indicates that other aspects in a child's personality and environment account far more for popularity with peers than do parents. One can think here of a child's partly genetic predisposition to shyness, extroversion, or leadership ability (Stoneman et al., 1999). One can also think in terms of a child's size, material possessions, race, and quality of peer group. For instance, an agreeable and prosocial child who is thrust into a classroom of children who are aggressive and have an "attitude" is quite unlikely to be well received. The child may actually become a victim, although there is obviously nothing wrong with this child or with his or her parents.

PEER ABUSE

An increasing segment of children and youth learn to be cruel, destructive, and even violent toward one another. They are allowed to be so because of a lack of adult concern and supervision. Such examples are mentioned in the newscasts on a weekly basis, and peer abuse as well as rejection has recently led youngsters to murder their schoolmates. Children who are victimized may create family dynamics that differ greatly from those encountered in families in which children are lucky with their peer group. The effect of children on parents varies accordingly.

How Prevalent Is Peer Abuse?

In research on students' written recollections of their childhood, I unexpectedly came across many accounts of abuse committed by students' peers when they were younger (Ambert, 1994). For many of the students, the impact of the peer group went beyond transitory unhappiness: it often led to dislike and avoidance of school (Kochenderfer and Ladd, 1996). In other instances, it contributed to poor school performance (Hodges, Malone, and Perry, 1997) as well as anxiety and depression (Egan and Perry, 1998). The contents of the autobiographies were tabulated for two different cohorts of students to see if peer impact had changed over the years. Looking only at the 0-14 age bracket, 17 percent in the 1974 class and 27 percent in the 1989 class of students recalled negative peer treatment they described as having had seriously detrimental and lasting consequences in their development; that is, these experiences had affected them negatively for several years, often up to the present time. When the 15-18 age bracket was included, the percentage increased to 37 percent for the 1989 cohort.

In contrast, 13 percent (1974) and 9 percent (1989) of students described negative—but not necessarily abusive—parental treatment and attitudes that had had a lasting detrimental impact. Far more negative treatment by peers than by parents was indicated in these autobiographies—and this is even more obvious for the 1989 than the 1974 cohort. This result, corroborated by other researchers, is startling considering the often single-minded focus of child-welfare professionals and researchers on parents while neglecting what is becoming the most salient source of psychological misery among youth—peer conflict, rejection, and maltreatment (Ambert, 2001).

In these autobiographies, one reads about the lives of students who had been happy and well adjusted, but quite rapidly began deteriorating psychologically, sometimes to the point of becoming physically ill and incompetent in school. This sudden deterioration followed experiences such as being rejected by peers, excluded, gossiped about, racially discriminated against, laughed at, sexually harassed, taunted, chased, or beaten. Even schoolwork was disrupted as a result as the children became too fearful and too distraught to focus on anything else.

Child and adolescent abuse at home has been estimated at approximately 3 percent, slightly more or less depending on the study (Finkelhor and Dziuba-Leatherman, 1994). Furthermore, there is some evidence that child abuse by parents is decreasing: it is, however, more often *reported* than in the past because we are more attuned to this problem. In contrast, child neglect may be increasing, both in terms of physical neglect and lack of supervision. Extrapolations from the data I have collected project a much higher rate of peer than parent abuse, as well as a rate that is *increasing*. Thus, a conservative estimate might be that a minimum of 20 percent of all children and adolescents are seriously abused by peers during their young lives— and we are not speaking here of normal conflicts, disagreements, or teasing. Moreover, recent surveys reported in the news media, both in Canada and the United States, present much higher estimates, often as high as 75 percent (Espelage et al., 1996). Child Help Lines report more calls related to fear of peers than to problems at home. During the school years, the peer environment definitely threatens children's development more than the aggregate of all negative parental environments does.

Context and Consequences of Peer Abuse

Although learning how to resolve *normal* peer conflict is useful, findings regarding peer abuse actually suggest that, in many instances, the consequences of abusive conflict are destructive. In fact, through abusive experiences with age mates, each child victim sees his or her competence as a social actor placed in question by the abuse; his or her self-esteem is shattered, and his or her fundamental right to a safe environment is violated. One can argue that the topic of peer socialization requires further theoretical and empirical scrutiny in light of the diversity of rapidly changing social contexts.

For instance, it is necessary that researchers realize that studying peer abuse no longer is a matter of delving into *victims'* characteristics. (This is akin to inquiring about the personal life of rape victims rather than prosecuting the rapist for his actions.) Nowadays, a child can become the victim of peer abuse through no fault of his own or of her family. A child may be beaten up because she wears a jacket that two bigger girls want. Or a boy can be assaulted because he refuses to hand over his brand-name sneakers. In other cases, children are "separated" from their lunch money by more powerful classmates. Peer abuse is not merely a psychological situation created by a victim and an abuser because of two sets of personality characteristics, nor it is merely a consequence of parenting practices, as often described in the literature (Finnegan, Hodges, and Perry, 1998).

Peer abuse is influenced by what children have learned elsewhere, including from the media—whether television or video games. For instance, Espelage and colleagues (1996) have found that adolescent bullies watch more violent television, are more difficult at home, spend less time with adults, and have more exposure to gang activities than other children. A third had a single parent while another third lived with a stepparent. Thus, it would seem that serious bullies escape adult influence and control; they surround themselves with negative role models, including what they learn by playing video games. Their family structure is lacking in terms of its ability to provide supervision. At a more macrosociological level, the culture of violence in the society at large is implicated along with reduced social control. Peer abuse is above all a *cultural phenomenon* and a reflection of a lack of an effective community. Indeed, as mentioned in Chapter 4, in a culture that rejects violence and that exerts effective social control over its children, even aggressive children will have few opportunities to indulge their inclinations, which are likely to die out for lack of reinforcement.

Peer Harassment and Sexual Abuse

Sexual harassment, mainly by boys toward girls, is a particularly pernicious form of abuse (Stein, 1995). It often starts very early, as described by a female student:

The boys of my elementary school were rude, disgusting, and held no respect for any of the girls. They felt that whenever they wanted to, they could grab you wherever they wanted. In addition to this they loved to fabricate stories about the girls and what they were able to do to them. So, in addition to having to feel insecure about yourself as you're going through such an unknown stage of life, you were under constant scrutiny of 13-year-old boys. I'd walk down the aisle to the teacher's desk and while the teacher turned their head someone would grab me at the closest location. No amount of insisting would convince these guys to stop.

Peer sexual abuse generally goes undetected, may even be approved of by boys' parents ("he's *all* boy"), and girls may be led to believe that it is flattering ("he *likes* you, silly") or simply the normal price one has to pay for popularity or to keep one's boyfriend. Many adolescents and even preadolescent girls are coerced into sexuality by male peers. The degree of coercion ranges from subtle pressure to outright rape in a relationship where the girl is afraid to lose her date. Adolescents are particularly at risk when they score high on scales of conformity to peers (Small and Kerns, 1993): they become vulnerable because they need their peers' approval more than less-conforming adolescents do. Although many young women are not forcibly raped, they nevertheless do not want sexual intercourse but comply because of peer pressure (Laumann, 1996). Some of this pressure comes from female peers who may already be sexually active or pretend to be in order to be "cool" in the eyes of their peers. This creates a cultural climate or peer pressure that is very potent; as a result, a teenager eager for peer acceptance will follow suit.

Victimization from severe forms of sexual abuse, rape, or coercion into unwanted sexuality is more likely to occur to female adolescents who live in neighborhoods that have a high rate of social problems and whose parents cannot supervise or protect them adequately. Thus, girls from single-parent families, particularly when they are poor, as well as those who have parents who suffer from alcoholism, for instance, are at a higher risk of sexual victimization in general, including by peers (Moore, Nord, and Peterson, 1989).

Peer sexual abuse, as is the case for peer abuse in general, is very much a *crime of opportunity*. It is done by and happens to children and adolescents while they are *unsupervised by adults,* whether at school, at home, in the community, or in a parked car. Too many parents are personally burdened as well as disempowered and therefore do not protect or supervise their children adequately. This is a form of child neglect. Peer sexual abuse is also the result of media influences and disengagement from adults, including teachers and parents—in other words, a generalized lack of an effective community.

THE EFFECT OF PEERS ON PARENTS

Peer abuse has indirect victims through the spillover effect from one system to another, in this case from the peer system to the family system of interactions. The ill-treated child's parents often suffer: they may suffer with their child when they learn of the victimization but they may also suffer indirectly. That is, the frustrated child often takes it out on his parents and siblings (Ambert, 1994). Parents inherit what one student called "the flak." In addition, as if to anticipate some of the material in the following chapter, the autobiographies revealed that some parents were even blamed by clinicians for traumas that had peers at their source. A male student's recollections illustrate this latter phenomenon quite vividly:

> Up to that age [11 years] I had been quite happy at school but then something happened to me; I stopped growing and I became in no time the shortest and skinniest and soon the pimpliest little runt at my grade level. The other boys used to pick on me, hide my coat, steal my lunches, and would never include me in their games. They'd laugh at me openly and the girls started avoiding me too because it wasn't cool to be seen with the most unpopular boy. . . . You can't imagine how many times my mother had to keep me home because I'd start throwing up. I became scared shitless . . . and to this day, I feel insecure around other guys. . . . The funny thing is that my parents had to send me to a psychiatrist and he turned around and blamed them for not being supportive and for whatever else. That's kind of sad when you think

that my problems had nothing to do with my parents. My parents were sort of being made miserable because of this little runt I was, and now by this psychiatrist and to this day they have never blamed me and have always been supportive.

The impact of the peer group continues to be effective even after the child returns home from school, as he or she keeps on reacting to what peers did or said or failed to say. Children and adolescents bring home the stress experienced via their peers and this stress spills over into their interactions with their parents (Ladd, 1992). Indeed, students frequently pointed out in the autobiographies that they used their parents as "scapegoats" and vented their peer-related frustrations on them as soon as one parent said or did something that the youngster could use as a trigger: "I used to sulk up and down the stairs, just to make them as miserable as I was," or "I would blow my top," or "I used to cry and yell and storm out." They would lash out at the surprised parent who then tried to reason out the situation, only to unwittingly provoke a sharp outburst from the youngster. Thus, the children had developed behavioral problems toward their parents as a result of peer abuse.

Furthermore, although the peer group may support parental teachings, it may also conflict with parents' values. Children whose peers' behaviors and values are so different from those they are taught within their families experience what Ladd (1992) refers to as *cross-pressures*. A child's socialization process is considerably easier when peers and parents agree, but is far more difficult when fundamental contradictions occur between the two reference groups. We can presume then that the greater the similarity between parents' values and those of their children's peers, the lower the level of parent-child conflict—and the more positive the child effect on parents.

Youngsters whose parents approve of their peers, and particularly of their close friends, get along better with their parents. Not only do they have more in common, but parents may need to exert less direct control over them, thus preempting conflict. Moreover, it is likely that these peers will, in turn, "approve" of the parents; this situation will reinforce both the connection between child and peers as well as the relationship between parents and child. In contrast, when parents disapprove of their children's friends, especially during adolescence, a great deal of tension may exist if parents voice their concerns. Fearing their children's outbursts, many parents learn to keep their opinions to themselves. This, in turn, deprives the children of effective adult feedback and may be construed as encouragement.

"Everybody is doing it" and "everybody has one" are powerful and often intimidating messages handed to parents (Ambert, 1997). What parent has not heard the following?

> "But all the others are going," indignantly protests a fourteen-year-old girl who wants to go to a nightclub. "I'm going to look like a loser leaving at eleven when everyone gets to stay until one and two a.m," plaintively objects another girl who has just received permission to attend a party. A fifteen-year-old boy whose father is inquiring about parental supervision at a house party informs him authoritatively : "Of course his parents aren't going to be there! Parents *always* leave for parties." And so on.

Thus, each parenting couple and, more and more, each single mother or father has to face what is presented by the child as a consensus, as a rule, as a normal entitlement among youngsters. Parents are made to feel that, if they do not conform, they will do a grave injustice and deprive the child. This alleged consensus among youngsters allows each individual child to speak with great authority to his or her parents because parents are generally more isolated than their children when it comes to tactical and moral support. Adolescent groups and subcultures are much more cohesive and less fragmented for each child than are adult subcultures for each parent. In reality, there is no such thing as a parent subculture or peer group, and this constitutes a disequilibrium that is detrimental to the parents' role (Small and Eastman, 1991). This disequilibrium stems from a lack of effective communities in the society at large, a theme we have already broached in the previous chapter. A single mother expresses the situation thusly when attempting to understand with hindsight how her teenage daughter became delinquent without her noticing it:

> My daughter has a lot of friends; some I know, some I don't. They talk on the phone on a daily basis even after they have been to school together; they make plans, they exchange clothes, they

cover up for each other, they watch each other's back against their parents. They come and they go and it's impossible to keep track of all of this. New clothes that she wears are borrowed from Mindy and if I ask Mindy, she'll say, "Don't I got good taste!" If Mindy's mother calls to find out where she is, all I can say is that they went to the movies together. That's what I was told. But they actually went to this boy's place. If Mindy's mother calls about clothes, I say that they exchange a lot while in reality they are all shoplifting. So you see you have to be a very, very clever parent to keep track of all of this and to add it all up together to one conclusion: my child is a shoplifter and she's barely fifteen and she's screwing around. But don't think for one minute that I added this up on my own—the police did it for me. These girls just protect each other. Protect for what? They're the ones who need protection against each other. Now I tell you that Mindy's mother, Jessie's mother, and I have all been fooled.

Along these lines, Steinberg and colleagues (1995:453) find that, when adolescents' peers have authoritative parents, the latter contribute to positive developmental outcomes above and beyond their own authoritativeness: "We believe that this may be due in part to the higher level of shared social control provided by a network of authoritative parents." Yet, in the mother's previous quote, the various parents are exhibiting all the "symptoms" of being authoritative and conscientious, but their children's delinquent peer group is far more clever and better organized. And, as pointed out at the outset of this chapter, it is an acquisitive and materialistic peer group which leads them to shoplift, among other things. Short of driving them to school and accompanying them wherever they go—an impossible task nowadays (such parents would, at any rate, be condemned as "overprotective")—it is impossible for these parents to supervise their children effectively.

CONCLUSIONS

Many parents, especially more educated ones, make an effort to become acquainted with their children's friends' parents (Muller and Kerbow, 1993). Parent networks can fulfill several functions both for parents and their children. When these are school based, parents are better informed, which can contribute to a smoother socialization process and norms that are more closely adhered to. It is, however, far more difficult for adolescents' parents than for young children's parents to know their children's peers' parents—at a time when such contacts would be the most helpful. Adolescents who have friends who are not exactly prosocial are not usually eager to introduce them to their parents. Those same friends would be upset if the two sets of parents became acquainted because these parents could exchange information that could curb these youngsters' freedom to behave antisocially or self-destructively. Unfortunately, parents are very busy making ends meet nowadays and they have far less time to devote to their children, least of all to their children's friends and these friends' parents.

This set of circumstances prevents parents from forming an effective community which would help them promote their children's healthy moral and psychological development. As children age, peer effect becomes more powerful and in turn affects parents. Parents fortunate enough to have positively motivated children who have equally positive peers and a high-quality living area may realize beneficial circumstances from peer effect. But rare are those families in which, at least at some point, parents do not clash with their children or are not obligated to patch up the damage done to their children because of peers. When we sum up all these facts, it is rather surprising that peer abuse, violence, and simple nastiness is not a topic of greater concern to clinical psychologists and the child-saving industry. Far more school-aged children need to be protected against abusive peers than abusive parents.

Chapter 8

Professionals and Parents

Professionals are part of the societal response described in Chapter 3. This rubric includes doctors, lawyers, psychiatrists, psychologists, and even social workers. We first examine how professionals can facilitate or burden parents' lives, and then present the history of the "schizophrenogenic" mother as an illustration of what can go terribly wrong in professionals' social construction of parents, particularly of mothers. Parent blaming is discussed and the merit of therapeutic interventions is examined. Parent effectiveness training is analyzed as a constructive as well as a potentially problematic method of intervention. The chapter concludes with an inquiry into the role, positive and negative, that researchers such as psychologists and sociologists may play in the relationships of the parents and children who participate in their studies.

PROFESSIONAL AUTHORITY OVER PARENTS

Since the beginning of the twentieth century, a variety of professionals have socially constructed or defined what good parenting is. At first, various religious leaders, and what has been called the child-saving industry, have brought their moral stamp to parenting. They were followed by physicians, who also took it upon themselves to reform parents. The parenting role became "medicalized," and parents were admonished to follow proper rules of hygiene in accordance with the morality and the knowledge of the day.

The interlude between the two world wars saw the appearance of psychologists and psychiatrists whose hegemony continues to this day, more recently aided by lawyers. Social workers have long been important members of these professions, but their standards and decisions are generally determined by the more powerful professions of psychiatry, psychology, medicine, and law. In tandem with the emergence of this series of experts, the nineteenth and twentieth centuries saw the emergence of what became a lucrative enterprise: books intended to teach parents how to take care of their children.

We live in a time when expert knowledge is given preeminence, fueled as it is by information technology. As a result of the social and media salience of professional knowledge, the lay public has gradually lost power over a variety of areas of life that have fallen under the aegis of science and the professions. The prominence given to experts and "pop" psychology in the media, including talk shows, has led people to follow a variety of trends in personal lifestyles. Thus, people have become dependent on various experts, not only for knowledge, but for their rights, their health, the education of their children, and, more recently, the definition of the quality of their sexual and conjugal life, and even the social construction of what constitutes happiness. People's lives have become "pop psychologized."

In addition, professionals have become highly valued by various state agencies. They are regularly consulted in matters that pertain to the family, over and above parents, and contribute to the enactment of laws and policies in this domain. Those laws and policies in turn enhance the power and enlarge the domain of the professions: "The manufacture of modern social problems is an industry in which professionals play major roles" (Sullivan, 1992:5). Experts are now so prominent in the definition and treatment of various problems that many thinkers are asking themselves whose best interest is being served, that of children and their parents or that of the professionals who define and oversee that "best interest"? Nelson (1984:17) makes this point by illustrating how alcoholism, considered a sin or a crime early in the twentieth century, is now defined as a disease: "Many behaviors with significantly aggressive or violent components have been similarly 'medicalized.' In addition to child abuse, examples include alcoholism, drug abuse, hyperkinesis, and to a lesser degree rape and domestic violence."

Professionals "police" the care parents give their children (Donzelot, 1979), assign blame to parents when youngsters develop problems, and, under the influence of systems theories, may even treat *parents* when children suffer from emotional or behavioral problems. Parents can no longer be just parents: they have to adhere to a set of professional norms and expectations. These, in turn, have also heavily influenced schoolteachers who then closely scrutinize parents when children do not meet their standards. Children and especially adolescents have not escaped from this cultural mentality: they have been schooled to accept these lean and useless versions of their parents' role—which too often place the onus of child outcome on parents and deprive youngsters of the assumption of responsibility for their own behaviors.

Professionals, especially psychiatrists, psychologists, and clinical case workers, become partners or yet intruders in family life (Lefley, 1997). The literature on disabled children well documents how parents are often led to feel helpless, as well as incompetent, when dealing with various service delivery personnel (Darling, 1987). It is not difficult to see how this could be even more so in the case of parents of emotionally disturbed or disruptive children, especially when the teaching and research literatures too frequently hold them responsible (Caplan and Hall-McQuorquodale, 1985). Many parents believe that mental health professionals do not have a realistic view of their child, whom they often see under very limited and artificial circumstances in their office. A mother had this to say on the topic:

> The psychiatrist has not the slightest inkling as to how difficult it is for us to care for Jimmy. Right now he thinks that he is doing better. I mean, he says that because these days Jimmy communicates better and he was able to have a good conversation with him [his psychiatrist]. But his behavior isn't any different. He doesn't see it. . . . At other times, we beg him to hospitalize him and he only tells us that we exaggerate. . . . You know, it's enough to drive parents to become schizophrenic themselves. (Ambert, 1992:119)

Professionals can either facilitate or complicate parents' lives as well as the parent-child relationship. They can contribute to child and adolescent development or they can unwittingly hinder it.

Fortunately, there are several movements among the helping professions and family scientists that critically study their own impact and constructions of reality (Paré, 1995). For instance, there is a growing awareness of cultural biases in determinations of therapeutic interventions (Gergen, 1992). There is greater recognition that clinicians and family scientists should receive more extensive training in cultural diversity (Ganong, Coleman, and Demo, 1995); such programs have already increased in number (Hills and Stozier, 1992). In addition, there is a growing awareness that some problems, such as depression, are partly genetic in nature, and it is therefore unlikely that purely environmental interventions will be successful (Bronfenbrenner and Ceci, 1993). Such a recognition is helpful to parents. Experts have criticized the tradition of parent blaming and urge greater compassion for parents of the emotionally disturbed, although similar sympathy has yet to be encouraged toward parents of difficult and delinquent children. Finally, others are encouraging a full partnership between professionals and families (Doherty, 2000).

THE "SCHIZOPHRENOGENIC" MOTHER

In the 1950s and 1960s, the "schizophrenogenic" mother was the buzzword in research and clinical work on children and adults with schizophrenia. It was widely disseminated in the lay media. This fashion began in 1948 with the publication of an article by psychoanalyst Freida Fromm-Reichmann. She defined the schizophrenogenic mother as one who, by her behavior and faulty mode of communication, *caused* her child to become schizophrenic. Given that psychoanalysis had already emphasized the negative role that mothers allegedly played in their children's development, the ground was fertile to receive a theory that placed blame solely on mothers. Consequently, a battalion of clinically oriented researchers began studying schizophrenics' families and family interactions, focusing on mothers and their "double bind" mode of communication (Bateson et al., 1958). Unavoidably, the results of their research showed that, in comparison to mothers of average children, mothers of children with schizophrenia suffered from a variety of personal problems and shortcomings. Hence the conclusion was drawn that these mothers caused schizophrenia.

Although the conclusion was totally wrong, the result arrived at by researchers was not unexpected and makes sense—but it makes sense for totally different reasons. First, studies of adopted children, as well as of identical and fraternal twins reared apart and separately, indicate a fairly high degree of heritability for schizophrenia, as discussed in Chapter 4 (Gottesman, 1991). It is therefore reasonable to assume that a certain number of mothers of persons with schizophrenia are either afflicted by this illness themselves or suffer from other emotional problems that can be genetically linked to schizophrenia. Consequently, the causality is a genetic one and does not stem from faulty mothering practices per se.

Second, it is likely that a certain number of fathers of persons with schizophrenia are also afflicted by the disease and could transmit this genetic propensity to their children. (These fathers, noticeably, were never implicated in this research—there was no such thing as a "schizophrenogenic" *father*.) In the scenario proposed here, the mother would experience stress from the simultaneous presence of a disturbed spouse and child; her own behaviors are bound to be affected negatively. As a consequence, researchers would observe a mother who is not perfecly normal because of the stressful familial environment created by her spouse's and her child's schizophrenia.

The third explanation resides in an elaboration of the previous scenario: it is difficult for a mother to care for and live with a child who suffers from schizophrenia. Hence, the causality may well be reversed: the mother's life becomes stressful because of the child rather than the child being "caused" to be schizophrenic by the mother. For instance, the researcher Beels (1974) had noticed that parents of people with schizophrenia exhibited better reasoning skills when he met with them separately from the patients. Thus, how professionals perceive parents may depend in large part on the circumstances under which they meet them.

A fourth explanation was provided by the psychiatrist Terkelsen (1983), who came to realize that some of the research carried out on families of persons with schizophrenia had taken place in the artificial environment of a laboratory and within a blaming atmosphere. These circumstances contributed to making parents feel blamed and ill at ease. They reacted with stress and at times with uncharacteristic behaviors and aberrant styles of communication. Unfortunately, researchers were not studying the effect of *their* own research methods on the hapless parents; the latter's atypical behaviors were seen as a cause of child abnormality rather than as a detrimental result of poorly designed research.

A final explanation is based on the fact that a mother with a schizophrenic child must *adapt* to him or her. She must learn to communicate with the child according to the child's mode of thinking and behaving, especially when he or she is in an acute phase. Therefore, the communication pattern of these mothers may be "disturbed" when in the child's presence. Many studies, reported in Chapter 5, have since shown how adults adapt to children; this has been particularly well illustrated in instances of children who are hyperactive or delayed. But, as we have seen with Beels's study, this also applies to mothers of children who suffer from a vast array of emotional problems.

This example of the "schizophrenogenic" mother serves to illustrate how research and professional fashions of an era can burden parents with useless blame and guilt for decades afterward. This notion of the schizophrenogenic mother was unsupported by all but the most superficial and biased evidence. It was abandoned in the mid-1970s, but not before it had inflicted much pain on these already-burdened women. Unfortunately, the myth is perpetuated to this day because some clinicians, especially those in private practice, believe it and continue to "treat" mothers in order to cure their children!

We should not conclude this section without mentioning that autism was once believed to be created by a "cold" mother, and that homosexuality was until fairly recently attributed in clinical circles to a domineering mother and an ineffectual father (Terry, 1998). In the meantime, we have learned that autism, like schizophrenia, is perhaps genetic or the result of an intrauterine infection and that, in some instances, homosexuality may also be genetic (Golombok and Tasker, 1996). In the case of homosexuality, this assumed pattern of maternal causality stemmed from a clinical ideology that defined or constructed homosexuality as pathological in nature, therefore subject to clinical intervention. This line of thinking still persists among a few clinicians.

PARENT BLAMING

By now it is evident that what too frequently happens with expert opinion on children and adolescents is that parents are marginalized, disempowered, and their role is consequently substantially reduced. The result is that conscientious parents can no longer be as effective as in previous generations because they have lost much of the moral authority that once belonged to them. Parents are placed in a dilemma. They may be told to "mind their business" when their child has problems and comes to the attention of various experts, but then they are often blamed for the problems. This is a "double whammy." During my fieldwork, I have discovered that many adolescents exploit this marginalization and blame of parents. They use it as a convenient excuse for avoiding any accountability for their actions and for continuing to pursue potentially self-destructive behaviors.

"Professionals under siege sometimes begin to fall back on their perception of parents to justify their desire to excuse themselves from their inability to respond to parents' concerns" (Rubin and Quinn-Curan, 1983:79). These two researchers point out that, when society cannot meet a parental request for services, the assumption is that there is something wrong with the parents. As they write, "seeing the parents as 'the problem' assumes that the parents are emotionally disturbed" (Rubin and Quinn-Curan, 1983:73). This rationalization preempts the need for an examination of systemic failures. Terkelsen (1983:191) points out the unfortunate consequence of such ideas: "When either therapist or family harbor the belief that schizophrenia is caused by personal experience with family members, therapeutic misalliance is bound to follow." He came to this conclusion, which applies to all problematic child behaviors, after having first misinterpreted the patients' parents' words. He describes how he "listened to the parents talk about life with the ill person, abstracting from their reports those interactional phenomena that I thought suggestive of parental pathology" (Terkelsen, 1983:192). He finally came to realize that abnormal patterns of family interaction were interpreted in terms of parental causality. In reality, these patterns constituted familial adaptations to the difficulties created by the disturbed child.

Although professionals and the workforce in mental hospitals and social agencies have chosen to care for the emotionally ill as their career, the patients' families have made no such choice. They have no alternative. Furthermore, the family's potential to contribute to the treatment of its mentally ill members is usually not actualized: the family is simply given a custodial role. As Falloon and Pederson

(1985:156) point out, "In this capacity, they are often denied access to information concerning the nature of the patient's illness and guidelines on its management." However, caution must be taken so that an increased role for the family, especially the parents, would not compound their burden. Falloon and Pederson show that an effective family management program on the part of the therapeutic community substantially reduces parental stress. In contrast, a program focusing intensively on patients does not relieve family burden.

THE MERIT
OF THERAPEUTIC INTERVENTIONS

Therapeutic intervention with children and adolescents has been found to be more successful in research or university settings than in private practice or clinics (Weisz, Donenberg, et al., 1995). As Suin (1993) pointedly remarks, too many clinicians, once installed in their practice, simply ignore literature that could inform them of new techniques, diagnostic improvements, and advances in the detection of causality. And, we might add, that would keep them within the boundaries of sound and ethical practice. Weisz, Weiss, and colleagues (1995) summarized the results of a variety of psychotherapeutic interventions with children and adolescents that were carried out mainly within a research setting where the therapist is closely monitored. Overall, the results show that about 75 percent of the children were functioning better after treatment than a comparative control group of children who had received no treatment. However, in attempts to replicate such results on therapy carried out in regular practice where there is little monitoring of clinicians and a more heterogeneous set of interventions exists, they found that outcomes ranged from detrimental to only minimally successful. These were clinical interventions for which a control group existed. In reality, very few clinicians use a control group or do research to measure the effectiveness of their interventions (Kendall and Stoutham-Gerow, 1995).

There are indications, supported in the Weisz, Weiss, et al. study (1995), that behaviorally focused interventions have a higher rate of success than other therapeutic programs (Piercy and Sprenkle, 1990).

Such treatments have been more extensively evaluated than others, perhaps because research clinicians utilize them more. It is not known, however, which features of their approach—that is, "targeting specific problems, use of explicit reinforcers, and direct teaching of coping skills"—are the most effective (Weiss and Weisz, 1995: 320). As in any other type of intervention, a therapist's interpersonal skills constitute an important element in treatment success.

Professionals not only treat children but may even request to treat *parents* when children suffer from emotional problems and physical ailments, as illustrated in the case below from my files (Ambert, 1998):

> In a first assessment, a fourteen-year-old boy with depression recalled being immediately asked questions about his parents and their relationship. Amidst these questions, according to the boy, the clinician interjected:
>
> "Isn't it possible that you feel very bad about this?" [parents' rare arguments]
>
> "No, not really, because it is never really serious. They make up right away."
>
> "But you know it's normal for children to be affected when their parents fight, so it's OK to say so."

Note here how the clinician tries to influence the child's way of seeing the effect of his parents' relationship on his own mental health. The suggestive nature of the therapist's approach continues:

> Later on [still according to the boy]:
>
> "It seems to me that a boy like you who feels so bad about life in general must have problems at home with his parents."
>
> "Well, yes; they aren't too happy about me being so sad all the time."
>
> "But don't you think that perhaps you don't want to say so but you're upset at your parents?"

The boy was very upset when he got out and told his mother: "What does he know about me that's helpful? He just wants to know about you." It is at this point that the mother decided to write the boy's account of his sessions. At his third interview the clinician told him:

> "Now, I'll have to tell your mother to take adult tests because there's got to be a reason why you feel so depressed."

As the reader can see, the clinician has relentlessly pursued his line of reasoning and tried to impose it on the boy, who, interestingly enough, strongly resists because that is not where his problem resides. But one can well imagine that many other children might give in to the suggestions, not only because they might find it convenient, but also because the clinician is an expert and an authority figure. Furthermore, it is noteworthy that the clinician did not suggest that the father participate in these tests.

> [confused] It seems to come on to me for nothing really. I don't think it's my mother, it's the whole world. I get really depressed at school.

The clinician never focused on the boy's peers, even though he wanted to talk about them as he felt most depressed following peer group activities. According to the mother, the boy was depressed about school issues, particularly peers, as he did not feel sufficiently accepted to participate in their activities. This isolation further contributed to the depression. Between the third and scheduled fourth interviews, the boy made a crude attempt at suicide. Alarmed, the parents located another therapist with the help of a friend. The new therapist did not see any indication that the symptomatology was home related (Ambert, 1998).

The transcript of the teenager's paraphrased report yields several themes all derived from a therapist's reductionist ideology of parental causality and mother blaming and do not address the child's need. In fact, the child cannot even talk about his problems as he experiences them. In contrast, the next therapist had no preconceived notions of blame and allowed the boy to focus on the sources of his problems, all of which were located extra-familially.

PARENT EFFECTIVENESS TRAINING

One type of behavioral intervention that has been extensively researched involves training parents to modify their children's behaviors. Parents are now at the front line of therapeutic interventions directed at redressing or alleviating their children's behavior problems, with a good measure of success with young children, but less so with adolescent offenders (Tate, Reppucci, and Mulvey, 1995). A variety of parent-effectiveness training programs have succeeded, at least temporarily, at breaking the cycle of coercion described in Chapter 5 (Bank et al., 1991). What happens in the long run is not generally studied.

Spitzer, Webster-Stratton, and Hollinsworth (1991) have documented the stages that parents enrolled in such a program go through, beginning with the admission that their three- to eight-year-old child has severe behavior problems, about which they feel helpless, ashamed, and even angry. As the chain of training sessions moves on, parents learn new coping skills and more appropriate methods of discipline and, as they regain a certain level of control, the children's coercive episodes diminish in number and severity. Parents feel great relief, as if a terrible burden has been lifted from their shoulders. They learn to utilize their support system more efficiently. When relevant, they are also encouraged to lower their expectations and to be more realistic concerning their children's behaviors and personalities.

Spitzer, Webster-Stratton, and Hollinsworth (1991) documented how, at one phase or another of the training cycle, a majority of parents "resist" the process, and setbacks follow. As these authors (1991:426) explain it, this resistance occurs because parents maintain unrealistic expectations: they hope that success will come rapidly and they generally underestimate "the commitment and energy needed." They are then frustrated over "having to deal continually with children who are aversive and nonreinforcing despite their best efforts." The authors sympathetically describe some of the pitfalls and frustrations that parents encounter during the weeks of the training process as they implement new techniques and use rewards and punishments more efficiently. I list a few to illustrate the magnitude of the difficulties facing such parents.

First, they evaluate themselves negatively and believe that they are the cause of their children's problems. They feel isolated because they cannot discuss their situation with others, such as relatives and teachers, who might blame or reject them. They are discouraged when they learn that their child has a chronic problem that will require continuous monitoring (Spitzer et al., 1991:422). It is difficult for parents to face the fact that the dysfunctional behaviors may remain, even though in a diminished form. Parents also experience unanticipated setbacks as siblings who have been easy become difficult in order to benefit from the problematic child's reward system, "thus taxing the already depleted resources and energy of these parents" (Spitzer et al., 1991:420). Then there are instances when a boyfriend or a grandmother who lives with the family, but does not participate in the training program, creates a conflictual situation by using inappropriate techniques or contradicting the mother in her attempts at controlling the child. In other instances, particularly resistant children use the reward system to find yet another way of controlling their parents: some children refuse to do anything without a reward. All in all, many parents feel that the time and patience they must invest in the child are excessive.

This litany of problems encountered by well-intentioned parents of young children is only magnified for parents of older children whose behavior is more entrenched and even potentially dangerous. Adolescents have additional means with which to confront their parents if they so wish: truancy from school, running away from home, breaking their curfew, being verbally or physically threatening, and even physically assaulting their parents—not to omit rationalizing their behaviors and blaming their parents. Appropriate reward systems can be nearly impossible to establish because such youngsters may prefer rewards from the streets to those from their parents. It is at that stage, one often leading to delinquency, that many parents become desperate and some turn to a parent support group.

This section illustrates how, because parents have to be involved in intervention programs aimed at helping their children, professionals wield a great deal of power over them, and their compliance is necessary if they are not to be judged "resistant." As discussed earlier, the success of the intervention, as assessed by the experts themselves, lies largely in parents' own resocialization progress: parents who accept the professionals' views are considered the most successful. But even accepting professionals' views is no guarantee that the children will change their behaviors. Moreover, not all parents can be reeducated, either because of their own personality problems, their lack of resources (transportation, babysitting, and money), and their right to disagree when they find the regime objectionable or the therapists unpleasant. Disturbed or poor parents are the most likely to drop out of such programs. Moreover, there is often a great deal of disagreement between professionals and families about goals and the causality of a child's problems. In view of the importance of the general environment in the etiology of behavioral problems, as seen in previous chapters, community-based intervention and education programs may be more appropriate. They might also reach a greater number of parents at a lower cost than therapy (Cunningham, Bremmer, and Boyle, 1995).

RESEARCHING PARENTS AND CHILDREN

Researchers can also become a part of the professional context of the parent-child relationship. Because studies often focus on negative child outcomes, parents who are problematic, have special-needs children, or are undergoing difficult transitions are probably more frequently researched than the average population. Few researchers return to ask respondents how they felt about the questionnaire, the interviews, or even the videotapes to which they contributed time. One such study by Russell and colleagues (1995) found that a small group of respondents and families had experienced strong negative emotions as a result of their participation in a research project, although the majority felt either no change in their lives as a result or felt that the change had been positive.

Although research is often beneficial to the persons studied, one can hypothesize that the more *intrusive* it is in parents' and children's lives, the less certain one can be of the participants' positive reaction, unless the direct purpose is to offer immediate help to the families in question. By intrusive, one means, in particular, methods that include several members of a family in a proposed discussion of *personal* topics, especially when videotaped. The closer these sessions are to a family therapy format, the greater the likelihood of creating unanticipated problems. The more family members are involved together in such a task, the more likely someone is to divulge something that will hurt at least one other member, possibly because the speaker feels that the research context grants total freedom of expression. The hurt feelings may linger on. A family member may suddenly disclose something that the others did not know and the abrupt revelation can have a devastating effect. Examples of such negative results from research are the impact on children of being openly discussed by their parents, the pain felt by parents upon hearing their children blame them, the revelations of spouses concerning negative feelings they harbor about each other, and stepparents discovering that they are not wanted in the family. Yet there is practically no examination of these research-created dangers or risk factors.

The reader may have noticed a parallel here with what takes place on many talk shows where the focus is on confessing problems and behaviors that are generally considered shameful, hurtful, or at the very least embarrassing in society at large. The talk-show hosts in effect attribute to themselves therapeutic, moralistic, and research roles. But they do it in public and they do not worry about the negative reactions that may occur when the participants return home and are all alone to face the consequences of their revelations. Furthermore, a good proportion of the guests who divulge their problems lack education and some are obviously poor: they certainly cannot afford professional help. Parents are often favorite targets of such shows: abusive parents, adoptive parents, birth parents, troubled parents—the list goes on. What appearing on talk show does to family dynamics is anyone's guess, but it has a good chance of being problematic.

In the scientific realm, one could also argue that even questionnaires given to children and adolescents should be carefully scrutinized from an ethical perspective. If not properly designed to balance the positive and the negative, the wording could influence vulnerable adolescents to interpret the questions as an encouragement to negatively evaluate their parents' childrearing approaches. In other words, even questionnaires and especially interviews can be problematic, either because of slanted wording or because a suggestible child reacts negatively. Unfortunately, it is not currently a concern of ethics committees that review research proposals to protect *parents*. In fact, at this stage, some consensus suggests that researchers should not need parental consent to distribute questionnaires in schools. The line of reasoning is that parents who object might have something to hide and their children's nonparticipation may bias the results. In other words, scientific goals are more important than parents' rights and familial integrity. This view might perhaps be acceptable were psychological and sociological research of great help to families. Unfortunately, too much of the research, although interesting, is of no great consequence for families' *well-being*. Therefore, researchers' wishes for free access may be more a matter of intellectual curiosity, professional promotion, and career advancement than of helpful consequences for families.

CONCLUSIONS

Professionals can either facilitate or complicate parents' lives as well as family dynamics. On the positive side, professionals have alerted us to child abuse and neglect by disturbed or uninvolved parents, for which we have to be very grateful. Unfortunately, it is perhaps also true that this achievement has resulted in a general mistrust of parents among professionals. The result is that conscientious parents can no longer be as effective as previous generations were because they have lost much of the moral authority that belonged to them in the past. Their moral authority is tainted by the stigma of child abuse, which, at any rate, does not apply to them. In fact, one could well argue that, because parents feel powerless, they become neglectful when they fail to properly monitor their adolescents' activities.

Although relatively few parents consult professionals directly, what is important here is that professionals constitute a key *cultural* context in the parent-child relationship in terms of defining what good parenting is. This is because of the wide public exposure and dissemination of their theories, the support that each group of experts gives to other groups, and the importance of science in our contemporary society. Reiterated otherwise, professionals socially construct and create a parenting climate. This power is accompanied with the prerogative to blame and even punish parents. The latter case can be illustrated by the possibility of having one's child unjustifiably taken away, although too many children are left in very dysfunctional families because of professional belief that natural parents are better than adoptive ones (see Chapter 11).

Some categories of parents are more vulnerable than others to professional control. Aside from parents whose children have obvious problems requiring help, the following are also particularly defenseless: parents who themselves have problems, impoverished single mothers, perhaps minority group single mothers, and all those who are most likely to come to the attention of welfare agencies and other intervention institutions. Middle-class parents who make it a point of following the latest trends in the popular "how to raise your child" literature may be particularly receptive to and, hence, affected by the opinions they encounter. Parental vulnerability and control by experts may produce good results or questionable ones. What is important to remember in the final analysis is that parents have been disempowered and have been "professionalized." One of the results of this situation is that they may be less effective at parenting.

The family is headed by parents and when they are the ones who suffer from serious emotional problems, their children are at risk of incurring a similar or related fate because of heredity and the stressful environment parents may create. Consequently, there is a huge body of research on the effect on children of nonnormative parents, whether alcoholic, depressed, or abusive, but far less exists when the situation is reversed. Yet when children are the afflicted ones, parents have to respond, adapt, seek help, and even suffer blame and a sense of failure. Family boundaries become permeable as help is sought or imposed. Parents can even become a disempowered "class" whose moral authority is effectively muted.

Chapter 9

The Effect of Adult Children on Parents

True or false?

1. As children grow up, their problems and difficulties no longer affect their parents. **False**
2. Aging parents help their adult children financially more than their adult children help them. **True**
3. Most elderly parents depend on their children for their care. **False**
4. Many senior parents help raise their grandchildren. **True**
5. Most adult children who live with their parents do so because they, not their parents, need it. **True**

In the "old days" and still in most countries of the world, there was a circular flow of intergenerational help. Parents raised children and invested in them for a few years and later on their children helped them, often for as many years, while parents contributed to the care of their grandchildren. Today, parents raise their children and invest in them, often to their last days. Adult children help a bit, some help a great deal for a few months or years, and a rare few devote themselves entirely to their parents' last years. But, in most cases when adult children help, parents are able to reciprocate in other ways, whether at the emotional level, as confidantes, as babysitters, or materially.

These facts are meant to help dispel myths. However, the truth about the effect of children on elderly adults is a complex pattern woven with threads of love, worries, shared joys, ambivalence, distancing, new duties, gratitude, ingratitude, help given and help received, loneliness, and fulfillment. Furthermore, no indications suggest that

childless seniors are less happy or healthy or more lonely than those
who are parents. However, a good relationship with a child is definitely an asset for any adult (Silverstein and Bengtson, 1991), and
seniors with children receive more help than childless seniors.

WHAT ADULT CHILDREN
DO FOR THEIR PARENTS

From an analytical perspective, one notes that there is a *huge*
amount of literature on the topic of what adult children do for their
aged parents. What is even more telling is the direction that this literature has taken. Much of that research has focused on the instrumental help that adult children give and on the stress that arises as a result
of the *caregiver burden.* These two words deserve some serious consideration and deconstruction. To begin with, few adult children are
their parents' caregivers in the true sense of the word. They help, certainly, but caregiving embodies connotations of feeding, bathing, and
toileting helpless seniors. In reality, few seniors require this type of
assistance. When they do, it is generally extended to them by a
spouse, an institution, or paid outsiders. Furthermore, most need this
type of care only during a few months or years before death. What
adult children generally do is supervise the care, run errands, clean
the house, transport the elderly, and manage their parents' finances.
This is a lot to do, especially when only one adult child is involved.
Thus, a more appropriate term might be *manager* in some cases,
helper in others; in only a portion is the term "caregiver" applicable.
Nevertheless, whatever the terminology, the parent who is by then
frail or suffers from Alzheimer's disease benefits greatly.

The word *burden* is even more problematic because it expresses a
double standard: one for parents and another for children. Consider
this: "burden" is a term that is never used for parents when they take
care of their young children or are taxed by a child with behavior problems or even deliquency. Burden implies a negative effect, and, as we
see in this text, many children are a real burden. Yet researchers even
refuse to consider child effect in these cases and certainly do not think
in terms of burden. The term burden is only starting to be used for parents who have the entire responsibility and care for adult children who

are seriously emotionally disturbed or mentally challenged. *If caring for one's problematic children does not qualify as a burden, why does caring for one's elderly parent qualify?* The answer can only lie in the way we socially construct what parenting means, which is devotion at whatever cost, and what being a child means, which is benefiting at whatever cost to the parents. The result of such a social construction of reality is that parents have to be at the giving end while children are at the receiving end. Thus, when the table is turned in old age, it is defined as a burden—even in instances in which the now-burdened adult children drove their parents to distraction and ill health during their protracted and very problematic youth.

Generally, when elderly (seventy-five years and older, often much older among whites and Asians but younger among blacks and Native Americans) parents' health falters and limitations are placed on their ability to be independent, adult children become their key support resources (Eggebeen and Hogan, 1990). When a parent falls prey to mental disabilities such as senility and Alzheimer's disease, the parent becomes the child and the child becomes the parent. This is when hardships arise from caring or supervising the care because the responsibilities multiply for the child, while meaningful verbal exchanges diminish until even recognition disappears. For the parent, the world, including her own children, fades little by little until it has entirely evaporated; this deterioration is very distressing for everyone involved. Children actually lose the parent long before biological death occurs.

In fact, adult children who care for a parent are far more stressed when the parent suffers from cognitive and/or behavioral problems than from physical disabilities (Starrels et al., 1997). This is an interesting parallel because, as we have seen in earlier chapters, it is also less stressful for parents to care for physically or mentally challenged children than for children who suffer from emotional and behavioral problems. It is the human-interaction nature of the latter two types of problems that make them so difficult to live with, whether one is a parent, a child, or even a sibling.

In contrast, when a parent's disabilities are strictly physical, the parent-child relationship often continues to include most of its previous elements. The research literature so far has emphasized the stress experienced by adult children, especially daughters, as a result of their role as caretakers of disabled parents (Gerstel and Gallagher,

1993). Comparatively little research shows the positive side of caring for one's elderly parents. In this respect, Pruchno, Patrick, and Burant (1997) have pointed out the importance of distinguishing between caregiving burden and caregiving satisfaction. Burden may lead to stress but the satisfaction derived from caring for a loved one and doing it well may counterbalance the potential stress.

Elderly parents are happier when they give than when they receive, and they accept help more readily when they can contribute something in return, particularly to their sons. When parents require a great deal of support from their children, they are less satisfied with the relationship. In part, this can be explained by the fact that contact with the child is necessitated by the parents' needs rather than by the child's desire to see the parents or by the spontaneity of a visit just to socialize. There may also be many cases of adult children who do not hide their dissatisfaction at having to help their parents. This can create a great deal of mental misery among seniors.

Lee, Netzer, and Coward (1995) find that older parents who receive more help are more depressed. As they point out, American elders value their independence, and dependence on children may be troublesome for them. But they also suggest the possibility of a reversed causality, that is, children might respond to their parents' depression by helping them more. It is not surprising, therefore, that when older parents are in better health, they report a more positive relationship with their children. But a family's value system and sense of morality is important. When the entire family, and not just the parents, have always valued reciprocity, elders may be comforted with the thought that their earlier parental efforts were appreciated. They may not be negatively affected if they are unable to reciprocate in their later years.

GENDER OF CHILDREN AND PARENTS

Studies unanimously find that *daughters* are far more likely to become their elderly parents' caretakers or helpers than sons (Silverstein, Parrott, and Bengtson, 1995). When a son has the responsibility for his parents, his wife often assumes this duty or, at the very least, contributes to it. Sons provide help mainly in the domains of transportation and finances; when parents become more needy in terms of personal care, sons frequently abdicate their role (Montgomery and Kamo, 1989). In fact, Spitze and Logan (1991) point out that the key to receiving help resides in having one daughter. This is because women are generally assigned nurturant roles in our society and learn to be responsible for the well-being of others from the time they are young (Montgomery, 1992). Consequently, parents may also expect more help from their daughters than their sons—although the reverse occurs in many other societies, such as China and Japan.

Starrels and colleagues (1997) have found that elderly parents who receive help from their children tend to reciprocate more with their sons than with their daughters, and provide less assistance to daughters than sons. Parents seem to appreciate their sons' caregiving more than their daughters', perhaps because it is taken for granted in this society that daughters are nurturant and dutiful. It is expected that they will help their elderly parents as part of their feminine role. This expectation and the greater reciprocity with sons may be reasons why daughters experience more stress than sons. The parallel with parents of children at home is that mothers are far more affected by their children than fathers, as seen in Chapters 5 and 6. Thus, the line of nurture and affect passes from mothers to adult daughters in the traditional division of care.

Gender is a factor not only in who gives help, but in who receives it. As their health deteriorates, widowed mothers in their seventies to nineties receive more help from their children than do widowed fathers. Perhaps children perceive their mothers to be more fragile or perhaps this is because mothers have cared for their children more than fathers in the past. Children are also generally more attached to mothers than fathers. Silverstein, Parrott, and Bengtson (1995) report that affection is a stronger motivator for help to older mothers while expectation of an inheritance is more frequently a factor for assistance to fathers, although this is more the case among sons than daughters.

WHAT PARENTS
DO FOR THEIR ADULT CHILDREN

From the time their offspring are young adults, parents continue to provide a great deal of moral, instrumental, and even financial assistance. This situation often continues for decades. The 1987 National

Survey of Families and Households indicated that only about 5 percent of adult children had given money to their parents in the past five years. In contrast, 20 percent of white adult children and 6 percent of African-American and Latino adult children had received over $200 from parents during the same period (Lee and Aytac, 1998). These figures would be far higher had smaller cash gifts been included. Furthermore, these numbers do not include what we could call "emancipated" children, that is, adolescent mothers who remain home with their children and other adolescents who are no longer in school but are unemployed and live at home. They coreside with their parents.

Coresidence is another form of help from which adult children benefit. In a recent survey, about 30 percent of adults aged twenty-five to fifty-four who had never married and 13 percent of those who were divorced lived in their parents' home (White and Peterson, 1995). The greater the number of children, the more likely senior parents are to have one who resides with them because of need. Some adult children have never left home while others have returned. Parents over sixty-five who have a coresident child (about 15 percent according to Aquilino, 1990) usually receive relatively little household or financial help from that child. Da Vanzo and Goldscheider (1990) show that male children are more likely to return home than female children; moreover, males do 20 percent less housework than females when they live with their parents. Hence, coresidence generally benefits the adult child more than the parents and reactivates parental duties in terms of food preparation and housework.

As parents age, they often do not or cannot disengage from the problems experienced by their adult children. Pillemer and Suitor (1991) report that 26 percent of senior parents mention that at least one of their children is experiencing serious physical or mental health problems or a high level of stress. These children's problems correlate significantly with depression in the older parents, and some studies find that older parents who have to help their children a lot feel more depressed (Mutran and Reitzes, 1984). These parents may be particularly worried about the future of children who fail to achieve a reasonable level of independence or of personal responsibility. Furthermore, many of these children may be too fixated on their problems to appreciate the extent of the demands they place on their parents; as a consequence, the latter may feel utterly unappreciated and even exploited. In addition, when children have mental health problems, they may need to receive advice that is not wanted or that they are unwilling or unable to put into practice. They may, as a result, resent their parents or openly defy them.

Emotional and behavioral disturbances experienced by children aged eight to ten relate twenty years later to a life that is on average more burdened with chronic stressors and negative events (Ronka and Pulkinen, 1995). From a life course perspective, Rutter and colleagues (1995:74) find that such individuals are less likely to "show planning in relation to key life transitions." This inability to plan, which often accompanies behavioral problems, in turn leads to additional negative events. For instance, children who had behavioral problems at age ten were far more likely to have entered a first union with a deviant partner, in part because such youngsters had congregated with antisocial peers and lived in areas where there was a higher ratio of antisocial persons (Quinton et al., 1993). No research documents the effect of such adult children's life courses on their middle-aged and elderly parents. Several students have reported older siblings who were still living at home or had just left who had been problematic all their lives. These students were very demoralized by what they considered injustices suffered by their parents. You may recall here a long student quote on page 85.

A certain proportion of parents of perturbed, troubled, or distressed and unsuccessful adults are themselves problematic persons: they were difficult persons as younger adults and were not very competent parents. They may have had an unsatisfying relationship with their children when the latter were growing up (Reiss, 1995). In addition, these children might have inherited temperamental disadvantages from them, such as tendencies toward irritability or depression. Hence, it is to be expected that a segment of distressed or difficult adults have parents who are or were similar to them because of a combination of heredity and familial adversity.

Of course, the type of help that parents provide to their adult children depends on their socioeconomic status. For instance, white parents provide much more financial help than do black parents. This is not a matter of race but rather one of income: white adults have on average a higher income and this allows them to pass this advantage on to their children. Black parents, particularly black grandmothers, help far more with their grandchildren. A greater proportion of them baby-sit their grandchildren, while others raise at least one of them for many years—far more often than do white grandparents. Again, this situation arises out of the dismal socioeconomic conditions in which too many African-American families raise their children, particularly in segregated, unsafe, and high-poverty inner-city neighborhoods. As a result, many black mothers become grandmothers prematurely (Burton, 1996). Their very young daughters need help and they have to give it. Too many of the grandchildren become their sole responsibility.

GRANDMOTHERS AS CHILD CARETAKERS

Thus, the effect of children on parents is pursued into the next generation as many grandparents help raise their grandchildren. A very small number take on this challenge out of their *own* unresolved sense of superiority over a child of whom they do not approve. For these few older adults, it is finally their chance to prove themselves to an adult child, particularly a daughter, who has "strayed" from conventions. But, in a majority of cases, grandparents simply see no other alternative: they must help. Therefore, for many women who become grandmothers, this transition more or less involves an extension of their maternal role.

Slightly over 40 percent of American grandmothers provide care for at least one grandchild on a regular basis (Baydar and Brooks-Gunn, 1998). Grandmothers often baby-sit while their daughters are at work, whether they live with them or nearby. Furthermore, as we see later, a little over 10 percent of grandparents are or have been at some point the primary caregivers of one or more grandchild (Fuller-Thomson, Minkler, and Driver, 1997).

It is difficult to say whether more grandmothers are now baby-sitting than was the case in the past, when fewer young mothers were in the labor force and the necessity for regular child care was less urgent. Now grandmothers are needed more than before because their daughters and daughters-in-law are employed. In fact, one-third of low-income women report that lack of child care is the main reason why they remain unemployed (Kisker and Ross, 1997). At the same time, however, young grandmothers are more likely to also be employed than in the past. Thus, it is difficult to predict the outcome of these trends because they involve conflicts of interest between the mother and grandmother generation in terms of economic needs.

Baydar and Brooks-Gunn (1998) have studied the characteristics of grandmothers who provide child care. A majority live with their spouses, have more education than those who do not provide care—in part because they belong to the younger cohorts of grandmothers—and about 45 percent are employed. Baby-sitting grandmothers are busy women who combine several roles and are often active in their communities. Some even care simultaneously for their older mother. They truly are the real "sandwich generation" (Ward and Spitze, 1998). Grandmothers who have several children and grandchildren have more opportunities to become caregivers. This opportunity increases when a teenage daughter who lives with them has a baby.

GRANDMOTHERS AS MOTHER SUBSTITUTES

In 1991, the U.S. Census Bureau estimated that 3.3 million children lived with their grandparents. This represented a 44 percent increase since 1980. Fifty percent of these grandchildren had only a mother, 28 percent had neither parent, 17 percent had two parents, and 5 percent had only a father (Saluter, 1992). In a national survey, 11 percent of grandparents reported that they had raised a grandchild for at least six months in their lifetime (Pearson et al., 1997). Grandparents who are given the custody of a grandchild no longer represent isolated cases. In fact, in some states, and particularly among African Americans (Pebley and Rudkin, 1999), over a quarter of the children in foster care are living with grandparents, generally a grandmother (Bonecutter and Gleeson, 1997).

Jendrek (1993) has studied the impact that these caretaking roles have on grandparents' lifestyles, especially the changes that grandparents have to bring to their own lives, the dreams they have to postpone or abandon altogether, and the physical and emotional demands that such a role places on them (Minkler, Roe, and Price, 1992). Jendrek reports that, in 73 percent of the sample, grandchildren live with their grandparents because the child's mother suffers from emotional problems. Maternal drug problems are also involved in half of the cases, and alcoholism in 44 percent of the cases (Burton, 1992). In half of the cases some overlap exists among the reasons, which means that the mothers suffer from a multiplicity of problems. Unfortunately, nothing is said of fathers. But we can presume that most are equally problematic or more so. Obviously, these grandparents are taking charge of children who have lived in deteriorating family circumstances as illustrated in the following student quote:

> I was raised by my grandparents who took me and my little brother in after my mother flipped after my father left her. We had had a hard life and all I remember about it is that my parents were scary [they were alcoholic]. Anyways, we were better off with my grandparents and we knew them because they had often kept us over weekends. . . . Now that we're older it's harder on them in a way because my brother grew up with lots of problems but at least I turned out just fine and this just makes up for it. . . . I love them like my own parents and we owe them everything and I am planning on making a lot of money to take care of them because they are getting on in years.

Given the reasons why they live with them, it can be expected that grandparents have to deal with grandchildren who are seriously at risk for emotional and behavioral problems. Their role may consequently be particularly difficult. The relationship that these grandparents maintain with the minors in their custody has to be parental if this family unit is to function. They give love, comfort, companionship, advice, supervision, and even mete out punishment just as parents do.

Solomon and Marx (1995) used the large National Health Interview Survey that included 448 households headed by grandparents to see how this type of family structure affected children's school and health outcomes. Children raised by grandparents were compared to children living with both biological parents and with children in single-parent families. The latter included families with a remarried parent. In terms of behavior at school as well as indicators of school achievement, children in two-parent families had an advantage over the other two groups. However, children raised by grandparents were doing better than those raised in single-parent families, despite the generally low educational level of these grandparents. In terms of health, there were few differences between children in two-parent and grandparent families, but children in single-parent families were less healthy. Grandparents who raised girls had an easier time than those who raised boys. In a nutshell, these results indicate that children raised by grandparents do quite well considering that many were neglected or mistreated by their parents before being more or less adopted by the senior generation. The devotion and level of maturity of the grandparents confer developmental advantages to the children.

Grandparents who provide child care assistance encounter fewer responsibilities, problems, and stressors than those who raise their grandchildren. While being raised by a grandparent is a reasonable alternative for children, it is a more problematic one for the grandparents. The grandparents often have a multiplicity of roles to fulfill in addition to childrearing, particularly when they are middle aged (Sands and Goldberg-Glen, 2000). They find themselves out of sync with the normal developmental stage of family life: people of their age do not raise children and this anomaly deprives them of moral as well as instrumental support at their grandchildren's schools and in the neighborhood, especially among whites (Pruchno, 1999). Hence, it is not surprising that support groups now exist for such grandparents; these groups constitute an indicator of changing times.

ABUSE OF ELDERLY PARENTS

Women tend to outlive men, and one of the consistent findings on elder abuse by children is that most victims are women (Whittaker, 1995). Until now, the study of elder abuse has emphasized the dependent elderly's caretakers. The reasoning behind this type of inquiry is that the frustrated caretaker lashes out at the frail dependent parent (Steinmetz, 1993). But self-sufficient elderly persons are also abused by an adult child who lives with them because of his or her own dependency (Wolf and Pillemer, 1989). In that case, the adult child depends on the parent financially or for shelter because he or she is unemployed, mentally delayed, physically challenged, or emotionally disturbed. Indeed, after discharge from hospital care, 85 percent of unmarried adult children who are mentally ill move in with their elderly parents (Greenberg, Seltzer, and Greenlay, 1993). The potential for abuse certainly exists (Lefley, 1997). Hence, Pillemer (1985) believes that research may have placed too much emphasis on the dependence of the elderly as a source of abuse and that those elderly who have a dependent and physically stronger spouse or child living with them should be considered.

It is difficult to know whether sons abuse their elderly parents more than daughters. The latter are more frequent caretakers, as seen earlier; consequently, they have more opportunities to be abusive and also more frustration to vent. They fit Steinmetz's (1993) theory better than sons. On the other hand, more sons live with their elderly parents because they are dependent. Males are more aggressive than females and are often not as emotionally attached to their parents as females are. These factors could contribute to more parental abuse by sons. One study in Florida discovered that males were more likely to practice physical abuse, while females were more likely to practice elderly neglect (Miller and Dodder, 1989).

Complicating the issue is the existence of verbal as well as material forms of abuse. The latter are motivated by greed, personal debts, or a spouse's or children's demands. It includes siphoning off parental revenues, walking out with the parents' possessions, or controlling the aged parents' house (Korbin, Anetzberger, and Austin, 1995). Medical abuse is at times perpetrated when the caregiving adult child does not seek assistance for an elderly parent who is suffering or is near death. The reason behind this form of abuse might be to hasten the death of a person who is a burden or to increase the chance that an earlier death will leave a larger inheritance.

Abuse of elderly parents is a relatively easy act to commit and can be less socially visible than abuse of school-age children. The elderly who are most at risk are often socially isolated: they are no longer connected to their social systems, such as church, work, or even friends. No one may notice the abuse and physicians who see bruises may be told that the senior person fell—which occurs quite often in old age. (The parallel with small children who are abused is obvious here.) Furthermore, elderly parents may be less likely to report the abuse than would a maltreated adolescent or even a child. Actually, perhaps as few as 5 percent report it (Tatara, 1993). They may be disabled and unable to use the phone. They may be ashamed of their situation and, at any rate, they may have no one else to turn to for help: an attempt to report it may fail and bring retaliation. Moreover, while abused children grow up and may eventually denounce their parents, the elderly parent dies with the secret.

There is little research on elder abuse among various ethnic and racial groups (Griffin, 1994). Comparisons between groups is important in view of the fact that black seniors, particularly grandmothers, take children and grandchildren in their homes more often than whites do. Thus, at least in theory, they are at a higher risk of abuse, not only from their children but from their grandchildren as well. To my knowledge, no research exists on this topic.

CONCLUSIONS

This chapter continues to highlight some of the biases inherent to the (lack of) research on the effect of children on parents, this time, the effect of adult children on their parents. Furthermore, a related issue that is becoming quite urgent in the wake of social change is the effect of foster grandchildren on the grandparents who assume their full responsibility.

Basically, child effect continues throughout parents' lives until they die. Even when we consider adult children, the combination of their own characteristics and those of their elderly parents contributes to explain the direction that child effect takes, that is, whether it is positive or negative. This is a field of inquiry that is practically untouched by research. Another particularly intriguing aspect is the type of sibling group. That is, are older parents more or less affected by an individual child when they have more than one offspring, several offspring, or a very large family? The offspring's social class and level of resources represents another intriguing variable as does the family's racial status. Adult children who experience rapid social mobility and move up in the class system may become very different from their parents and espouse values that are not shared with them. Furthermore, social mobility is often accompanied by geographic mobility, thus a double potential for distancing from parents. These phenomena would constitute interesting research topics in terms of child effect.

Chapter 10

Immigrant and Minority Parents

Immigrant and minority parents are often affected by their children in ways that differ from those of native-born families of white ancestry. This child effect may be particularly evident when parents are not well acquainted with the English language and when they come from a rural country and settle in a large North American city where the lifestyle is totally different from the one they left behind. Children will be at a cultural advantage over their parents as they become assimilated through the school system.

Among visible minorities, negative child effect is often fostered by the detrimental neighborhood and school environment in which families are forced to live because of discrimination and consequent segregation. In this chapter, we discuss immigrant and minority parents in general as well as in certain specific domains of life. Unfortunately, the literature on child effect among minority families is practically nonexistent so that these discussions are by necessity brief. Once again, this forces us to point out what needs to be done in terms of research and why it has to be done or, in other words, to summarize what does not exist.

At the end of the nineteenth and the beginning of the twentieth centuries, most immigrants were white but they spoke a variety of languages, such as Italian, Polish, Yiddish, German, and Spanish. They were discriminated against because of their poor clothes, improper English, "dark" appearance in the case of Italians, lack of education, and rural origins. Even the Irish were singled out for prejudicial treatment because they were largely poor, unskilled, and Catholic (Coontz, 2000). Early in the twentieth century, children of immigrant families, including Jews, were definitely not attending school as long as old-stock American children, nor were they doing well academically. High delinquency rates prevailed, while some of the adults were heavily involved in criminality because of blocked educational, occupational, and residential opportunities after arrival.

For instance, in 1905 in New York, over a third of correctional institution inmates were Jewish (Gold and Phillips, 1996). Yet this group did not have a history of criminality in the old countries—their opportunities in the United States were limited by discrimination. Today, immigrants' great-grandchildren are part of the American majority, both in terms of values and language, as well as occupational skills. Therefore, each century witnesses discrimination against immigrant families of different origins. Currently, nonwhite minorities are the target of discriminatory practices.

WHAT HAPPENS TO CHILDREN?

Immigrant families whose children do well combine economic and educational adaptation while retaining core family and religious values as well as a sense of ethnic identity. The children become bicultural, at least for a generation or two (Kim and Choi, 1994). They develop a positive dual frame of reference. Parents encourage them to respect teachers and learn English. But for many other families, the next generation does less well in school than expected by parents. Many arrive poor and, particularly when they are racially distinct, are forced to live in segregated, high-poverty areas. These areas often have elevated rates of school dropout, nonmarital pregnancy, and unemployment. As a consequence, these children of immigrants and of U.S.-born minority groups do less well than the American average, a factor that must give rise to a great deal of disappointment and even regrets on the parents' part.

Alejandro Portes has coined the term *downward assimilation* (1995). This concept describes what happens when immigrant families are both poor and belong to a visible minority. These families have migrated to secure a better future for their children and have high aspirations. But they have to settle in neighborhoods harboring social problems. While the parents work hard, often at minimal wages, their children attend a school where attitudes toward education and work are "adversarial," as

Portes and Zhou (1993) have put it, where dropping out is acceptable, where language skills are not mainstream, and where hanging out around the corner courting trouble is the main form of social activity. These immigrant children learn about American culture through their neighbors' social isolation from mainstream society. Thus, they learn and accept the norms and ways of behaving of locally born children, who are themselves members of visible minorities and as such have been cut off from mainstream society and its educational as well as occupational opportunities.

These children's immigrant parents may not yet be well acquainted with American ways, and may not know English sufficiently well to counterbalance the influence of this external environment on their offspring. Their own cultural community either possesses too few social resources or the children no longer identify with their parents' origins. The result is that the second generation may be as poor, or even poorer, than the first one. It is, at the very least, less motivated. These youth are not willing to do the "dirty" work that their parents have done, but are unqualified for the better-paying jobs to which they aspire (Gans, 1992). Consequently, many of these children, as adults, have higher rates of unemployment, single-mother families, drug use, and criminality than the parent generation. Their lifestyle and achievement level are bound to disappoint their parents. These youths have assimilated themselves within an educational and economic poverty context: this is what is referred to as downward assimilation.

The opposite occurs when the second generation attaches itself to a neighborhood or a school where the English spoken is mainstream, where students do well, expect to go to college, and consequently have low rates of early parenthood and school dropout. This could be called *mainstream assimilation;* it is likely to lead to upward rather than downward social mobility and to be rewarding for parents who feel that their move away from their country or, in the case of Native Americans, from the reservations, has been justified.

INTERGENERATIONAL CONFLICT

For immigrant parents, family cohesiveness may be more important than it is for native-born parents because immigrants often leave everything behind. Their children are their main source of happiness. Intergenerational conflict may thus be particularly painful for them. At the risk of simplifying matters, there is less conflict between parents and growing/grown children when the family originates from an urban area of an economically advanced society. Such families have less adaptation to make and fewer aspects of their lives require change. The various facets of American society resemble to some extent what the parents had already been exposed to in their country of origin. But when families originate from rural areas of underdeveloped countries, the fit between life in the United States or Canada and that in their country of origin diminishes. A great deal of adaptation is necessary and, although this may not be unpleasant, not all the family members adapt at an equal rate and on the same matters. In some contexts, parents adapt faster than children, especially if they are educated and then preserve their traditional role. But generally the contrary occurs. Children and adolescents are immersed in American culture through school systems and peer groups as well as television; they adapt more quickly. *The problem lies in what they adapt to:* they may abandon "old" cultural practices and language as well as educational aspirations, all of which create conflict between parents and children.

Not surprisingly, Rumbaut (1996) reports that parent-child conflict is more likely when parents are less educated, struggle financially, and when the child prefers English, watches a great deal of television, and does not do well at school. Adolescents who experience discrimination may also have more conflict with their parents, as they may bring home the stressors that are school and peer-driven, as explained in Chapter 7 on peers. While their parents believe in the results of doing well at school, these children's only desire is to be accepted by their peers. At that point, there is a divergence of immediate goals between the two generations. Indeed, immigrant children have perhaps a greater need than others to be accepted by their peers. They are consequently eager to immerse themselves into the new American lifestyle. Girls in particular crave the freedom that their locally born peers enjoy or appear to be enjoying. This may not be so acceptable to parents, and parent-daughter conflict occasionally arises, as described by one student:

It was so hard for a twelve-year-old girl who came from a small town to fit in this big city in a school where every child was so different than the children back home. They all seemed to have more freedom, clothes, money. I felt so deprived and lonely because no one accepted me. I was dressed weird by my parents and I wasn't allowed to go out like the other teenagers. I began rebelling against my parents but this didn't improve my situation because I lost the support of the only people who truly loved me. But, at the time, all I wanted was to be accepted by my peers and my parents didn't count in this picture.

Immigrant parents, therefore, often feel rejected by their adolescent children, particularly when the latter adopt ways of living and thinking that go against their norms.

The child's *gender* is an important variable in this respect. The majority of current immigrant families originate from societies that are patriarchal, thus father and male dominated. In these societies, girls are generally more closely supervised than boys, especially in terms of contact with the opposite sex, activities outside the home, and clothing. American adolescents start dating at a very young age compared to the norm in most countries of the world. In fact, in many cultures, particularly in Asia, Africa, and even Latin America, dating as it is known here does not exist. Courting takes place, but generally not in the early teens, usually under some sibling or adult supervision, and with the goal of marriage in mind. Elsewhere, marriages are arranged between families, with or without consulting the couple. When such families settle in the United States or Canada, the freedom that North American women enjoy may lead to dissatisfaction and conflict between parents and children, particularly fathers who are vested with the protection of the family's honor.

In other instances, adolescent males have more conflict with their parents than their sisters have. This generally occurs when they integrate themselves into peer groups that have low educational aspirations, high rates of dropout, and may even be delinquent. Although this can take place at all social class levels, it is more likely to happen when immigrant families settle in disadvantaged neighborhoods where street gangs have visibility and where downward assimilation is consequently the rule.

INTERGENERATIONAL CONTINUITY

In contrast, other immigrant families experience little intergenerational conflict. This happier situation often is the result of living in a community of their group, whether Korean, Chinese, Cuban, or Mexican. This community provides youth with a great deal of contact with similar peers and with other adults of their ethnic group who become role models. These contacts reinforce what they are taught at home and provide social support to parents. Although these youths may attend a school that has a wide diversity of students, their community provides them the security of same-culture peers whose parents' expectations are similar to their parents'. Thus, some collective socialization takes place, as these children belong to an effective community (Coleman and Hoffer, 1987) with a certain degree of insulation from the rest of society. A Chinese student from a poor family explains this situation:

> There were several other Chinese students at my school and we all clung to each other desperately because we didn't fit in with the other students. They were all rich or so it appeared but we were all poor and had to help our parents and worked long hours during weekends in addition to doing our homework. This could have been the worse time of my life if I had gone to another school. But my Chinese friends all had the same problems and we all wanted to make our parents proud of us while too many of the other students who were popular didn't seem to respect their parents. We studied hard, learned English diligently, and visited at each other's homes. I know that everyone thought that we were eggheads but we made it and we were basically happy because we had each other for moral support and to look up to.

In fact, evidence supports that a certain degree of cultural continuity between the parent and child generations is functional both at the familial and individual levels. Children who do not reject their parents' culture benefit from emotional support at home. These same children retain greater respect for parental authority than do their more assimilated peers. This allows them to work harder at school and meet parental expectations. Such children are in turn more likely to go on to postsecondary education and earn high incomes later on. Thus, child effect is far more positive under these circumstances.

Bilingualism, or the speaking of one's language at home while being fluent in English, is an indicator both of generational, cultural continuity, and ability to adapt. Children who are thoroughly bilingual, whether they are Mexican or Asian American, do better at school than those of the same origins who no longer speak their language or who do not know English well (Blair and Qian, 1998). For instance, the dropout rates are higher among Latinos who are totally assimilated at the linguistic level and no longer speak Spanish at home (Rumberger and Larson, 1998). It seems that children and youth who have retained part of their cultural heritage are more influenced by higher parental aspirations on their behalf and less by peers who have lost their heritage and whose educational aspirations may be lower. Thus, cultural heritage, particularly linguistic, fosters positive child effect on parents, in part because it allows for communication between the two generations and the maintenance of parental authority (Mouw and Xie, 1999). In fact, adolescents who use the family's native language at home tend to experience a better relationship with their parents (Tseng and Fuligni, 2000).

SPECIFIC EXAMPLES
OF CONTINUITY AND DISCONTINUITY

In this section, we look at two immigrant minorities, Mexican Americans and Chinese Americans, in terms of what occurs between the generations as children adapt. The comparison of first generations and subsequent generations of Mexican Americans leads to the conclusion that, while a substantial proportion of these families have progressed economically with their American children (slightly lower birth rate, more college education, home ownership, and less poverty), another proportion have acquired American habits that are more problematic, such as higher rates of single mothers, youthful parents, and welfare assistance. For instance, in 1997, the Mexican-American teen birth rate surpassed that of blacks (Ventura et al., 1999). Thus, a segment of Mexican-American children has downwardly assimilated, a situation that will affect their parents negatively depending on the latter's expectations.

As they become more Americanized, second- and third-generation Mexican-American youth identify less with their country of origin and have fewer contacts with relatives "back home." A proportion reject their parents' work ethics and some of their family's values (Buriel and De Ment, 1997). When this occurs, assimilation is subtractive because the children lose valuable aspects of their culture of origin and have either not replaced them with anything or have replaced them with American patterns that are considered deviant in mainstream America and are not conducive to a reasonable level of success in this society (Portes and Rumbaut, 1996).

These might include a devaluation of school, of hard work, of respect for authority, as well as pregnancy without a reasonable income support. As one can see, while cultural assimilation of immigrants may appear to be a worthwhile goal, it can only be so to the extent that the immigrant families are placed in a situation where their children have the opportunity to learn the positive rather than the negative aspects of their host society. Thus, for immigrant parents who arrive poor, the quality of the societal response or, in this case, of the environment that society provides their family is the key variable through which child effect takes place.

The situation of Chinese immigrant children is often quite different. Indeed, Chinese-American families are fairly effective at the double task of giving their children the tools with which to be educationally and to some extent financially successful in the United States and Canada while retaining some core cultural values. These same values themselves contribute to achievement. Feldman and Rosenthal (1990) have compared the age expectations for autonomy in various life domains of fifteen- through eighteen-year-old adolescents of Chinese origins, including a sample living in Hong Kong, first generation, and second generation Chinese-American samples, as well as a sample of white Americans. They found that white American adolescents had the earliest age expectations for the initiation of dating, boy-girl parties, and so on. First-generation Chinese-Americans and Hong Kong students had the latest age expectations, with second-generation Chinese being somewhat in the middle. Feldman and Rosenthal suggest that Chinese-American adolescents are slow to shift their expectations toward the American model of early auton- omy because of the effectiveness of the family in transmitting its val- ues. The cultural environment of the Chinese-American adolescents thus postpones large-scale intergenerational conflict.

As well, Chinese-American students experience less nonconform- ing peer pressure than whites because they are often excluded from the activities of their more emancipated peers, whether white or black. These combined factors in turn contribute to reduce intergenerational conflict among Chinese-American families. Nevertheless, Chinese- American teenagers still perceive their family environment as less accepting and more demanding than do white teenagers (Rosenthal and Feldman, 1990). However, the difference is not large and could be the result of a comparison on the part of the Chinese of their families with what they perceive to be the norm in America (Pyke, 2000). Over- all, the level of life satisfaction is as high among Chinese Americans and Canadians as it is in the rest of the population (Ying, 1992).

As among other immigrants, Chinese children often play the role of cultural brokers (Buriel and De Ment, 1997). This occurs mainly because in many families one or both parents may not be proficient in the English language. This role begins when children must translate instructions for their mother, for instance, or help her at the checkout counter in stores, or make phone calls for her. Later on, the more edu- cated sibling tends to be the one who is the most relied on by parents or grandparents for information or as an interpreter.

AFRICAN-AMERICAN PARENTS: THE EFFECT OF A NEGATIVE ENVIRONMENT

Black parents are the most likely to suffer from negative child effect on a large scale because of the characteristics of the societal response. As framed in Chapter 3, their environment rather than their own or their children's characteristics are the key determinants of child development and effect. Therefore, in the next paragraphs, we describe how African Americans' living conditions often defeat black parents' aspirations for a better life for their children.

To begin with, black children usually are raised in close geo- graphic proximity to many other black children; in contrast, proportionally more white children live in single-home dwellings in suburbs with lower child density. Black children are often surrounded by siblings, cousins, young aunts and uncles, same-floor neighbors, building peers, and street peers, all of whom contribute to their socialization. In contrast, white children have more adults around them, so that peer effect may be somewhat diluted. One survival strategy that black children learn in many neighborhoods is to be "cool," what Richard Majors and Janet Billson (1993) refer to, in their book title, as the *Cool Pose*. It is a front, a self-presentation with the purpose of establishing one's style, one's status, and giving black males a sense of self-confidence. The authors find that this cool pose, which emphasizes posturing, shuts out life alternatives and contributes to wife or girlfriend abuse and detachment from obligations toward one's children. The "cool cat" is also less likely to value school and go into legitimate occupations. Parental aspirations can be defeated. The following excerpt is from a black mother who is part of a racially mixed support group for parents who have difficult adolescents:

> Oh, my boy is soooo cool [she imitates her son's language here]; you know, I don't think he even knows who he is. There is nothing real in him and all the dudes around him. I tell you I really resent these boys; they get away with everything. They act tough so all the other children are afraid of them at school and let them do what they want. . . . Then their parents—mothers, really—ah, I don't know what they think or do. Some of them act real cool too so what can you expect from the boys and even the girls? Now these girls are tough, real tough too. . . . So between these girls who act cool and these stupid white 'trash girls who are wannabees and want a black baby, well, my boy thinks he's God's gift to girls so he struts his stuff and the police know his stuff, see what I mean? . . . A mother can't do a thing and even my brother has tried to talk some sense into him, but he's soooo cool that my brother feels like punching him. So, yeah, I see jail time soon. That's cool, ain't it? [shakes her head sadly]

Parents' approach to child socialization differs according to the place they occupy in the resource structure of their society and the cultural tasks that the realities of their environment place upon them

(Ogbu, 1985). Black parents face the fact that their children's chances in the opportunity structure of society are fairly low, especially in comparison to what white parents can expect for their children. Many have accepted alternative strategies of child orientation to success through unconventional means. Raising children to be competent inner-city adults involves different skills than raising children to be competent middle-class, white suburban adults. For instance, disadvantaged inner-city black parents may actually raise their children to develop "attitudes," to be defiant, self-reliant, able to fight back, and acquire a certain dose of mistrust (Ogbu, 1985). Thus, there is likely to be a great deal of difference in the ways African Americans raise their children, depending on their own socioeconomic status and neighborhood situation. What we would want to know for the purpose of this book is the extent to which such socialization practices then impact the quality of the parent-child relationship, whether negatively or positively.

Despite positive neighborhood characteristics, middle-class African-American families do not live in a context that is ecologically equal to middle-class whites, and that is the rule rather than the exception (Sampson and Wilson, 1995). Most affluent blacks are not able to escape from visible social problems because they reside in communities that are the equivalent of those housing the poorest whites (Alba, Logan, and Bellair, 1994:427) and are as crime prone (Logan and Stults, 1999). Patillo (1998) has carried out an observation study of a black neighborhood in a large metropolitan area. In this neighborhood, 60 percent of the population is white collar and most families live in single-dwelling homes on well-maintained streets. A majority of the families have resided in the area for two or three generations.

But "Groveland," as Patillo called the area, is also the home of gang leaders who grew up in the neighborhood and want to keep it safe for their own families. Therefore, most of the drug selling is done outside of the immediate area and gang leaders join with the legitimate leaders who went to school with them to keep the area clean and safe. The length of residence and the fact that the children went to the same schools result in the interlocking of legitimate and illegitimate networks. This mutual familiarity means that residents, especially youth, are exposed to antisocial networks along with legitimate ones. This mixture of influences involves cross-pressures that are not a concern of most white middle-class parents. Furthermore, because many of the middle-class black families have reached that level only recently, a greater proportion of blacks than whites have poor relatives (Billingsley, 1992). Others have relatives who have served time in jail, are on welfare, or are addicted to drugs. Therefore, even *within* the extended families themselves, it is often difficult to insulate children against negative socialization forces.

Overall, the average African-American family is faced with many problems that are foreign to the average white family. Besides having to contend with prejudice and discrimination, they have to shelter their children against negative peer behaviors and neighborhood dangers. Many solve this problem by enrolling their children in private religious schools. In contrast, the average white family sends its children to the neighborhood school without worrying about its quality. Thus, African-American families face a higher financial burden: they pay public school taxes and also pay for private school tuition fees, often at great personal sacrifice because their income is usually lower.

Unfortunately, the private school may be in another neighborhood. This means that the black students often have few or no friends they can socialize with in their immediate neighborhood. Their parents must become overprotective and cannot allow them to play in the streets because they may meet bad peers, or they will be picked on by gang members, or will be caught in the crossfire of street violence. These parents must be constantly vigilant and find alternative leisure activities for their children outside their neighborhoods or else keep them at home. In her autobiography, a student describes her reaction to her parents' efforts:

> We lived in a cramped apartment near a subsidized project and there were kids, kids, kids everywhere. We were always with kids and I think that after a while our parents couldn't tell us apart (smile!). We had a lot of fun some days but my parents didn't. They were trying to raise us well, but the other kids we were always hanging around with would have none of it. And their parents weren't always the best either. They'd let them stay out late at night, go wherever, invade and control the hallways, parking lots, you name it. They were up to no good

but my sister, brother, and myself couldn't appreciate that our parents were trying to protect us from this mayhem. I resented my parents but at the same time I loved them . . .

Maton and Hrabowski (1998) report that African-American males who are very successful in school are raised in families that are very involved in their children's lives, so as to counterbalance the negative influence of the neighborhood and peers as well as social stereotypes. These parents are strict, nurturant, and well connected to a community of teachers, church members, and extracurricular activities.

Although both children and parental characteristics are no doubt important determining variables in terms of the effect of children on parents, one senses that the characteristics of the African-American environment may be more important than for whites and perhaps even Asian-American families. There are many exceptions, but, overall, the environment in which white families live is more advantageous in terms of the achievement of mainstream abilities and aspirations. White parents generally need to exert less effort and make fewer sacrifices while raising their children. Thus, one could well wonder whether black children may not have a more negative effect on their parents than white children in some areas of parents' lives, while in other areas they may have a more positive effect. The research evidence indicates that blacks, particularly women, experience their marriage and family life less positively than whites (Aldous and Ganey, 1999). But it is impossible at this juncture to relate these findings to child effect, as we do not have sufficient information.

CONCLUSIONS

This chapter, as is the case for most of the others in this book, raises more research questions than it provides facts and answers. It is only recently that immigrant and minority families have been included in studies; as a result, we know relatively little about the quality of their parent-child relationship, family dynamics, parenting, and child development. The statistics generated by surveys too often follow a deficit model whereby only the problems affecting these families are documented. This material gives us very little basis to study the effect of children on parents as well as the interaction between child and parent characteristics in this respect.

However, this chapter highlights one conclusion: the characteristics of the societal response are probably more important determinants of child effect on parents (and parental effect on children as well) among immigrant and minority families. Immigrant and particularly poor minority families are plunged into an environment that can be rather overwhelming. It is like being suddenly thrown fully clothed into a hot tub. Forces bear down on these families that do not exist for whites—particularly middle-class whites.

Minority parents need to be allowed to recover their right to raise their children according to their dreams and to become reempowered by schools, social agencies, and even the welfare and justice systems. Their neighborhoods would often need massive social reinvestment so that they can raise their children in a hopeful rather than defeatist climate. This, of course, includes Native Americans, whether they live in an urban environment or on reservations. The rates of social problems are very high among many visible minority groups, both native and immigrant, and we need to have far more information on parent-child relationships. The topic of child effect may need to be studied somewhat differently in these situations. It is an entirely unexplored land.

Chapter 11

Adoptive Parents

Although relatively few children are adopted by nonkin each year, adoption nevertheless constitutes an important sociological basis from which to analyze the effect of children on parents. Adoption is shrouded in social constructions that have specific consequences for both adoptive parents and children. This topic is very enlightening in the context of this book because, as we have seen throughout, the fact that the effect of children on parents is rarely studied depends in large measure on general social definitions of parenting and childhood. Adoption reflects this pattern, but in a more acute form: adoptive parents experience child effect, mainly indirectly, that is not experienced by biological parents. This situation largely stems from the negative social construction of adoption in North America.

HOW IS ADOPTION SOCIALLY DEFINED?

In societies of European origins such as ours where family is equated with biology and kinship with blood ties, a great deal of ambivalence exists concerning adoption (Wegar, 1992). In contrast, in other societies, adoption is more widespread and the adoption of kin may be routine. In North America, a woman's fertility is still considered an important mark of self-esteem and social recognition despite a general liberalization of gender role norms (Letherby, 1994). Biological motherhood is often considered superior to adoptive motherhood, even by some feminists such as Phylis Chesler (1989). This new alliance of biology with feminism presents an anomalous situation at the ideological level because feminist theories generally reject gender roles based on biological constraints (Rothman, 1989). Who has not heard the well-known feminist slogan "biology is not destiny"? Yet infertility and adoption are stigmatized even from these same well-meaning quarters (Bartholet, 1993). Other feminists, however, point out that "we can recognize and appreciate the genetic tie without making it the determining connection" (Rothman, 1989:39). Still other feminists and scholars such as Arlene Skolnick (1998) critique this "new biologism" as a cultural phenomenon with policy implications.

It is probably because of this ambivalence and even duality between what is natural versus different or natural versus biological that adoption has captured the public interest. Wegar (1997:97) reveals that, in 1993, adoption was featured 113 times in nationwide radio and television programs in comparison to 186 times for abortion, 95 times for divorce, and 31 times for birth control. Furthermore, adoption is often portrayed in television soap operas. This large number of mentions and portrayals reflects a preoccupation rather than a reality because adoption by nonkin is far less frequent in our society than either divorce, abortion, or particularly birth control. Adoption obviously has dramatic and mediatic value, in part because it is socially constructed in an ambivalent way. In another society with a different social construction of family life and ties, adoption would go unnoticed.

Adoption is a topic that has been newsworthy for several decades, but each decade puts a different spin on the matter. The focus in the 1950s was more practical and centered on advice given to prospective adoptive parents. The realities of the baby shortage as well as international and transracial adoption did not surface until the 1960s. By 1974, sealed adoption records had become an issue and by the early 1980s this focus was accompanied by one on the search for biological parents and subsequent reunions. Birth parents became more visible socially and more acceptable (Wegar, 1997). They were also given more rights by the courts. In the 1990s, newscasts reported on several heartbreaking cases of small children taken away from the only family they had ever known, crying and totally devastated emotionally, to be given to a natural parent who had reappeared in their lives and sued for custody.

Therefore, an evolution has occurred in the cultural description of issues surrounding adoption and in the consequences for the children involved. This evolution in itself well illustrates that ideas about adoption change and are cultural rather than "natural." At any rate, even something natural, such as mothering, is redefined or reconstituted as we go along. The more recent development of reunions of adopted children with their birth mothers is a case in point. It has seized the public's interest and has been constructed within the language of other values that are currently prevailing in our culture. First, the language used reaffirms the merits of biological over social parenting (Rothman, 1989; Skolnick, 1998). It equates biology or genes with nurturance and, as such, accords with the new scientific trends in molecular genetics. This is referred to as "the DNA mystique" by Nelkin and Lindee (1995).

Second, search and reunion have come to be equated with the triumph of nature over the oppression of the adoption system. Search-movement activists have depicted the psychological need to search as a universal one, while there are indications to the contrary (Wegar, 1997): in other words, not every adopted child feels a need to search or will remain "incomplete" without a reunion. What "incomplete" means is also a social construction but it is an effective imagery because it currently has high value in our "psychobabble." Furthermore, this presumed universal "need" to locate one's roots is couched within other very modern psychological and individualistic themes such as the need to "find oneself," for "self-fulfillment," "freedom," "choice," and the presumed personal problems and "repression" of those who do not search. As Bartholet (1993) points out, the search movement has inadvertently contributed to the further stigmatization of adoption and particularly adoptive parents, as well as of adopted children who are not interested in finding their birth parents.

THE PROFESSIONAL REPRESENTATION OF ADOPTED CHILDREN

The literature on adoption is divided between those researchers who have not found any significant difference in adjustment levels and outcomes between adopted and nonadopted persons and those who do (for a review, see Sharma, McGue, and Benson, 1998). A few studies even find that adopted children show certain ego strengths and resilience (Benson, Sharma, and Roehlkepartain, 1994). But, overall, adopted children and their parents do not show any appreciable deficit that is consistent and would warrant concern (Bartholet, 1993). Nevertheless, superficial reviews of the research reported in popular outlets tend to highlight the negative rather that the positive, a focus which is unlikely to make adoptive parents feel secure in their role and adopted children secure in their sense of belongingness.

The deficits and strengths that are detected in the studies depend largely on the methodology used; that is, the type of adopted children included in the sample (for example, their age at adoption), the comparison group, and the outcomes measured. As a result of this research ambivalence, professionals who come into contact with troubled adopted children or adolescents may be too hasty to attribute the problems to adoption (Miall, 1996). These youngsters may not be treated for the real problems that affect them: instead, they may be queried about "how you feel about being adopted." Such a line of inquiry simply reinforces the adopted child's thinking that something is wrong with being adopted. This will not solve whatever other problems they might have.

More adopted than nonadopted children, including adoptions of older children, are found among the psychologists' and psychiatrists' clientele (Brodzinsky, 1993). The explanations that have been offered are twofold. First, some adopted children may have a more difficult time growing up because of identity problems or because their parents may not have properly bonded with them. Here, "bonding theories" constitute a great disservice to adoptive parents because such theories often posit the necessity of bearing a child as well as touching an infant immediately after birth so that attachment can take place. If we extended this line of reasoning, one could well say that husbands and wives cannot bond because they were not together at birth!

The second explanation posits that there may be no real developmental difference between adopted and nonadopted children. Rather, what may actually occur is that adoptive parents are of higher socioeconomic status and are more familiar with mental health services. Consequently, they may be more inclined to consult professionals as soon as their children evidence some problems (Warren, 1992). They may also consult professionals quickly because they have heard that adopted children "have more problems." Biological parents, in contrast, may seek help only after more serious problems have developed. Hence, comparatively fewer nonadopted children would appear in the psychologists' statistics.

A third explanation has not been highlighted: it is cultural and stems from the negative social construction of adoption. Although adopted children may feel as loved and as accepted by their parents as nonadopted children, their peers and even other adults often openly express doubts to them on this topic.

> A respondent in March's (1995:656) study said that outside the family people "never believe that your adoptive parents love you like their parents love them. Because you aren't biological." One of my students recalls returning home one day quite distressed around age ten and asking her mother, "Is it true that you can't love me as much because I am adopted?" The mother was shocked and found it difficult to accept the cruelty or incomprehension of other children. A twelve-year-old girl received this reaction from a classmate; "Oh, no, you're adopted! You, poor, poor thing. You don't have *real* parents." The classmate shrieked while covering her mouth with her hands, to the bewilderment of the adopted girl who then told her mother, "You can imagine that this did not make me feel very good." Another girl has been asked about her "fake" mother.

And, of course, parents feel very sorry for their children and have to explain that adoption is not common enough for people to be used to it and that they do not understand it, and so on. Nevertheless, parental explanations and reassurances may not be sufficient to offset the damage created by peers' reactions. After all, as we have seen in Chapter 7, peers are an extremely important reference group in the formation of a child's self-definition. Thus, this stigmatization may constitute a heavy mental burden for some adoptees and may perhaps explain all of the problems that adoption causes to children's adjustment in life. Instead, if children received the message that adoption is either neutral or natural or good, they would experience fewer feelings of ambivalence.

Other parents are saddened when their own parents prefer grandchildren who are of their "own blood." Or parents become upset when a teacher says, "Of course, your child is difficult, but you never know what you get when you adopt them." Or another points out, "Well, I understand, you can't quite love them as much as if they were your own." Then there is the case of a new acquaintance who insists upon asking, "What about children of your *own?*" In other words, the social response constitutes a form of discrimination, and it is somewhat surprising that researchers have failed to grasp this phenomenon and its effects on parents and children.

The view on adoptive parents is equally mixed (Groze, 1996). Some writers have suggested that adoptive parents may be less confident, more anxious, and harbor feelings of stigmatization because of their infertility, while other researchers have not found any support for this "at-risk" perspective (for a review, see Borders, Black, and Pasley, 1998). Research questions are unfortunately framed within a pathological or deficit view of adoption. Such questions assume a social construction of adoption that creates problems rather than prevents them. It may perhaps not be surprising that the results are what they are: the social constructions create the very problems attributed to the adoption itself.

TRANSRACIAL ADOPTION

Approximately 50,000 children are available for adoption and, of these, approximately half are nonwhite, primarily black (Child Welfare League of America, 1993). Even though transracial adoptions constitute only a tiny fraction of all adoptions, about 4 percent in 1993, much research is devoted to this topic. This research "surplus" or overrepresentation stems from the fact that race is such a salient aspect of the structure of American society and anything that goes with it gives rise to ideological controversies. One can then well imagine that, if being an adoptive parent is considered anomalous, adopting transracially is an even greater deviation from the average. Thus, it is likely to present even more situations that are less than optimal, both for parents and children. Such families are highly visible: they stand out visually. They are often inspected in public places with great curiosity and at other times with obvious animosity by children and adults alike. Both parents and children have to develop a level of resilience and a good sense of humor to cope with this "interest."

Much of the controversy surrounding transracial adoption arises because most of the children are African American while most adoptive parents are white. Many blacks, including social workers belonging to the National Association of Black Social Workers, have condemned this type of adoption as a form of cultural genocide. They have advanced the notion that black children placed in white families will lose their African-American identity and will suffer an identity crisis. The NABSW also wanted to force the adoption system to stop discriminating against black couples as potential adoptive parents. On the other side of the ideological spectrum, it has been argued that a child needs parents who love him or her in order to develop a secure sense of self; whatever their race, children simply have a right to have parents.

On which side of the debate does the evidence fall? There is absolutely no indication in the research literature that black children adopted by white parents turn out much differently than those adopted in black families (Silverman, 1993). The same results have been replicated in Great Britain (Bagley, 1993). Vroegh (1997) reports from a longitudinal study that, by adolescence, transracially adopted children are still well adjusted and enjoy a high level of self-esteem. These results are rather amazing when one considers the double anomaly that these families find themselves in: adoptive and transracial. Furthermore, most children grow up identifying as black and most parents conscientiously promote their children's African-American identity (Vroegh, 1997).

There is certainly a lack of sound research on transracially adoptive parents' experiences. It would be interesting to compare the effect of adoption depending on the race of the child adopted, not only black and white children, but Asian as well as Native-American ones. The social construction of racial acceptability probably affects parents as it does children. Furthermore, when a white father or mother are separately alone in public with their black child, reactions may differ. Thus, again, the impact may vary depending on the sex of the parent: strangers often think that the white parent has a black partner and this situation may not be socially acceptable to everyone. Furthermore, transracial adoptive parents face the notion that they have to enhance their child's cultural heritage and perhaps racial identity. This is a task other parents do not have to face. Yet none of this has been addressed in the research literature in terms of impact on the family.

STEPCHILD ADOPTION

Levine and Sallee (1990) have estimated that 100,000 stepchildren are adopted by their stepparents, generally a stepfather, each year. This number far surpasses regular adoptions of a nonrelated child. While a few similarities exist between regular adoptions and adoptions by a stepparent, important differences as well as motives are specific to each situation (Ganong et al., 1998). Adults usually adopt because they want to start a family but are infertile. A stepparent already has a family; he or she may actually have children living elsewhere. Rather, the main reasons for stepadoptions after divorce reside in a desire to be a "regular" family, to sever the relationship with the nonresidential parent, particularly when he or she does not contribute child support nor has much do to with the child, and to legitimize the roles and relationships within the reconstituted family.

The nonresidential parent either consents to the adoption or the case can go to court. A judge will rule in favor of the adoption only if the parent is deemed unfit or if it is in the child's best interest to sever the relationship (Mahoney, 1994). The long-term consequences of stepadoption after divorce are unknown. On one hand, in terms of systems theories, it constitutes a reaffirmation of the impermeability of the boundaries of the nuclear family. On the other hand, it may give rise to a great deal of pain and resentment when the child reaches adulthood, both on the natural parent's part and on the child's part. The latter may come to feel that the stepparent "stole" him or her from the nonresidential parent. The child may also resent the nonresidential parent for having given his or her rights away so easily. At this stage, longitudinal studies of step-adoptions are required, examining child effect on the adoptive stepparent as well as on the biological parent who loses children legally.

OPEN ADOPTION

More and more agencies are moving toward open adoption. This concept involves some level of communication between biological and adoptive parents. Under this system, birth mothers relinquish their infant for adoption only under certain circumstances that allow them greater control over the adoption process and access to the child. To begin with, they participate in the selection of couples and may meet them.

Several types of contractual agreements may be arranged between a birth mother (and occasionally a birth father) and adoptive parents, and much depends on the mother. She may simply request to receive pictures and letters explaining how the child is doing. She may request yearly visitations with the parents or both the parents and the biological child. In Etter's (1993) study of seventy-two open adoptions, the biological parents had not pressured the adoptive parents for more visits than agreed upon.

When the process is totally open, biological parents more or less enter the adoptive parents' family system as they enjoy regular visits and participation in decision making concerning their child's health (Grotevant et al., 1994). Many cases of weekly contacts have been described by the media in California but it is not possible to know how widespread this phenomenon is nor how well it works out in reality. Although both sets of parents declared themselves very happy in media interviews, it is unlikely that dissatisfied adoptive parents would discuss their case with the media, as this might not be in their child's best interest. They might also fear a negative reaction from the biological mother and the potential loss of their child.

The few studies that exist on open adoptions seem to indicate that most of the adoptive and biological parents are satisfied with their relationship (Etter, 1993). But slightly more biological than adoptive parents are happy about this arrangement, which concurs with Berry's (1991) conclusion that most of the benefits accrue to biological parents. However, adoptive parents are generally comfortable with the situation and may even gain a greater sense of permanency (Grotevant et al., 1994). Although most studies indicate that this arrangement is satisfactory (Gross, 1993), it is difficult to draw solid conclusions on the basis of the existing research.

First, some of the studies are carried out by the social workers involved in the process and who favor open adoption. This preference could color their data gathering and subsequent interpretations. Second, the samples are very small and do not allow for a comparison of adoptive families depending on the frequency of the biological mother's visits to see how satisfaction on the part of adoptive parents changes by the frequency and type of contact. Of particular importance is the extent of the contacts between biological mother and the adopted child. At this stage, it is impossible to determine how adolescent children function with two sets of parents and how the adoptive parents who have the responsibility of raising them are affected. There is a certain parallel here with children in stepfamilies who visit their noncustodial parent. Obviously, open adoptions are a relatively new phenomenon and longitudinal studies are necessary in terms of effect on children, birth parents, and adoptive parents. The social construction of birth parents relative to that of adoptive parents may play an important role in this respect—and currently the public is more fascinated by the former than the latter.

CONSEQUENCES OF REUNIONS

A combination of a greater emphasis on children's rights, on biological origins, on biological parents' rights, including fathers' rights, and on a change in the balance of the supply "market" of children has led to an acceptance and even encouragement of reunion of birth parents and biological child. With sealed records, total confidentiality concerning the birth mother's identity, and a greater protection of the adoptive family, children in the past were not encouraged or even allowed to locate their birth parents. Today many adoption agencies allow basic information to be given to an adult child about birth parents while others encourage search and reunion.

Birth parents as well as children and even siblings can enter information about themselves and specify whom they are searching for in registries. Mothers and daughters are the most common clientele of such registries (Pacheco and Eme, 1993:55). The gender difference may be the result of women being more biologically involved in reproduction and also because women are socialized to be more nurturant and family oriented than males. Women are generally more attached to their mothers than to their fathers. In fact, young women at times search for their birth parents only after they have become mothers themselves.

What functions do search and reunion fulfill and what are the consequences of reunions? The answers to these questions largely depend on which part of the family unit is considered. There can be functions and consequences for the child, the birth parent, the birth parent's family, and the adoptive family. The few studies that exist on this topic indicate that a majority of the adoptees who have been reunited with their biological family see this as a positive experience. But, as Pacheco and Eme (1993:55) point out, this high success rate, which was at 86 percent in their sample, is somewhat inflated: the possibility exists that the individuals who do not respond or refuse to participate in the research have had a negative experience. Furthermore, all reunions studied were initiated by the adoptees, and when the biological parents initiate the reunion, the adoptees' responses are less positive (Sachdev, 1992). An additional complication occurs because most of the studies, including those of the three authors cited in this paragraph, have obtained their samples from support groups with a strong advocacy position in favor of the benefits of reunions. Adoptees who might believe otherwise or do not search are excluded from these support groups and the sample. This presents a research bias that may distort reality.

For the adopted child, the most obvious advantage is to gain knowledge about physical resemblance and genetic factors that could predispose to illness and to integrate this information into his or her self-identity. A second function of reunions allows the adoptees to explain their background to others who may have stigmatized them because of their adoptive status (March, 1995). A third function that reunions fulfill, when they are emotionally successful, is to provide an additional emotional outlet both for the child and birth mother—an extension of the kinship system. Some become friends, others feel like sisters because of the narrow age difference, others simply feel like another set of relatives, while in fewer cases a real parent-child bond is formed. The latter is more likely to occur when the adoptive relationship is not satisfying to the child.

For some children, a search is initiated because of a distant or conflictual parent-child relationship in their adoptive family. The birth parents may have been idealized for years and the youth entertains notions that, "If only they (the adoptive parents) were my *real* parents, they'd love me more." So far, the research indicates that adoptive parents love their children as much as natural parents do. However, as in natural families, exceptions do occur. In such a case, a reunion with a loving birth parent can be a solution. Fortunately, studies also show that 90 percent of the adoptees who search feel loved by and love their adoptive parents (Sachdev, 1992). Furthermore, half of the adoptees who initiate a search wait until they are older because they are concerned about upsetting their adoptive parents. To alleviate these concerns, perhaps a third of the adoptees keep the search secret from their adoptive parents, at least until after the reunion (Pacheco and Eme, 1993). How the timing of their learning about the search and reunion affects adoptive parents is not known. One can presume that, for many, the news initially constitutes an emotional blow.

For birth parents, the functions fulfilled by a reunion may be very similar to those of the child in terms of informing them about what their child looks like and how he or she has grown up. A reunion also extends their kinship system. In addition, birth mothers may carry guilt feelings that can be alleviated when they see how successful in life the child has become. For others, however, suppressed guilt is reactivated (Sachdev, 1992). One can immediately sense a danger for those cases when the child is seeking a reunion because the adoption relationship has not worked out. Upon reunion, this young person may be either very vulnerable, or yet very troubled, even quite disturbed and malfunctioning; unless the birth parent is equally disturbed (a possibility in terms of genetic inheritance), a healthy birth parent will suddenly acquire a load of guilt: "if only I had kept her with me, she would have turned out better." Probably not, but the doubt and the guilt may nevertheless remain.

In the Pacheco and Eme study, 71 percent of the respondents felt that the biological parent had reacted positively to the reunion, which is a lower figure than that of the adopted adults themselves. Many adoptees admitted that they had held expectations that were unrealistic; several were reunited with biological parents suffering from an assortment of problems, such as alcoholism, poverty, and mental illness. A proportion of the adoptees have only one meeting with the birth parent, while half settle for occasional contacts. In only about a quarter of the cases are relationships actively and regularly maintained over time. Approximately 35 percent of these adoptees describe the new relationship as a close one (Gladstone and Westhues, 1998).

What is the effect on the adoptive parents? Here, a far greater risk for unhappiness probably exists, at least in the short term. Only about half of adoptive parents are perceived by their children as being

entirely positive about the reunion. Sachdev (1992) found that 64 percent of the parents in his sample had reactions other than being
"pleased." However, the parent-child relationship itself did not suffer
and a substantial number of adoptees "realized that they had had a
much better life than they would have had with the biological parent"
(Pacheco and Eme, 1993:64).

While many adoptive parents are more accepting of reunions than
others, it nevertheless gives rise to a host of conflicting emotions.
Parents tend to be somewhat apprehensive about the reunion because
they are concerned about their child's well-being (Sachdev, 1992):
they may fear that the child will be hurt, disappointed, or even emotionally exploited. As well, in many cases, parents feel left out, even
if this is only temporary. They may fear losing their child emotionally, a fear that rarely materializes but may nevertheless be traumatic
in some instances. Many of these parents are rewarded when they
realize how much their children appreciate the home they have been
given compared to what they might otherwise have had. Their child's
continued attachment may then more than compensate for whatever
anxieties they might have initially experienced.

Several of my students have discussed reunions, either in their
autobiographies or within the context of a class seminar. (Since 1974,
I have encountered only three instances of problematic adoption outcomes as perceived by students.) In 1996, a young woman in a seminar recounted the day she met her birth mother for the first time:

> "I was motivated by curiosity as I wanted to know if I looked
> like her and if I shared personality characteristics with her."
>
> "So what happened?"
>
> "I decided to bring my mom along so she would not feel left out
> because I could tell that she was more concerned than my father
> was; after all, I was not searching for my birth father, so he had
> no competition. So I met this woman at the Children's Aid Soci-
> ety, and she was introduced to us as my birth mother. It was re-
> ally awkward. I introduced myself and said to her, 'This is my
> mom,' and they shook hands and we all sat together. To make a
> long story short, I have met her alone a couple of other times but
> things just didn't click. I do look like her somewhat, but I think

that I share my parents' values more. To me, she feels like a cousin, a distant family member. That's all."

Another woman recounted a somewhat more emotionally charged reunion where both cried tears of joy:

> Yes, I definitely found my biological roots with her. We are so much alike that it's amazing. But she is so much younger than my real [her word] parents that she feels more like a sister to me. I just can't think of her as my mom. My [adoptive] mom is really it but it's a fun relationship because she has little kids so this means that I now have half-brothers and I baby-sit for her once in a while.

These are the happy cases in terms of the adoptive parents. But the potential exists for different scenarios of late adolescents or young adults who become more attached to the birth parent and distance themselves from adoptive parents who have bonded with them and have been very good to them.

> One such case emerged in a mature student's autobiography as her fourteen-year-old daughter had accidentally come upon her twenty-nine-year-old birth mother. The girl had been problematic all her life, and had even run away. The twenty-nine-year-old birth mother was equally footloose, and eagerly took in her birth daughter to live with her and her boyfriend. The giddy threesome then moved from Toronto to Los Angeles. The adoptive parents were devastated because they were very attached to their daughter and, in the mother's words, "We had given her so much. I still can't believe it." They were, in effect, bereaved. They were also very concerned because, under their care, their daughter was largely protected from the negative consequences of her actions and was channeled into more prosocial behaviors. With the young birth mother, the daughter received no guidance, was rarely attending school, and had already begun experimenting with sex and drugs.

It is also noteworthy that none of the studies on search and reunions included instances of transracial adoptions. It appears, at least intuitively, correct to presume that the reunion of a black child with her black birth mother may be more threatening to the white adoptive parents because of racial identity issues. On the other side of the coin, as adoptive parents tend to be of higher socioeconomic status than birth parents, this social status gap may unfortunately be even more evident in these instances, so that the children may identify less with the disadvantaged birth mothers. Furthermore, many of the cases of transracial adoptions involve a white birth mother and a black birth father. Twenty years later, the white birth mother may have rebuilt her life entirely within a white context, with a white husband and children. The arrival of the racially mixed birth child may give rise to complications. These issues are bold and raw, and that is perhaps why they are not discussed—and that is perhaps why we do not hear of transracial search and reunions: they may not actually occur frequently.

CONCLUSIONS

Adoption can be problematic in our society, in terms of effect both on parents and children, because it is not widely practiced and is socially constructed as a less desirable form of parent-child relationship. Therefore, if and when there are negative effects on children and adoptive parents, the explanation has to be found in the *cultural interpretation* and social perception of the situation. The negative effects do not originate from biology or a lack of biological ties. Rather, they depend on how biological ties are constructed and on how much preference they are given in people's minds over adoption, as well as how many legal rights are granted adoptive parents.

So long as professionals and the lay public think of adoption within a deficit model, adoptive parents, and particularly their children, will be negatively affected. Adopted children are far more likely to acquire doubts about their parents' attachment to them from their peers and insensitive adults than they are from their parents. The latter rarely treat them less well than they would their biological children and are rarely less attached to them. When children perceive the contrary, this perception can only arise as a result of society's reaction to the adoptive situation.

Thus, again, as predicted in Chapter 3, it is possible that the negative societal reaction to adoption is currently a far more potent variable in terms of consequences both for adopted children and their parents. It would be interesting to know how this chapter applies to international adoptions of children from poor countries. The adoptive parents in question may be viewed more positively (they have not taken a child away from another American or Canadian mother) and the children may grow up with a collective understanding of how lucky they have been—which is not currently what regularly adopted children are made to feel.

Chapter 12

Let's Not Forget Genes!

In several chapters, we have alluded to genetic variables in the development of personality or temperament as well as emotional and behavioral problems. Indeed, the study of the effect of children on parents and the parent-child relationship cannot be complete without a more comprehensive discussion of the genetic realm. But we have also seen that the larger environment frequently is responsible for children's problems, particularly variables such as poverty, peers, and the media. Thus, although the focus of this chapter is on genetic contribution to child effect, this contribution is itself circumscribed and encouraged by the environment. In others words, every human being is born with a set of genes which interact with one another and with the child's environment to create the child's personality, abilities, coping mechanisms, and reactions to his or her parents.

At birth, each baby arrives in the world with its predispositions, physical appearance, and health status, all of which are entirely innate. The term "innate" includes both genetic and intrauterine influences, as well as birthing conditions and accidents. For instance, a mother who smokes, drinks, uses drugs, or is malnourished while pregnant inadvertently alters some of her child's potential abilities and compromises his or her health status. It is also possible that viral infections that affect her only slightly interact with a fetus's genetic makeup to make it vulnerable to certain disorders or illnesses after birth. With multiple births, each twin's intrauterine environment is more crowded and less optimal. As they grow, multiple fetuses become so overcrowded in the womb that the mother's system is heavily taxed and she gives birth prematurely to human beings who face the world often not fully formed and totally dependent on medical technology to survive.

HOW GENETIC INHERITANCE WORKS

Each baby inherits half of its genes from each parent: 50 percent from the mother's ovum and 50 percent from the father's sperm. But parents have thousands of genes and they never transmit a perfect copy of all these genes to their offspring. Rather, each ovum contains a combination of a mother's genes; thus, the pattern that she transmits is somewhat different from her own genetic makeup. Then, this combination of genes present in her ovum makes contact with the pattern available in the one spermatozoid that fertilizes her ovum. The fertilized ovum transforms itself into a fetus that contains the interaction of genes, half of which were inherited from the mother and half inherited from the father. Therefore, a child inherits a *configuration of genes* that is both similar and different from that of its parents.

In other words, there is a great deal of chance or randomness in genetic inheritance. No two ova carry exactly the same genetic pattern and neither do two spermatozoids. This is why siblings are both similar and different, and this is why children are both similar to and different from their parents. In some families, all the children look more like the father and in others, they resemble the mother, and some look like neither. In terms of abilities and temperaments, the patterns of genetic inheritance are even more complex.

To begin with, temperamental predispositions seem to be polygenic, that is, they result from several genes rather than just one. This means that parents have to transmit a particular *set* of genes so that their children can be predisposed to agreeableness, for example. Furthermore, a parent can carry genes and transmit them without having ever been affected by them. If the other parent is not a carrier, then even if the child inherits the carrier set of genes, they may produce no effect. But if the other parent is also a carrier and then passes the genes to the child, the child now has the two copies needed to produce a given trait, quality, or even mental illness. This perhaps explains why most persons who suffer from schizophrenia have normal parents. The parents may individually be carriers of the related genes: their own mental health has not been affected but now that their child has the two copies or the two complementary sets of genes, that child is at a higher risk of becoming schizophrenic. If this child has an identical twin, he or she also inherits the same vulnerability. In fact, as we have seen in Chapter 5, when one identical twin suffers from schizophrenia as an adult, so does the other in a great proportion of the cases.

Furthermore, a child may inherit a mother's predisposition for aggressiveness but also inherits at the same time the father's predisposition for self-control. The potential effect of one set of genes either cancels the potential effect of the other or the two compensatory sets of genes combine to form a new predisposition for what we could call "drive" or leadership.

In a nutshell, the previous paragraphs explain how children inherit genes and the consequences of such inheritance. The process of genetic inheritance is still not fully understood, nor do we yet know which sets of genes create certain abilities and temperamental predispositions. Neither do we yet know which sets of genes interact to produce severe mental disorders such as bipolar disorder and schizophrenia.

Nevertheless, the fact remains that the closer the genetic bond between two persons, the more alike they are *on average*. Thus, each child on average shares 50 percent of his or her genes with each parent. Identical twins share all of their genes, full siblings half, and half-siblings share 25 percent of their genes. In comparison, a child shares no genes with the next-door neighbor, except those that are random in a population. Thus, while siblings are often different from each other on the basis of their genes, they are even more different from their neighbor's children.

However, as children grow up and as their personalities and preferences stabilize, they tend to *choose* friends who may be similar to them in certain dimensions. For instance, studious children gravitate toward similarly inclined peers. So it may happen that, in a family, one child is more similar to his or her best friends than he or she is to a sibling who dislikes school and books and does not do well academically.

The process of selecting peers on the basis of one's preferences and personality inclinations also means that, given the opportunity, people often select mates or partners on the same basis. Although a great deal of randomness occurs in the way we meet and select partners, we meet most through schools, colleges, hobbies, and employment environments. Such contexts allow people to select others who share similar interests, at least in some dimensions. By the same token, men's and women's choices are based either on similarity or complementariness of genetic inheritance. Rarely does a person with a high IQ mate with a person who has a very low IQ, for instance. Thus, in families where parents are similar in some abilities and personality traits (this is called *assortative mating*), their children are more likely to inherit genes that reinforce one another. The siblings will be more similar to one another and to their parents than in a family where the two parents are utterly different.

This can be illustrated with hair color. When two adults coming from families where black hair predominates produce children, the offspring have a near perfect chance of having black hair. In contrast, if a blond man mates with a dark-haired woman, and assuming their own families are similar to them in hair color, each of this couple's children will be a surprise at birth. They could have black, or blond, or brown hair and various shades of any of these.

HOW DO GENES INTERACT WITH ENVIRONMENT?

Most of the studies that have found correlations between, say, a child's aggressiveness and parents' harsh, inconsistent, or even permissive childrearing conclude that a cause and effect exists. That is, the improper socialization practices have caused child aggressiveness. Of course, this happens in some families. But there are *other* causes for aggressiveness and for whatever else ails or benefits a child's personality and abilities such as siblings, peers, teachers, other adults, the media, and life course occurrences such as a severe car accident, a viral infection, a fall, and, in other countries, wars. In other words, many causes generally combine to produce a given outcome in a person (Steinberg and Avenevoli, 2000). Thus, it is not surprising that the results of these studies linking childrearing to child outcomes generally yield, at best, small to moderate correlations or statistics. The results would be much more reliable and valid were both environmental and genetic information included (Collins et al.,

2000). But they generally are not because studies are not yet designed with this integrative approach in mind. Furthermore, we need to await advances in molecular genetics for this purpose.

This traditional method of imputing causality to parents' socialization patterns confounds genetic and environmental influences (Scarr, 1993). Indeed, in biological families, parenting behaviors and child outcomes may have one common factor: the fact that parents and children share genes (Rowe, 1994). These genes in part influence personality development through which both the parenting practices and the children's behaviors are affected. It is not surprising, therefore, that there is a correlation between the two in many, but not all, families. But a correlation can mean a variety of causality paths, and, as I have pointed out, these correlations are not very substantial.

For example, parents who punish harshly or angrily and are easily irritated by their children may possess genetic predispositions for aggressiveness or impulsivity (this, of course, does not excuse their behavior, because genetic predispositions should not be equated with inevitability). In turn, the children themselves are predisposed to aggressiveness and start misbehaving, in part because of the same genetic inheritance. In other words, both parents and children may be genetically predisposed to aggressiveness (or to agreeableness, or to high intelligence). This would explain a portion of the observed correlation between parents' irritable childrearing practices and offspring's aggressiveness. Furthermore, the harsh parenting practices become part of the familial climate or the children's environment; thus incompetent parenting may trigger or reinforce negative predispositions in children (O'Connor et al., 1998). Moreover, when parents are irritable and unstable, stressors such as a difficult marriage or poverty exacerbate their negative style of parenting and further impact detrimentally on the child's aggressive tendencies. As you can see, there is an overlap between genetic and environmental causality and the pathways are multiple (Horowitz, 2000). Unfortunately, researchers have paid scant attention to the genetic aspect and attributed the entire causality to parents' behaviors.

In addition to this partly genetically produced environment, there is another mechanism involved in the causality chain. Parents *react* to their children's behaviors, as do peers, siblings, and teachers. For instance, faced with an aggressive and noncompliant child, many parents who are not themselves aggressive are somewhat astounded. They may not plan on reacting negatively but the child's outbursts, taunting, and disobedience may trigger adverse parental reactions. Without thinking, they may slap in anger. Now, an average child will usually learn from this and cease his or her difficult behavior. But, as we have seen in Chapters 5 and 6, an aggressive child may simply become more aggressive. Other parents may react by becoming more controlling. Others give up and become permissive (Ambert, 1997).

In the above scenarios, which are very frequent nowadays, what researchers obtain from questionnaires distributed to parents or to adolescents are negative types of parenting coexisting with aggressive child behaviors. But these questionnaires fail to inquire into the trajectory of this pattern, which is more likely to originate from the child than from the parents, especially among adolescents. The parents are reacting to the child, and it is unlikely that the questionnaires will show this—in great part because such questions are *not* asked. In many cases, this negative child behavior and parenting behavior has a common genetic source. In other instances, a family happens to live in an area where there is a great deal of violence and abuse among youth; the child learns to behave aggressively and brings this attitude home. The child may have no genetic predispositions for aggressiveness: it is a matter of social learning here. His or her aggressiveness is environmentally caused and may trigger adverse parental reactions.

Parents who are also somewhat aggressive may immediately respond negatively and with great irritation, while others may fail to notice the aggressive behaviors because they are also immersed in a violent environment and have come to accept aggressiveness as a normal way of interacting. In all instances, the child's environment at home would reinforce his or her newly acquired antisocial behavior.

Good genetic predispositions, such as intelligence, can be diluted or extinguished by strong environmental forces. Poverty is an environmental force well known for its negative impact on the development of children's cognitive abilities (McLoyd, 1998). Poverty can also affect temperamental predispositions, but this linkage is not yet well documented. However, children who are born with good temperamental predispositions and are "easy" as well as pleasant may better overcome negative environmental forces than other children who have a "short fuse" and are easily defeated by life's challenges.

Thus, as children develop, a constant interaction takes place between their innate predispositions and the environment in which they live (Ambert, 1997). The more numerous a child's personal resources (or human capital), the more resilient the child is to environmental pressure. But the more numerous the deficits that exist in a child's environment (familial ruptures, poverty, dangerous neighborhood, antisocial peers), the more at risk this child is to succumb to negative predispositions and to fail to actualize his or her positive predispositions or potential (Luthar, 1993).

DO GENES MEAN
THAT PARENTING IS USELESS?

Now, let's look more specifically at the parental contribution to child outcomes and life, otherwise the reader might be led to believe that parents have little to do in this respect (Ambert, 1997). The point this chapter makes is that parents' role is less deterministic than is generally described in the research. But this is not synonymous with a lack of parental effect other than by genetic transmission. It is certainly not the intent of this chapter to encourage parents to abandon their duties. Furthermore, a small proportion of parents are less than ideal and do affect their children negatively, at least in terms of happiness and, for others, development of negative traits and behaviors. For instance, a minority of parents, at most 1 to 3 percent, are abusive (Finkelhor and Dziuba-Leatherman, 1994). Such parents are detrimental and should be held responsible. Perhaps another 5 to 20 percent have abdicated the most difficult part of their role, which is rule setting and supervision, while a number of them provide their children with poor examples and teach them values that are antisocial (Ambert, 2001). As the reader can see, an emphasis on child effect does not preclude the belief that there *are* some very incompetent parents out there. Nevertheless, the fact remains that a large majority are conscientious and devoted. Unfortunately, it is this majority of parents who bear the brunt of being held responsible for child outcomes with which they have nothing to do. Moreover, some of the abdicating parents mentioned earlier have given up because they felt that there was nothing they could do: both their adolescent children and the "system" prevent them from fulfilling their responsibilities and they are afraid to assert themselves.

Parenting is important first of all because not all human characteristics and behaviors are equally affected by genes. Genetic influence may be near zero for some aspects of personality and particularly for behaviors. For instance, impulsiveness that appears during childhood but is easily "cured" suggests a less genetically based characteristic but rather a more environmentally induced one. Beliefs, values, religiosity, manners, study and work habits, among others, are greatly influenced by the environment, and particularly by parents (see, for example, Kelley and De Graaf, 1997). Therefore, parents' task remains quite formidable in domains other than personality development.

Second, even personality traits that have a high genetic component can at the very least be improved or tempered by proper parental practices and a good extrafamilial environment, such as a stable and resourceful neighborhood (Bronfenbrenner and Ceci, 1994; Collins et al., 2000). This proposition is important to keep in mind because many objections are brought to bear on ideological grounds against the science of behavior genetics and against what is erroneously interpreted as insurmountable determinism: *heredity does not mean irrevocability,* as already mentioned. A child who is mildly to moderately hyperactive (which may be innate)* can be given opportunities to "vent" surplus energy through activities such as karate or gymnastics and can be given enough structure to lower the hyperactivity. In contrast, when such children live in a stressful family situation, where parents do not get along, are erratic, too punitive, or too permissive, and the house is noisy and overcrowded, the child's hyperactivity may increase, along with other problems. Therefore, such children are likely to achieve more optimal results in a home that is better than average. However, when a characteristic is genetic *and extreme*, parents can do very little to change it. They may be, at best, able to channel it, contain it, or encourage it if it is a positive characteristic, such as intellectual ability or a talent for music.

---

*Hyperactivity, often called ADHD, may be genetic in some instances. However, the fact that the number of these cases has increased so much since the 1970s implies some environmental causality (whether in the cultural or physical environment). The gene pool in a population does not change abruptly in two generations. Such a change would generally take hundreds of years.

Third, even in extreme cases, parents can play another role. As an example, one can think of a child with a very low IQ. While IQ is perhaps the most genetically grounded ability, a very low or a very high IQ may even be more genetically fixed than an average one (Brody, 1993). Parents can do little to change the child's intellectual ability. But they can facilitate functioning and they can prevent the child from becoming even more incompetent by teaching him or her basic social skills. Parents may also affect other aspects of the child's life, and, consequently, add to the child's well-being. For instance, they may nurture the child's affective qualities and encourage the development of motor skills when the latter are within normal range. Once again, this indicates that children who are subnormal in one dimension can still benefit from their parents' guidance in others. They may especially benefit from *love* and may live quite happily as a result. (All the while, however, their parents may be terribly stressed and worried about the child.)

Fourth, when children possess partly hereditary traits that are deemed positive in a society, parents can contribute to the enhancement of these traits (Bronfenbrenner and Ceci, 1994). A child may be musically gifted, but if parents discourage this talent, the child may not persist and the "gift" will not be utilized. When parents encourage a natural ability and provide compatible resources, that gift will go much further and the child may also be happier and more fulfilled. In turn, this enhancement of an ability may result in a positive impact on other child characteristics such as self-esteem and sociability. It may also counterbalance the potential effect of negative characteristics such as impulsivity or shyness. Thus, parents can contribute to the child achieving balance—of course, they accomplish this within the range of the child's potential, but they nevertheless do contribute.

Fifth, in many cases, parents can prevent a youngster from being negatively influenced by detrimental forces in the external environment, such as a delinquent peer group, a poor school system, violent mass media, or neighborhood criminality. But here we have to recall that parents are not all-powerful. Child cooperation is required. As we have seen in Chapter 5, many children, even small ones, can be very "allergic" to any effort made by their parents to socialize them. This is a reality that law enforcement agencies and a variety of professionals often fail to grasp.

Sixth, parents are a great source of social support and, in our society, the main origin of love and attachment for their children: without support and attachment children would not fare so well nor be so happy. This may well be parents' foremost contribution to their offspring. Parents provide a haven that serves as a respite "from the frenzied world of peers and the demands of school" (Larson and Richards, 1994:99). Thus, whatever a child's genetic constitution, loving parents who invest in their children in terms of time, attention, and teachings are likely to provide a healthier platform for emotional security than is the case with unavailable parents.

LIMITATIONS TO PARENTAL INFLUENCE

We have just mentioned six reasons why parents are important in their children's development and well-being. But, as we know by now, this should not be taken to mean that parents can always accomplish miracles. We review five of the main reasons why their influence is limited, especially in some instances. To begin with, as emphasized in this chapter, there is the matter of genes: each personality benefits from inherent abilities and suffers from limitations that are difficult to overcome. These can either be enhanced or improved, as we have seen, but abilities cannot be created by parents as one would design a dress; nor can limitations be entirely ignored or even eradicated. Hence, at the negative level, genes constitute the first limitation to parental influence (Rowe, 1994). However, at the positive level, good genetic predispositions, such as certain talents, may lead a child to be particularly welcoming of parental influence.

In the literature, discussion and some supportive data indicate that a viewpoint emphasizing genetics might discourage parents and lower their motivation to improve their children's negative behavior. However, such reactions are due to the fact that the topic of genes gives rise to a great deal of misinterpretation and is often erroneously perceived as deterministic (Horowitz, 2000). Hence, presenting a better-balanced picture, as done in this text, can eliminate these biased reactions and yet have the advantage of lowering the burden of guilt that parents often carry. A properly interpreted behavior genetics perspective is no more deterministic and discouraging than an environmental one. It is very difficult to change the environment around us, whether we think in terms of neighborhood criminality or media violence. As our environment becomes more technological, it may become even more deterministic than in the past—more deterministic than genes. So it is an error to think of genetic causes as hopeless ones and environmental causes as the only ones that are solvable. Currently, much research is devoted to solving problems of a genetic nature while, paradoxically, at the commercial level, money is poured into creating a technological environment that will sell products detrimental to children's moral and emotional development.

A second factor that limits parents' influence has also been widely discussed in this text. The interactional perspective proposes that, while parents influence children, the effectiveness of this influence depends in great part on how children, and particularly adolescents, perceive and react to their parents' efforts to help them, socialize them, and monitor them. Even a very small child can choose to ignore requests made by parents. Parents actually need a child's cooperation in parenting, as do teachers as well as clinicians who engage in any form of psychotherapy. True, there are indirect routes that adults can utilize to attempt to defeat children's self-destructive resistance. It is for this reason that some parents whose difficult children rule the home can be trained to become more effective. This is what was referred to as parent effectiveness training in Chapter 8. But this training does not produce miracles. Children's responses to parents remain a potential mitigating factor in parental authority.

Thus, a third restriction to parental influence resides in the shortcomings of interventions, such as parent effectiveness training:

1. They are too costly to reach and benefit most parents.
2. Parents who are highly dysfunctional cannot be trained.
3. Children who are very problematic on many fronts cannot be changed.
4. The rest of the environment frequently fails to reinforce parents' newly acquired effectiveness.

Interventions are not a panacea for all ills affecting all parents and children. In extreme cases, nature is deterministic or, yet, what the combination of an unfortunate nature with a bad environment has created is irreversible. There are limits to interventions and social engineering once they occur *after* a situation has arisen. This is why preventive measures are more effective.

A fourth limitation to parental influence stems from the fact that children create their environment to some extent, which was discussed earlier. Depending on their abilities and deficiencies, children actively choose certain courses of action that reinforce their characteristics. Hence, while very bright children may receive much encouragement from their parents, they alone create, without any help, many facets of their experience. They may teach themselves to read; they may linger over books long after their parents have finished reading to them; they may utilize their imagination to dream up all stories that enliven their world. "Bright children can use the stimulus of an empty room to think about the geometric configuration of its corners" (Plomin, 1994:157). Children who have an easy temperament may similarly find sources of happiness in minor details of life, with or without parental help. At the negative end of the spectrum, parents could uselessly exhaust themselves trying to satisfy children who constantly want more, or are dissatisfied with what they have, or have an unhappy streak. Such children have the habit of focusing on what displeases them and what they do not have—even when they have everything else. These children are not ones who count their blessings.

A fifth limitation occurs as a result of parents and children not living in a closed environment. They are bombarded by a variety of external influences that particularly affect vulnerable children. Good socialization practices can be defeated by a negative peer-school-neighborhood-media environment. This can occur even in otherwise good schools if children with behavioral problems seek out the only two or three similarly deviant peers available in the entire school. Unknown to parents and staff, such children create a little world of their own, manage to avoid supervision, and often "sneak" out for illegal drug use, shoplifting, and other questionable activities, to the detriment of their schoolwork. In the long run, when this behavior comes to light, some of these youngsters straighten out but others remain deviant. As we have seen in Chapter 7, children and adolescents bring home their peer group's joys and frustrations, ideas and values, as well as their lifestyles. Being like the others is a very important element for American and Canadian youngsters, and only the stronger ones are able to resist the lure of peer acceptance. Parents are often rendered useless in the face of such conformity to peer values. Moreover, parents suffer from this spillover of the negative environment into family life, or benefit from it when it is positive, which may, again, augment or damage their ability to influence their children positively (Ambert, 1994).

CONCLUSIONS

A child's genetic inheritance in part helps explain his or her personality. It also contributes to the explanation of child effect on parents from two perspectives. First, the societal reaction to parents of children with behavioral and emotional problems has been largely negative and guilt inducing. Thus, the societal response has increased these children's negative impact on their parents and reduced parents' ability to help their children. When the role of genetic inheritance is better understood, then parents can be exonerated for their offspring's severe problems. This exoneration may provide them with much-needed social support and, in turn, may lower negative child effect. As a further consequence, children would inherit a more secure structure that could counteract their negative predispositions.

Second, taking the role of genes into consideration also clarifies that parental childrearing practices should not be the only focus of research attention, whether children's outcomes are positive or negative. Genes interact with the environment and parents constitute an important aspect of this environment. However, the very diverse, technological and market-driven environment in which we live presents more negative options to children than in the past. This environment may be less suitable to the development of children's prosocial predispositions and more suitable to the development of their negative predispositions.

Chapter 13

Conclusions:
What Is Wrong
with Parenting Today?

Throughout this book, we have examined how the social definition of parents and children impacts on their relationship and their respective duties, and causes a great deal of negative and useless child effect on parents. In this chapter, we pursue the theme of the lack of societal support for parents' role, the lack of recognition for the difficulties they face, and how these two deficits magnify negative child effect. Furthermore, these deficits in the societal response actually prevent children themselves from taking responsibility for the role they play in their own development.

CULTURAL AND SOCIAL ROADBLOCKS TO EFFECTIVE PARENTING

There are several structural and cultural roadblocks that dilute parents' capacity to assume their full responsibility. These roadblocks prevent children from actualizing their abilities and positive characteristics in their entirety. They also foster negative child effect on parents. Six are examined here, although many more could be added (Ambert, 1997).

The first roadblock stems from a combination of recent demographic changes, especially those changes that are accompanied by poverty. High divorce rates and nonmarital childbearing have resulted in widespread single parenting under particularly difficult circumstances. Single parents, by all measures, are generally at a disadvantage financially as well as in terms of social capital (Coley and Chase-Lansdale, 1998). They are not sufficiently supported by society and, as a result, are less able than others to invest in their children. This is evident in the vast literature documenting more negative outcomes for children of single parents than those in two-parent families. The necessity for many parents to be employed long hours is another structural barrier to parents' involvement with their children—or perhaps to simply enjoying that involvement.

These changes cumulatively mean that adults are too often emotionally distressed, socially isolated, financially disadvantaged, overworked, and have too little time at home, while others are frequently too young and ill-equipped to parent adequately. These circumstances take time and energy away from the parenting role, while some even cause a decline in parenting skills, thus reducing the level of support and monitoring that children and adolescents can receive.

Moreover, so many of these same parents live in neighborhoods with a high concentration of similarly underprivileged families as well as criminality and juvenile gangs. Living in such neighborhoods places parents and children at risk (Garbarino and Kostelny, 1992). As Patterson, Reid, and Dishion (1992:105) point out, such areas "require a very *high* level of parenting skills just to keep their children out of the juvenile court system." They add that "there is no sense in which it is fair for our society to expose these families to such adverse conditions." Poverty and the noxious environment it generally creates is probably one of the most serious roadblocks to effective parenting, to positive child outcomes (McLoyd, 1998), and consequently to positive child effect on parents.

The third roadblock preventing children from receiving parental support and control is less often discussed: It stems from a combination of the effect of what Schwartz (2000) calls the "tyranny of freedom and the surfeit of life options," as well as individualism and materialism on the family system, whereby individual choices, rights, and satisfaction rather than mutual obligations take precedence (Etzioni, 1994). One simply cannot assume that parents are immune to these trends—nor are their children. We can logically presume that this mentality leads some adults to be less willing to make a commitment to adequate parenting when the cost is too high, the reward too low, and the alternatives too numerous. It is one of the reasons why our society should find ways to make parenting easier and more effective so that it is a more rewarding experience. Materialism and individualism also affect children directly and encourage them to focus on rights, gratification, and acquisition rather than on their responsibilities. This situation makes it less easy to raise them within a prosocial set of goals.

The fourth roadblock is both social and cultural; it pertains to all the extraneous influences that bear on children and encourage them to prevent their parents from fulfilling their role adequately. These influences or cross-pressures range from detrimental contents of television programs and video games to deleterious peer groups, dangerous neighborhoods, and the easy availability of drugs and weapons. In our society, children are presented with too many opportunities to develop their negative tendencies or to engage in behaviors that are antisocial in one form or another. Children and adolescents are actually cheated out of an optimal development. This situation prevents parents from fulfilling their duties as they see fit and creates detrimental child effect.

The fifth roadblock stems from a widespread cultural reliance on philosophies of life, outdated scientific theories, and clinical practices that fail to make adolescents accountable and that blame parents (Maziade, 1994:71). This situation will persist as long as the view is maintained that adolescents and children are tabula rasa for their parents. Lopsided and ineffective clinical practices and interventions will be pursued as long as theories continue to deprive adolescents of their responsibility vis-à-vis their parents. To compound this difficulty, parents do not enjoy a cultural climate that bestows upon them a sense of personal efficacy and moral authority. As discussed in Chapter 8, professionals have effectively granted themselves the right to define what proper parenting is, thus disempowering parents.

The last roadblock to be mentioned is described by Bronfenbrenner (1985:377) as the "unraveling of the social fabric in which families, schools, and other immediate contexts of development are embedded." For the purposes of our discussion, the result of this unraveling of the social fabric is that parents become more socially isolated. They no longer belong to a neighborhood or community with a high value consensus, an element that would facilitate their task and enhance their moral authority (Coleman and Hoffer, 1987). They do not have any subculture of their own, nor any lobby group. The lack of a functional community also means that parents are solely responsible for the supervision of their adolescents. In reality, what is needed is collective socialization of children, whereby all adults in a neighborhood make it their responsibility to keep an eye out for the welfare and behavior of all children.

STRENGTHENING PARENTAL INFLUENCE

Of course, parents are very busy, some are quite preoccupied, others are poor, and many are single. But one could argue that these would be ample reasons to *help* parents rather than berate their shortcomings. Several suggestions are summarized below; they flow from the contents of previous chapters.

Parents need an effective *moral* authority in order to fulfill their role in an environment that has become more difficult (Elshtain, 1990). Parents' authority has been eroded, and this loss is related to other weakening aspects of our culture because, in fact, no one is left with great moral authority—neither teachers, clergy, nor elected officials. Parents should be in a position to request that their child respect and follow rules of behavior, secure in the knowledge that they are supported by other institutions in this endeavor.

Parental authority has become synonymous with a breach of children's rights in certain quarters, and it can be observed on a daily basis that children take advantage of this obvious lack of support for their parents. A proportion of the calls children place to Child Help Lines, for instance, are from youngsters who complain about parental rules such as curfews. Others want to know how to find a lawyer to sue their parents because they are not allowed to smoke or participate in other desired activities. Such calls are indicators not only that children are less isolated than in the past (a heartening point) but also that they perceive the erosion of parental authority and the increase in social support they themselves can obtain when complaining (even unjustly) about their parents. Moreover, it is reasonable to suggest that it is those parents who would most need to see their authority valued who are the most likely to be deprived of it and castigated—single mothers and the poor; too often, these two are synonymous.

If we lived in a society in which parents were respected and socially supported (by schools, professionals, welfare agencies, and law enforcement personnel), and where children were encouraged from all quarters, including the media, to respect their parents, the family would become a more effective institution—whatever its size and structure. Generally speaking, parent-child relations would be facilitated and child development enhanced. Within such a context, children would more easily accept and internalize norms of behavior and would be more inclined to cooperate in their upbringing. (Basically, I am echoing some of the implications of James Coleman's functional community—Coleman and Hoffer, 1987.) In contrast to this ideal, our children are bombarded from the time they are very small by conflicting and discouraging messages concerning parental authority.

Faced with often contradictory how-to advice, constrained by a variety of professionals whose blame they fear, and muzzled by a better organized peer group at their doorstep—far better organized than their own social support is—many parents become indecisive, unsure of themselves, and unable to say no. They may be afraid to displease their children. Some fear that their youngsters will run away; at any rate, they frequently threaten to do so. This threat instills the potent and realistic specter of their youngster ending up as a street kid immersed in drugs and prostitution. Therefore, within this context, many parents find it easier to disengage from the parental role and reduce it to one of being their child's "friend." This role confusion may work well with adolescents who are self-controlled, have an easy personality or are achievement oriented, and benefit from a prosocial peer group. But this type of "egalitarian" relationship, which resembles the permissive parenting style and even has elements of neglect, can be disastrous with children who have less favorable personality characteristics and belong to a deviant peer group.

A new role for teachers, professionals caring for children/adolescents, police, and welfare workers suggests itself. It would consist of encouraging children and adolescents to develop behaviors that are more altruistic and collectivist, or less individualistic and self-centered. Youngsters could be encouraged to turn to their parents for advice and to cooperate with them in their upbringing. Professionals may object to this suggestion with the following: "But if these teen-agers feel that no one understands them, what will happen to them?" It can be argued that this concern is exaggerated, given that many adolescents themselves place barriers to others "understanding" them. Also, the question is defeatist from the perspective of the parent-child relationship because it implies that only people, preferably profes-sionals, *other than parents* can understand adolescents. *It is an indi-rect and poorly camouflaged condemnation of parents* that does not escape adolescents' attention.

PARENTAL GRATIFICATION: WHY NOT?

In the technological world of today, children remain dependent upon their parents longer than in other societies and longer than in the nontechnologized past. The main reason for this is that children have to be schooled and trained to hold the complex jobs the economy needs. Consequently, adolescents have been transformed into teen-agers. Teenagers are a category of people, between thirteen and nine-teen, who, in our culture, are supposed to learn to be independent from their parents, go to school, and hopefully have a good time. They are also expected to be rebellious, go through a "phase" of parental rejection, while for their protection remaining under the responsibility of their parents. Teenage years are expected to be "tumultuous," "a search for one's identity," "conflictual," and "full of risks" for adolescents. In these years the "peer group" becomes "more important" than the parents. Often, in low-income areas and among certain subgroups, teenagers are expected to earn their living and, in the case of girls, even to get married or have babies.

In terms of middle-class social constructions, there is obviously a clear-cut dichotomy in the division of labor here: parents who sup-port children on one side and said children who generally would rather be with other children than with their parents. Or, stated another way, there are parents whose main purpose in these young persons' lives is to support them and teenagers whose main purpose for being with their parents is to be supported. Fortunately, not all parents or all teenagers follow this ideology. Indeed, many parents expect their teenagers to contribute to their maintenance by performing certain household duties, and many do. Moreover, many families with adolescents experience a great deal of closeness and sharing. But, overall, in terms of social construction of reality, middle-class society has definitely created a situation of imbalance and intergenerational separation. Even in terms of exchange theory, the imbalance is very tilted: parents give and teenagers receive. What is in it for the parents, one may ask?

Fortunately, most parents are reasonably altruistic, have been well conditioned to accept their role, and believe that this is the way things unavoidably have to be. It is their "duty." Writing about mothers, Elaine Heffner (1978:27) pointed out that no one "suggests that it is permissible for her to consider herself, or indicate that she is as important as the child." This applies to both parents, and she adds that parents in our society are not allowed to exhibit negative feelings concerning their role or their children. This was well illustrated in the chapter on delinquency, in which we saw that parents who confide about their children's misbehaviors are often ostracized socially. Basically, parents are socialized to believe that they owe everything to their children. If they do perceive an imbalance, society provides them with a multitude of rationalizations: "it will pass"; "it's a phase"; "they will outgrow it". Such parents are at a *waiting* stage: waiting for the "phase" (often a very long one) to end, waiting for the teenager to come back to his or her senses, waiting for him or her to become a responsible adult. Such parents' *own lives* are suspended while their adolescents go through their series of phases, some minor, some major, some positive, some negative—but most negative ones are avoidable, as they are dictated by the cultural context.

Even parents who have demanding and difficult teenagers are expected to derive satisfaction from their role. At the very least, they should "accept their lot." They should "stand by" their child. Should it then be surprising if many parents are relieved when their children are on their own? In the past, the "empty-nest syndrome" involved expectations of loneliness and purposelessness by parents who found themselves alone. More recent studies clearly indicate that such parents may have suffered from an overflowing nest before and the new state of their nest suits them just fine. In the recent past, women had no other purpose in life except to be housewives and mothers. They may indeed have keenly felt the loss of their central and core role when children left. But today's parents are usually both employed, have an enormous amount of financial responsibilities (one of the largest is the maintenance of their adolescent and young adult children), have more complicated personal lives (higher divorce/remarriage/stepparenting rates), have many extrafamilial "distractions," and can look to postparenthood and still be in a state of good health for many years to come.

An imbalance therefore exists against parents in terms of exchange theory. The result of this imbalance is reflected in the drastic decline in the birth rate in this century. As children's schooling has extended, as urbanization has outpaced rural life, as adolescents have become teenagers, and as experts have told parents that difficulties are quite normal, couples have had fewer and fewer children. The *use* of children has diminished. The *costs* of children have skyrocketed. Why, otherwise, would more people choose not to have children and most others choose to have only one or two? If children were as useful and as gratifying as they were or *could* be, people would have them in greater numbers. If children were not so costly, more people would have them or have more of them.

Our society is more egocentric, individualistic, and hedonistic than in the centuries past. Such characteristics can also explain why adults prefer to minimize child encumbrance. But the vicious circle can only keep spinning if one encourages teens to be egocentric as opposed to family oriented. If one encourages adolescents to receive from their parents with no reciprocity involved, these teens will grow into additional individualistic persons who later on will not want to be responsible for children either, nor perhaps even for their aging parents. Teenagers do look back occasionally and see the life their parents had—and reject such a life for themselves; paradoxically, they were its chief beneficiaries.

Adults have a great *need* for gratification, yet they see that parenthood may supply very little of it. It has become an emotionally draining experience and can isolate socially when outcomes are negative. The perceived imbalance leads adults to other forms of gratification instead of parenthood. A career, traveling, or a single lifestyle are such sources of alternate gratification. Consequently, unless we have an influx of very young immigrants who will have large numbers of children, we will have, in twenty to thirty years, a severe imbalance in the ratio of children and young adults to seniors.

Allowing adults the "right" to seek emotional gratification *as parents* from their children, whom they now have to support into young adulthood, may encourage parents in their role, and may even encourage others to have more than one child. Whatever the fertility outcome is (as we have to keep overpopulation in mind), such policies would certainly make parents' lives more fair and equitable. Of course, such a simple statement does require the entire restructuring of our society . . . a task that is easier said than done.

Currently in many societies, and fifty years ago in most Western societies, adolescents were young adults with rights but with duties. They probably gave as much to their parents as they received: both parties reciprocated. Each had a need for the other—economic and/or emotional. Adolescents were not dependents. In contrast, teenagers are dependents. But as long as they are, why can't those who pay their way have the pleasure of their cooperation, their help, their smile, their occasional company, and, why not—their gratitude? The relationship would be reciprocal, interdependent rather than dependent, and obligated with immediate returns for both parties involved. Adolescents would harvest greater emotional and moral benefits from their parents. The effect of children on parents would become more positive.

TO CONCLUDE

The effect of children on parents, as we have seen in the previous chapters, is a valid topic of research and sociological inquiry. Child effect exists. Parents and children interact with one another and impact one anothers' lives. Unfortunately, it is possible that the research methods most commonly used in sociology and psychology may not adequately depict this interactional reality. Closed-ended or multiple-choice questionnaires and surveys, even when longitudinal, have serious limitations. They do not allow researchers to see the links between what happens before, during, and after an event or interaction.

But, above all, the lack of social acceptance of child effect is detrimental to parents' ability to carry out their role and to socialize their children. Indeed, children and adolescents would be the prime beneficiaries in terms of responsible and healthy development were parents empowered and supported in their socialization efforts.

Bibliography

Adler, P. A. and Adler, P. 1998. *Peer power: Preadolescent culture and identity.* New Brunswick, NJ: Rutgers University Press.

Agnew, R. and Huguley, S. 1989. Adolescent violence toward parents. *Journal of Marriage and the Family,* 51, 699-711.

Alba, R. D., Logan, J. R., and Bellair, P. E. 1994. Living with crime: The implications of racial/ethnic differences in suburban location. *Social Forces,* 73, 395-434.

Aldous, J. and Ganey, R. F. 1999. Family life and the pursuit of happiness: The influence of gender and race. *Journal of Family Issues,* 20, 155-180.

Amato, P. R. and Booth, A. 1997. *A generation at risk: Growing up in an era of family upheaval.* Cambridge, MA: Harvard University Press.

Ambert, A.-M. 1992. *The effect of children on parents.* Binghamton, NY: The Haworth Press.

Ambert, A.-M. 1994. A qualitative study of peer abuse and its effects: Theoretical and empirical implications. *Journal of Marriage and the Family,* 56, 119-130.

Ambert, A.-M. 1997. *Parents, children, and adolescents: Interactive relationships and development in context.* Binghamton, NY: The Haworth Press.

Ambert, A.-M. 1998. *Parent-blaming by clinicians: The effect on mothers.* Paper presented at the Mother-Son Symposium, York University, Toronto, September.

Ambert, A.-M. 1999. The effect of male delinquency on mothers and fathers: A heuristic study. *Sociological Inquiry,* 69, 621-640.

Ambert, A.-M. 2001. *Families in the new millennium.* Boston: Allyn and Bacon.

Ambert, A.-M. and Gagnon, L. D. 1995. Que sait-on de l'expérience existentielle des parents des jeunes contrevenants? *Criminologie,* 28, 131-142.

American Psychiatric Association. 1994. *Diagnostic and statistical manual of mental disorders,* Fourth edition (DSM-IV). Washington, DC: American Psychiatric Association.

Aneshensel, C. S. and Sucoff, C. A. 1996. The neighborhood context of adolescent mental health. *Journal of Health and Social Behavior,* 37, 293-310.

Angold, A. 1993. Why do we not know the cause of depression in children? In D. F. Hay and A. Angold (Eds.), *Precursors and causes in development and psychopathology* (pp. 265-292). Chichester, UK: John Wiley.

Apfel, R. J. and Handel, M. H. 1993. *Madness and loss of motherhood.* Washington, DC: American Psychiatric Press.

Aquilino, W. S. 1990. The likelihood of parent-adult child co-residence: Effects of family structure and parental characteristics. *Journal of Marriage and the Family*, 52, 405-419.

Ariès, P. 1962. *Centuries of childhood: A social history of family life*. New York: Knopf and Random House.

Arnett, J. J. 2000. Emerging adulthood: A theory of development from the late teens through the twenties. *American Psychologist*, 55, 469-480.

Asarnow, J. R. 1994. Annotation: Childhood-onset schizophrenia. *Journal of Child Psychology and Psychiatry*, 35, 1345-1371.

Bagley, C. 1993. Transracial adoption in Britain: A follow-up study, with policy considerations. *Child Welfare*, 72, 285-299.

Baldwin, S. and Glendinning, C. 1983. Employment, women and their disabled children. In J. Finch and D. Groves (Eds.), *A labour of love: Women, work, and caring*. London: Routledge and Kegan Paul.

Bank, L., Marlowe, J. H., Reid, J. B., Patterson, G. R., and Weinrott, M. R. 1991. A comparative evaluation of parent training interventions for families of chronic delinquents. *Journal of Abnormal Child Psychology*, 19, 15-33.

Barkley, R. A. 1997. Behavioral inhibition, sustained attention, and executive functions: Constructing a unifying theory of ADHD. *Psychological Bulletin*, 121, 65-94.

Bartholet, E. 1993. *Family bonds: Adoption and the politics of parenting*. Boston: Houghton Mifflin.

Bates, J. E. 1987. Temperament in infancy. In J. D. Osofsky (Ed.), *Handbook of infant development*, Second edition (pp. 1101-1149). New York: Wiley.

Bates, J., Pettit, G., Dodge, K., and Ridge, B. 1998. Interaction of temperamental resistance to control and restrictive parenting in the development of externalizing behavior. *Developmental Psychology*, 34, 982-995.

Bateson, G. et al. 1958. Toward a theory of schizophrenia. *Behavioral Sciences*, 1, 251-261.

Baumeister, R. F. 1999. Low self-esteem does not cause aggression. APA *Monitor*, 30, January, p. 7.

Baydar, N. and Brooks-Gunn, J. 1998. Profiles of grandmothers who help care for their grandchildren in the United States. *Family Relations*, 47, 385-393.

Beardsall, L. and Dunn, J. 1992. Adversities in childhood: Siblings' experience, and their relations to self-esteem. *Journal of Child Psychology*, 33, 349-359.

Beels, C. C. 1974. Family and social management of schizophrenia. In P. Guerin (Ed.), *Family therapy: Theory and practice*. New York: Gardner Press.

Bell, C. C. and Jenkins, E. J. 1993. Community violence and children on Chicago's southside. *Psychiatry*, 56, 46-54.

Bell, R. Q. and Harper, L. V. 1977. *Child effects on adults*. Hillsdale, NJ: Erlbaum.

Belsky, J., Robins, E., and Gamble, W. 1984. The determinants of parental competence. In M. Lewis (Ed.), *Beyond the dyad* (pp. 251-279). New York: Plenum.

Benson, P. L., Sharma, A. R., and Roehlkepartain, E. C. 1994. *Growing up adopted: A portrait of adolescents and their families*. Minneapolis, MN: Search Institute.

Berry, M. 1991. The effects of open adoption on biological and adoptive parents and the children: The arguments and the evidence. *Child Welfare*, 70, 637-651.

Billingsley, A. 1992. *Climbing Jacob's ladder: The enduring legacy of African-American families.* New York: Simon and Schuster.

Blair, S. L. and Qian, Z. 1998. Family and Asian students' educational performance: A consideration of diversity. *Journal of Family Issues*, 19, 355-374.

Bloom, A. 1987. *The closing of the American mind.* New York: Simon and Schuster.

Bohman, M. 1996. Predispositions to criminality: Swedish adoption studies in retrospect. In G. R. Bock and J. A. Goode (Eds.), *Genetics of criminal and antisocial behavior. Ciba Foundation Symposium* 194 (pp. 99-114). Chichester, UK: Wiley.

Bonecutter, F. J. and Gleeson, J. P. 1997. Broadening our view: Lessons from kinship foster care. In G. R. Anderson, A. S. Ryan, and B. R. Leashore (Eds.), *The challenge of permanency planning in a multicultural society* (pp. 99-119). Binghamton, NY: The Haworth Press.

Boocock, S. S. 1976. Children and society. In A. Skolnick (Ed.), *Rethinking childhood.* Boston: Little, Brown.

Borders, L. D., Black, L. K., and Pasley, B. K. 1998. Are adopted children and their parents at greater risk for negative outcomes? *Family Relations*, 47, 237-241.

Boyd, M. and Norris, D. 1995. Leaving the nest? The impact of family structure. *Canadian Social Trends*, 38, Autumn, 14-19.

Braungart-Rieker, J. et al. 1995. Genetic mediation of longitudinal associations between family environment and childhood behavior problems. *Developmental Psychopathology*, 7, 233-245.

Brim, O. G. Jr. 1968. Adult socialization. In J. A. Clausen (Ed.), *Socialization and society.* Boston: Little, Brown.

Brody, N. 1993. Intelligence and the behavioral genetics of personality. In R. Plomin and G. E. McClearn (Eds.), *Nature, nurture, and psychology* (pp. 161-178). Washington, DC: American Psychological Association.

Brodzinsky, D. M. 1993. Long-term outcomes in adoption. In R. E. Behrman (Ed.), *The future of children: Adoption* (pp. 153-166). Los Altos, CA: Center for the Future of Children, the Davis and Lucille Packard Foundation.

Bronfenbrenner, U. 1985. Freedom and discipline across the decades. In G. Becker, H. Becker, and L. Huber (Eds.), *Ordnung und Unordnung (Order and disorder)* (pp. 326-339). Berlin: Beltz.

Bronfenbrenner, U. and Ceci, S. J. 1993. Heredity, environment, and the question "how?"—A first approximation. In R. Plomin and G. E. McClearn (Eds.), *Nature, nurture, and psychology* (pp. 313-324). Washington, DC: American Psychological Association.

Bronfenbrenner, U. and Ceci, S. J. 1994. Nature-nurture reconceptualized in developmental perspective: A bioecological model. *Psychological Review*, 101, 568-586.

Brooks-Gunn, J., Klebanov, P., Liaw, F., and Duncan, G. J. 1995. Towards an understanding of the effect of poverty upon children. In H. E. Fitzgerald, B. M. Lester, and B. Zuckerman (Eds.), *Children of poverty* (pp. 3-36). New York: Garland.

Brunk, M. A. and Henggeler, S. W. 1984. Child influences on adult controls: An experimental investigation. *Developmental Psychology*, 20, 1074-1081.

Buehler, C., Krishnakumar, A., Stone, G., Anthony, C., Pemberton, S., Gerard, J., and Barber, B. K. 1998. Interparental conflict styles and youth problem behaviors: A two-sample replication study. *Journal of Marriage and the Family*, 60, 119-132.

Buriel, R. and De Ment, T. 1997. Immigration and sociocultural change in Mexican, Chinese, and Vietnamese American families. In A. Booth, A. C. Crouter, and N. Landale (Eds.), *Immigration and the family: Research and policy on U.S. immigrants* (pp. 165-200). Mahwah, NJ: Erlbaum.

Burke, K. C., Burke, J. D., Regier, D. A., and Rae, D. S. 1990. Age at onset of selected mental disorders in five community populations. *Archives of General Psychiatry*, 47, 511-518.

Burton, L. M. 1992. Black grandparents rearing children of drug-addicted parents: Stressors, outcomes, and the social service needs. *The Gerontologist*, 32, 744-751.

Burton, L. M. 1996. Age norms, the timing of family role transitions, and intergenerational caregiving among aging African American women. *The Gerontologist*, 36, 199-208.

Butterfield, F. 1999. As inmate population grows, so does a focus on children. *The New York Times*, April 7, A1, A18.

Cabrera, N. J., Tamis-LeMonda, C. S., Bradley, R. H., Hofferth, S., and Lamb, M. E. 2000. Fatherhood in the twenty-first century. *Child Development*, 71, 127-136.

Call, V., Sprecher, S., and Schwartz, P. 1995. The incidence and frequency of marital sex in a national sample. *Journal of Marriage and the Family*, 57, 639-652.

Capaldi, D. M., Crosby, L., and Stoolmiller, M. 1996. Predicting the timing of first sexual intercourse for at-risk adolescent males. *Child Development*, 67, 344-359.

Caplan, P. J. and Hall-McCorquodale, I. 1985. Mother-blaming in major clinical journals. *American Journal of Orthopsychiatry*, 55, 345-359.

Carr, J. 1988. Six weeks to twenty-one years old: A longitudinal study of children with Down's syndrome and their families. *Journal of Child Psychology and Psychiatry*, 29, 407-431.

Casper, L. M. and O'Connell, M. 1998. Work, income, the economy, and married fathers as child-care providers. *Demography*, 35, 243-250.

Caspi, A. 2000. The child is father to the man: Personality continuities from childhood to adulthood. *Journal of Personality and Social Psychology*, 78, 158-172.

Caspi, A., Entmer Wright, B. R., Moffitt, T. E., and Silva, P. A. 1998. Childhood predictors of unemployment in early adulthood. *American Sociological Review*, 63, 424-451.

Caspi, A. and Moffitt, T. 1991. The continuity of maladaptive behavior: From description to understanding in the study of antisocial behavior. In D. Cicchetti and D. Cohen (Eds.), *Manual of developmental psychopathology*. New York: Wiley.

Cawthron, P., James, A., Dell, J., and Seagroatt, V. 1994. Adolescent onset psychosis: A clinical outcome study. *Journal of Child Psychology and Psychiatry*, 35, 1321-1332.

Chesler, P. 1989. *The sacred bond: The legacy of Baby M*. New York: Vintage.

Child Welfare League of America. 1993. *Charting the new course: Children's legislative agenda.* Washington, DC: Child Welfare League of America.

Chodorow, N. and Contratto, S. 1982. The fantasy of the perfect mother. In B. Thorne and M. Yalom (Eds.), *Rethinking the family: Some feminist questions.* New York: Longman.

Clarke-Stewart, K. A. 1973. Interaction between mothers and their young children: Characteristics and consequences. *Monographs of the Society for Research in Child Development,* 153, 6-7.

Coleman, J. S. and Hoffer, T. 1987. *Public and private schools: The impact of communities.* New York: Basic Books.

Coley, R. L. and Chase-Lansdale, P. L. 1998. Adolescent pregnancy and parenthood: Recent evidence and future directions. *American Psychologist,* 53, 152-166.

Collins, W. A., Maccoby, E. E., Steinberg, L., Hetherington, E. M., and Bornstein, M. H. 2000. Contemporary research on parenting: The case for nature and nurture. *American Psychologist,* 55, 218-222.

Cook, J. A. 1988. Who "mothers" the chronically mentally ill? *Family Relations,* 37, 42-49.

Cook, W. L. et al. 1990. Mother-child dynamics in early-onset depression and childhood schizophrenia spectrum disorders. *Development and Psychopathology,* 2, 71-84.

Coontz, S. 2000. Historical perspectives on family studies. *Journal of Marriage and the Family,* 62, 283-297.

Corsaro, W. A. 1997. *The sociology of childhood.* Thousand Oaks, CA: Pine Forge Press.

Cowan, C. P. and Cowan, P. A. 1992. *When partners become parents: The big life change for couples.* New York: Basic Books.

Cowan, C. P. and Cowan, P. A. 1997. Working with couples during stressful transitions. In S. Dreman (Ed.), *The family on the threshold of the 21st century* (pp. 17-48). Mahwah, NJ: Erlbaum.

Crnic, K. A. and Greenberg, M. 1987. Maternal stress, social support, and coping: Influences on the early mother-infant relationship. In C. F. Zachariah Boukydis (Ed.), *Research on support for parents and infants in the postnatal period.* Norwood, NJ: Ablex Publishing.

Crnic, K. A., Greenberg, M. T., Ragozin, A. S., Robinson, W. M., and Basham, R. 1983. Effects of stress and social support on mothers and premature and full-term infants. *Child Development,* 54, 209-217.

Crockenberg, S. B. 1981. Infant instability, mother responsiveness, and social support influences on the security of the infant-mother attachment. *Child Development,* 52, 857-865.

Crouter, A. C., Helms-Erikson, H., Updegraff, K., and McHale, S. M. 1999. Conditions underlying parents' knowledge about children's daily lives in middle childhood: Between and within-family comparisons. *Child Development,* 70, 246-259.

Cummings, J. S., Pellegrini, D. S., Clifford, I., and Cummings, E. M. 1989. Children's responses to angry adult behavior as a function of marital distress and interparent hostility. *Child Development,* 670, 1035-1043.

Cummings, S. T. 1976. The impact of child deficiency on the father: A study of fathers of mentally retarded and chronically ill children. *American Journal of Orthopsychiatry*, 46, 246-255.

Cummings, S. T., Bayley, H. C., and Rie, H. E. 1966. Effects of the child's deficiency on the mother: A study of mothers of mentally retarded, chronically ill, and neurotic children. *American Journal of Orthopsychiatry*, 36, 595-608.

Cunningham, C. E., Bremmer, R., and Boyle, M. 1995. Large group community-based parenting programs for families of preschoolers at risk for disruptive behavior disorders: Utilization, cost effectiveness, and outcome. *Journal of Child Psychology and Psychiatry*, 36, 1141-1159.

Da Vanzo, J. and Goldscheider, F. K. 1990. Coming home again: Returns to the parental home of young adults. *Population Studies*, 44, 241-255.

Darling, R. B. 1987. The economic and psychosocial consequences of disability: Family-society relationships. *Marriage and Family Review*, 11, 45-61.

Deater-Deckard, K., Pickering, K., Dunn, J. F., Golding, D., and the Avon Longitudinal Study of Pregnancy and Childhood Study Team. 1998. Family structure and depressive symptoms in men preceding and following the birth of a child. *American Journal of Psychiatry*, 155, 818-823.

Demos, J. 1974. The American family in past time. *American Scholar*, 63, 422-446.

Dinnerstein, D. 1976. *The mermaid and the minotaur*. New York: Harper and Row.

Dix, T. 1991. The affective organization of parenting: Adaptive and maladaptive processes. *Psychological Bulletin*, 110, 3-25.

Doherty, W. J. 2000. Family science and family citizenship: Toward a model of community partnership with families. *Family Relations*, 49, 319-325.

Doherty, W. J., Kouneski, E. F., and Erickson, M. F. 1998. Responsible fathering: An overview and conceptual framework. *Journal of Marriage and the Family*, 60, 277-292.

Donzelot, J. 1979. *The policing of families*. New York: Random House.

Dornbusch, S. M. and Gray, K. D. 1988. Single-parent families. In S. M. Dornbusch and M. H. Strober (Eds.), *Feminism, children, and the new families*. New York: Guilford.

Downey, D. B. 1995. When bigger is not better: Family size, parental resources, and children's educational performance. *American Sociological Review*, 60, 746-761.

Dubow, E. F., Edwards, S., and Ippolito, M. F. 1997. Life stressors, neighborhood disadvantage, and resources: A focus on inner-city children's adjustment. *Journal of Clinical Child Psychology*, 26, 130-144.

Duncan, G. J. and Brooks-Gunn, J. 2000. Family poverty, welfare reform, and child development. *Child Development*, 71, 188-196.

Earls, F. 1994. Oppositional-defiant and conduct disorders. In M. Rutter, E. Taylor, and L. Hersov (Eds.), *Child and adolescent psychiatry*, Third edition (pp. 308-329). Oxford: Blackwell.

Edin, K. and Lein, L. 1997. *Making ends meet: How single mothers survive welfare and low-wage work*. New York: Sage.

Egan, S. K. and Perry, D. G. 1998. Does low self-regard invite victimization? *Developmental Psychology,* 34, 299-309.

Eggebeen, D. J. and Hogan, D. P. 1990. Giving between generations in American families. *Human Nature,* 1, 211-232.

Elder, G. H. Jr., Liker, J. K., and Cross, C. E. 1984. Parent-child behavior in the Great Depression: Life course and intergenerational influences. In P. B. Baltes and O. G. Brim Jr. (Eds.), *Life-span development and behavior,* Vol. 6. New York: Academic Press.

Eley, T. C., Lichtenstein, P., and Stevenson, J. 1999. Sex differences in the etiology of aggressive and nonaggressive antisocial behavior: Results from two twin studies. *Child Development,* 70, 155-168.

Elshtain, J. B. 1990. The family and civic life. In D. Blankenhorn et al. (Eds), *Rebuilding the nest: A new commitment to the American family* (pp. 119-132). Milwaukee: Family Service America.

Elster, A. B., Ketterlinus, R., and Lamb, M. E. 1990. Association between parenthood and problem behavior in a national sample of adolescents. *Pediatrics,* 85, 1044-1050.

Entwisle, D. R., Alexander, K. L., and Olson, L. S. 1997. *Children, schools, and inequality.* Boulder, CO: Westview Press.

Etter, J. 1993. Levels of cooperation and satisfaction in 56 open adoptions. *Child Welfare,* 72, 257-267.

Etzioni, A. 1994. *The spirit of community: Rights, responsibilities, and the new communitarian agenda.* New York: Crown.

Fagot, B. I., Pears, K. C., Capaldi, D. M., Crosby, L., and Leve, C. S. 1998. Becoming an adolescent father: Precursors and parenting. *Developmental Psychology,* 34, 1209-1219.

Falloon, I. R. H. and Pederson, J. 1985. Family management in the prevention of morbidity of schizophrenia: The adjustment of the family unit. *British Journal of Psychiatry,* 147, 156-163.

Farrington, D. P. 1995. The development of frequent offending and antisocial behavior from childhood: Key findings from the Cambridge Study of Delinquent Development. *Journal of Child Psychology and Psychiatry,* 360, 929-964.

Feldman, S. S. and Rosenthal, D. A. 1990. The acculturation of autonomy expectations in Chinese highschoolers residing in two Western nations. *International Journal of Psychology,* 25, 259-281.

Fergusson, D. M., Horwood, L. J., and Lynskey, M. T. 1994. Culture makes a difference . . . or does it? A comparison of adolescents in Hong Kong, Australia, and the United States. In R. K. Silbereisen and E. Todt (Eds.), *Adolescents in context* (pp. 99-113). New York: Springer-Verlag.

Fincham, F. D. 1994. Understanding the association between marital conflict and child adjustment: Overview. *Journal of Family Psychology,* 8, 123-127.

Finkelhor, D. and Dziuba-Leatherman, J. 1994. Victimization of children. *American Psychologist,* 49, 173-183.

Finnegan, R. A., Hodges, E. V. E., and Perry, D. G. 1998. Victimization by peers: Associations with children's reports of mother-child interaction. *Journal of Personality and Social Psychology*, 75, 1076-1086.

Firestone, S. 1970. *The dialectic of sex: The case for feminist revolution*. New York: Bantam Books.

Floyd, F. J. and Gallagher, E. M. 1997. Parental stress, care demands, and the use of support services for school-age children with disabilities and behavior problems. *Family Relations*, 46, 359-371.

Forcier, K. I. 1990. Management and care of pregnant psychiatric patients. *Journal of Psychosocial Nursing*, 28, 11-16.

Forgatch, M. S. 1989. Patterns and outcomes in family problem solving: The disrupting effect of negative emotion. *Journal of Marriage and the Family*, 51, 115-124.

Fox, G. L. 1999. Families in the media: Reflections on the public scrutiny of private behavior. *Journal of Marriage and the Family*, 61, 821-830.

Frick, P. J. et al. 1992. Familial risk factors to oppositional defiant disorder and conduct disorder: Parental psychopathology and maternal parenting. *Journal of Consulting and Clinical Psychology*, 60, 49-55.

Fromm-Reichmann, F. 1948. Notes on the development of treatment of schizophrenics by psychoanalytic psychotherapy. *Psychiatry*, 11, 263-273.

Fuller-Thomson, E., Minkler, M., and Driver, D. 1997. A profile of grandparents raising grandchildren in the United States. *The Gerontologist*, 37, 406-411.

Furstenberg, F. F. Jr. et al. 1994. How families manage risk and opportunity in dangerous neighborhoods. In W. J. Wilson (Ed.), *Sociology and the public agenda* (pp. 231-258). Newbury Park, CA: Sage.

Galambos, N. L. and Lerner, J. V. 1987. Child characteristics and the employment of mothers with young children: A longitudinal study. *Journal of Child Psychology and Psychiatry*, 28, 87-98.

Ganong, L. H. and Coleman, M. 1987. Effects of children on parental sex-role orientation. *Journal of Family Issues*, 8, 278-290.

Ganong, L. H., Coleman, M., and Demo, D. H. 1995. Issues in training family scientists. *Family Relations*, 44, 501-508.

Ganong, L. H., Coleman, M., Fine, M., and McDaniel, A. K. 1998. Issues considered in contemplating stepchild adoption. *Family Relations*, 47, 63-71.

Gans, H. J. 1992. Second generation decline: Scenarios for the economic and ethnic futures of post-1965 American immigrants. *Ethnic and Racial Studies*, 15, 173-192.

Garbarino, J. 1999. *Lost boys: Why our sons turn violent and how we can save them*. New York: The Free Press.

Garbarino, J. and Kostelny, K. 1992. Child maltreatment as a community problem. *Child Abuse & Neglect*, 16, 455-464.

Garmezy, N. and Masten, A. S. 1994. Chronic adversities. In M. Rutter, E. Taylor, and L. Hersov (Eds.), *Child and adolescent psychiatry*, Third edition (pp. 191-208). Oxford: Blackwell.

Garrison, M. E. B., Blalock, L. B., Zarski, J. J., and Merritt, P. B. 1997. Delayed parenthood: An exploratory study of family functioning. *Family Relations,* 46, 281-290.

Gecas, V. and Seff, M. A. 1990. Families and adolescents: A review of the 1980s. *Journal of Marriage and the Family,* 52, 941-958.

Gergen, K. J. 1992. Toward a postmodern psychology. In S. Kvale (Ed.), *Psychology and postmodernism* (pp. 1-16). Newbury Park, CA: Sage.

Gerstel, N. and Gallagher, S. K. 1993. Kinkeeping and distress: Gender, recipients of care, and work-family conflict. *Journal of Marriage and the Family,* 55, 598-607.

Gillis, J. R. 1981. *Youth and history. Tradition and change in European age relations, 1770-present.* New York: Academic Press.

Gladstone, J. and Westhues, A. 1998. Adoption reunions. A new side to intergenerational family relationships. *Family Relations,* 47, 177-184.

Gold, S. J. and Phillips, B. 1996. Mobility and continuity among Eastern European Jews. In S. Pedreza and R. G. Rumbaut (Eds.), *Origins and destinies: Immigration, race, and ethnicity in America* (pp. 182-194). Belmont, CA: Wadsworth.

Goldstein, M. J., Talovic, S. A., Nvechterlein, K. H., Fogelson, D. L., Subotnik, K. L., and Asarnow, R. F. 1992. Family interaction versus individual psychopathology: Do they indicate the same processes in the families of schizophrenics? *British Journal of Psychiatry,* 161, 97-102.

Golombok, S. and Tasker, F. 1996. Do parents influence the sexual orientation of their children? Findings from a longitudinal study of lesbian mothers. *Developmental Psychology,* 32, 3-11.

Gonzales, N. A., Cauce, A. M., Friedman, R. J., and Mason, C. A. 1996. Family, peer, and neighborhood influences on academic achievement among African-American adolescents: One-year prospective effects. *American Journal of Community Psychology,* 29, 365-387.

Gorman, E. H. 1999. Bringing home the bacon: Marital allocation of income-earning responsibility, job shifts, and men's wages. *Journal of Marriage and the Family,* 61, 110-122.

Gottesman, I. I. 1991. *Schizophrenia genesis: The origins of madness.* New York: W. H. Freeman.

Graff, H. J. 1995. *Conflicting paths: Growing up in America.* Cambridge, MA: Harvard University Press.

Grant, L., Simpson, L. A., Rong, X., and Peters-Golden, H. 1990. Gender, parenthood, and work hours of physicians. *Journal of Marriage and the Family,* 52, 39-49.

Greenberg, J. S., Seltzer, M. M., and Greenlay, J. R. 1993. Aging parents of adults with disabilities: The gratifications and frustration of later-life caregiving. *The Gerontologist,* 33, 542-549.

Griffin, L. W. 1994. Elder maltreatment among rural African-Americans. *Journal of Elder Abuse & Neglect,* 6, 1-27.

Gross, H. E. 1993. Open adoption: A research-based literature review and new data. *Child Welfare,* 72, 269-294.

Grotevant, J., McRoy, R., Elde, C., and Fravel, D. 1994. Adoptive family system dynamics: Variations by level of openness in the adoption. *Family Process, 33,* 125-146.

Groze, V. 1996. *Successful adoptive families: A longitudinal study.* Westport, CT: Praeger.

Grusec, J. E., Goodnow, J. J., and Kuczynski, L. 2000. New directions in analyses of parenting contributions for children's acquisition of values. *Child Development, 71,* 204-211.

Hanson, T. L., McLanahan, S., and Thomson, E. 1997. Economic resources, parental practices, and children's well-being. In G. J. Duncan and J. Brooks-Gunn (Eds.), *Consequences of growing up poor* (pp. 190-238). New York: Russell Sage.

Harrington, R. C., Fudge, H., Rutter, M. L., Bredenkamp, D., Groothues, C., and Pridham, J. 1993. Child and adult depression: A test of continuities with data from a family study. *British Journal of Psychiatry, 162,* 627-633.

Hawkins, A. J. and Dollahite, D. C. (Eds.). 1997. *Generative fathering: Beyond deficit perspectives.* Thousand Oaks, CA: Sage.

Hays, S. 1996. *The cultural contradictions of motherhood.* New Haven, CT: Yale University Press.

Heath, D. T. 1995. The impact of delayed fatherhood on the father-child relationship. *The Journal of Genetic Psychology, 155,* 511-530.

Heffner, E. 1978. *The emotional experience of motherhood after Freud and feminism.* New York: Doubleday.

Heller, T., Hsieh, K., and Rowitz, L. 1997. Maternal and paternal caregiving of persons with mental retardation across the life span. *Family Relations, 46,* 407-415.

Heston, L. L. 1966. *Family interaction and psychopathology: Theories, methods, and findings.* New York: Plenum.

Hills, H. I. and Stozier, A. L. 1992. Multicultural training in APA-approved counseling psychology programs: A survey. *Professional Psychology: Research and Practice, 23,* 43-51.

Hochschild, A. R. 1983. *The managed heart.* Berkeley: University of California Press.

Hochschild, A. R. 1997. *The time bind.* New York: Metropolitan Books.

Hodges, E. V. E., Malone, M. J., and Perry, D. G. 1997. Individual risk and social risk as interacting determinants of victimization in the peer group. *Developmental Psychology, 33,* 1032-1039.

Hofferth, S. et al. 1998. Reported in *Time,* November 25, p. 44.

Hogan, D. P. and Kitagawa, E. M. 1985. The impact of social status, family structure, and neigborhood on the fertility of black adolescents. *American Journal of Sociology, 90,* 825-855.

Horowitz, F. D. 2000. Child development and the PITS: Simple questions, complex answers, and developmental theory. *Child Development, 71,* 1-10.

Jang, S. J. and Smith, C. A. 1997. A test of reciprocal causal relationships among parental supervision, affective ties, and delinquency. *Journal of Research in Crime and Delinquency,* 34, 307-336.

Jendrek, M. P. 1993. Grandparents who parent their grandchildren: Effects on lifestyle. *Journal of Marriage and the Family,* 55, 609-621.

Johnson, M. E. and Huston, T. L. 1998. The perils of love, or why wives adapt to husbands during the transition to parenthood. *Journal of Marriage and the Family,* 60, 195-204.

Johnston, C. and Pelham, W. E. 1990. Maternal characteristics, ratings of child behavior, and mother-child interactions in families of children with externalizing disorders. *Journal of Abnormal Child Psychology,* 18, 407-417.

Kallman, F. J. and Roth, B. 1986. Genetic aspects of preadolescent schizophrenia. *American Journal of Psychiatry,* 112, 599-606.

Kaufman, G. and Uhlenberg, P. 2000. The influence of parenthood on the work effort of married men and women. *Social Forces,* 78, 931-949.

Kelley, J. and De Graaf, N. D. 1997. National context, parental socialization, and religious belief: Results from 15 nations. *American Sociological Review,* 62, 639-659.

Kendall, P. C. and Stoutham-Gerow, M. A. 1995. Issues in the transportability of treatment: The case of anxiety disorders in youths. *Journal of Consulting and Clinical Psychology,* 63, 702-708.

Kendler, K. S. 1995. Genetic epidemiology in psychiatry. Taking both genes and environment seriously. *Archives of General Psychiatry,* 52, 895-899.

Kendler, K. S. et al. 1992. Life events and depressive symptoms: A twin study perspective. In P. McGriffin and R. Murray (Eds.), *The new genetics of mental illness* (pp. 146-164). Oxford: Butterworth-Heinemann.

Kendler, K. S., Karkowski, L. M., and Prescott, C. A. 1999. Causal relationships between stressful life events and the onset of major depression. *American Journal of Psychiatry,* 156, 837-841.

Kett, J. F. 1977. *Rites of passage: Adolescence in America 1790 to present.* New York: Basic Books.

Kim, U. and Choi, S. H. 1994. Individualism, collectivism, and child development: A Korean perspective. In P. M. Greenfield and R. R. Cocking (Eds.), *Cross-cultural roots of minority child development* (pp. 227-257). Hillsdale, NJ: Erlbaum.

Kisker, E. E. and Ross, C. M. 1997. Arranging child care. *Future of Children,* 7, 99-109.

Kochenderfer, B. J. and Ladd, G. W. 1996. Peer victimization: Cause or consequence of school maladjustment? *Child Development,* 67, 1305-1317.

Koller, M. R. 1974. *Families: A multigenerational approach.* New York: McGraw-Hill.

Korbin, J. E., Anetzberger, G., and Austin, C. 1995. The intergenerational cycle of violence in children and elder abuse. *Journal of Elder Abuse & Neglect,* 7, 1-15.

Korner, A. F. 1971. Individual differences at birth: Implications for early experience and later development. *American Journal of Orthopsychiatry,* 41, 608-619.

Krueger, R. F., Schmutte, P. S., Caspi, A., and Moffitt, T. 1994. Personality traits linked to crime among men and women: Evidence from a birth cohort. *Journal of Abnormal Psychology,* 103, 328-338.

Kupersmidt, J. B. et al. 1995. Childhood aggression and peer relations in the context of family and neighborhood factors. *Child Development,* 66, 360-375.

Kurdek, L. A. 1993. The allocation of household labor in gay, lesbian, and heterosexual married couples. *Journal of Social Issues,* 49, 127-139.

Ladd, G. W. 1992. Themes and theories: Perspectives on processes in family-peer relationships. In R. D. Parke and G. W. Ladd (Eds.), *Family-peer relationships: Modes of linkage* (pp. 1-34). Hillsdale, NJ: Erlbaum.

Lamb, M. E. 1997. *The role of the father in child development.* New York: Wiley.

LaRossa, R. 1997. *The modernization of fatherhood: A social and political history.* Chicago: University of Chicago Press.

Larson, R. W. and Richards, M. H. 1994. *Divergent realities: The emotional lives of mothers, fathers, and adolescents.* New York: Basic Books.

Laumann, E. O. 1996. Early sexual experiences: How voluntary? How violent? In M. D. Smith et al. (Eds.), *Sexuality and American social policy.* Menlo Park, CA: Henry J. Kaiser Family Foundation.

Lavigueur, S., Tremblay, R. E., and Saucier, J.-F. 1995. Interactional processes in families with disruptive boys: Patterns of direct and indirect influence. *Journal of Abnormal Child Psychology,* 23, 359-378.

Lee, G. R., Netzer, J. K., and Coward, R. T. 1995. Depression among older parents: The role of intergenerational exchange. *Journal of Marriage and the Family,* 57, 823-833.

Lee, Y.-J. and Aytac, I. A. 1998. Intergenerational financial support among whites, African Americans, and Latinos. *Journal of Marriage and the Family,* 60, 426-441.

Lefley, H. P. 1997. Synthesizing the family caregiving studies: Implications for service planning, social policy, and further research. *Family Relations,* 46, 443-450.

Lerner, R. M. 1988. Personality development: A life-span perspective. In E. M. Hetherington, R. M. Lerner, and M. Perlmutter (Eds.), *Child development and the life-span perspective.* Hillsdale, NJ: Erlbaum.

Lerner, R. M. 1995. *America's youth in crisis.* Thousand Oaks, CA: Sage.

Lerner, R. M. and Busch-Rossnagel, N. A. 1981. Individuals as producers of their development: Conceptual and empirical bases. In R. M. Lerner and N. A. Busch-Rossnagel (Eds.), *Individuals as producers of their development: A life-span perspective* (pp. 1-36). San Diego, CA: Academic Press.

Lerner, R. M., Fisher, C. B., and Weinberg, R. A. 2000. Toward a science for and of the people: Promoting civil society through the application of developmental science. *Child Development,* 71, 11-20.

Letherby, G. 1994. Mother or not, mother or what? Problems of definition and identity. *Women's Studies International Forum,* 17, 525-532.

Levine, E. S. and Sallee, A. L. 1990. Critical phases among adoptees and their families: Implications for therapy. *Child and Adolescent Social Work,* 7, 217-232.

LeVine, S. and LeVine, R. A. 1985. Age, gender, and the demographic transition: The life course in agrarian societies. In A. S. Rossi (Ed.), *Gender and the life course*. New York: Aldine.

Liem, J. H. 1974. Effects of verbal communications of parents and children: A comparison of normal and schizophrenic families. *Journal of Consulting and Clinical Psychology*, 42, 438-450.

Loeber, R. and Stouthamer-Loeber, M. 1986. Family factors as correlates and predictors of juvenile conduct problems and delinquency. In M. Tonry and N. Morris (Eds.), *Crime and justice*, Vol. 7. Chicago: University of Chicago Press.

Logan, J. R. and Stults, B. J. 1999. Racial differences in exposure to crime: The city and suburbs of Cleveland in 1990. *Criminology*, 37, 251-276.

Lowry, D. T. and Towles, D. W. 1989. Soap opera portrayals of sex, contraception, and sexually transmitted diseases. *Journal of Communication*, 39, 76-83.

Luthar, S. S. 1993. Methodological and conceptual issues in research on childhood resilience. *Journal of Child Psychology and Psychiatry*, 34, 441-453.

Lytton, H. 1980. *Parent-child interaction: The socialization process observed in twin and singleton families*. New York: Plenum.

Maccoby, E. E. 1992. Commentary. Family structure and children's adjustment: Is quality of parenting the major mediator? In E. M. Hetherington et al. (Eds.), Coping with marital transitions. *Monographs of the Society for Research in Child Development*, 57, Nos. 2-3, 230-238.

Maccoby, E. E. and Martin, J. 1983. Socialization in the context of the family: Parent-child interaction. In E. M. Hetherington (Ed.), *Handbook of child psychology: Vol. 4. Socialization, personality, and social development* (pp. 1-101). New York: Wiley.

Machamer, A. M. and Gruber, E. 1998. Secondary school, family, and educational risk: Comparing American Indian adolescents and their peers. *Journal of Educational Research*, 6, 357-369.

MacLeod, C., Mathews, A., and Tata, P. 1986. Attentional bias in emotional disorders. *Journal of Abnormal Psychology*, 95, 15-20.

Magnusson, D. 1995. Individual development: A holistic, integrated model. In P. Moen, G. H. Elder Jr. and K. Lüscher (Eds.), *Examining lives in context* (pp. 19-60). Washington, DC: American Psychological Association.

Mahoney, M. M. 1994. *Stepfamilies and the law*. Ann Arbor, MI: University of Michigan Press.

Majors, R. and Billson, J. M. 1993. *Cool pose: The dilemma of black manhood in America*. New York: Simon and Schuster.

March, K. 1995. Perception of adoption as social stigma: Motivation for search and reunion. *Journal of Marriage and the Family*, 57, 653-660.

Maton, K. I. and Hrabowski, F. A., III. 1998. Preparing the way: A qualitative study of high-achieving African American males and the role of the family. *American Journal of Community Psychology*, 26, 639-668.

Maziade, M. 1994. Temperament research and practical implications for clinicians. In W. B. Carey and S. C. McDevitt (Eds.), *Prevention and early intervention: In-*

dividual differences as risk factors for the mental health of children (pp. 69-91). New York: Brunner/Mazel.

McBride, B. A. and Rane, T. R. 1998. Parenting alliance as a predictor of father involvement: An exploratory study. *Family Relations,* 47, 229-236.

McCrae, R. R. et al. 1999. Age differences in personality across the adult life span: Parallels in five cultures. *Developmental Psychology,* 35, 466-477.

McGee, R., Feehan, M., Williams, S., and Anderson, J. 1992. DSM-III disorders from age 11 to 15 years. *Journal of the American Academy of Child and Adolescent Psychiatry,* 31, 50-59.

McGuffin, P. and Katz, R. 1993. Genes, adversity, and depression. In R. Plomin and G. E. McClearn (Eds.), *Nature, nurture, and psychology* (pp. 217-230). Washington, DC: American Psychological Association.

McKeever, P. 1992. Mothering children who have severe chronic illnesses. In A.-M. Ambert, *The effect of children on parents* (pp. 170-190). Binghamton, NY: The Haworth Press.

McLoyd, V. C. 1995. Poverty, parenting, and policy: Meeting the support needs of poor parents. In H. E. Fitzgerald, B. M. Lester, and B. Zuckerman (Eds.), *Children of poverty* (pp. 269-298). New York: Garland.

McLoyd, V. C. 1998. Socioeconomic disadvantage and child development. *American Psychologist,* 53, 185-204.

Mead, M. 1928. *Coming of age in Samoa.* New York: William Morrow.

Miall, C. E. 1996. The social construction of adoption: Clinical and community perspectives. *Family Relations,* 36, 34-39.

Miller, K. S., Forehand, R., and Kotchick, B. A. 1999. Adolescent sexual behavior in two ethnic minority samples: The role of family variables. *Journal of Marriage and the Family,* 61, 85-98.

Miller, R. B. and Dodder, R. A. 1989. The abused-abuser dyad: Elder abuse in the state of Florida. In S. R. Ingmore and R. Filinson (Eds.), *Elder abuse: Practice and policy.* New York: Human Sciences Press.

Minkler, M., Roe, K. M., and Price, M. 1992. The physical and emotional health of grandmothers raising grandchildren in the crack cocaine epidemic. *The Gerontologist,* 32, 752-761.

Minton, C. J., Kagan, J., and Levine, J. 1971. Maternal control and obedience in the two-year-old. *Child Development,* 42, 1873-1894.

Mintz, S. and Kellogg, S. 1988. *Domestic revolution: A social history of American family life.* New York: Free Press.

Mirrlees-Black, C., Mayhew, P., and Percy, A. 1996. *The 1996 British Crime Survey: England and Wales.* London: Home Office Statistical Bulletin no. 19-96.

Montgomery, R. J. 1992. Gender differences in patterns of child-parent caregiving relationships. In J. W. Dwyer and R. T. Coward (Eds.), *Gender, families, and elder care* (pp. 65-83). Newbury Park, CA: Sage.

Montgomery, R. J. V. and Kamo, Y. 1989. Parent care by sons and daughters. In J. A. Mancini (Eds.), *Aging parents and adult children* (pp. 213-230). Lexington, MA: Lexington Books.

Moore, K. A., Nord, C. W., and Peterson, J. L. 1989. Nonvoluntary sexual activity among adolescents. *Family Planning Perspectives, 21*, 110-114.

Mounts, N. S. and Steinberg, L. 1995. An ecological analysis of peer influence on adolescent grade point average and drug use. *Developmental Psychology, 31*, 915-922.

Mouw, T. and Xie, Y. 1999. Bilingualism and the academic achievement of first- and second-generation Asian Americans: Accommodation with or without assimilation? *American Sociological Review, 54*, 232-252.

Muller, C. and Kerbow, D. 1993. Parent involvement in the home, school, and community. In B. Schneider and J. S. Coleman (Eds.), *Parents, their children and schools* (pp. 13-42). San Francisco: Westview Press.

Munch, A., McPherson, J. M., and Smith-Lovin, L. 1997. Gender, children, and social contact: The effects of childrearing for men and women. *American Sociological Review, 62*, 509-520.

Musgrove, F. 1964. *Youth and the social order.* Bloomington: Indiana University Press.

Mutran, E. and Reitzes, D. G. 1984. Intergenerational support activities and well-being among the elderly: A convergence of exchange and symbolic interaction perspectives. *American Sociological Review, 49*, 117-130.

Nagin, D. S., Farrington, D. P., and Moffitt, T. E. 1995. Life-course trajectories of different types of offenders. *Criminology, 33*, 111-139.

Nagin, D. S. and Land, K. C. 1993. Age, criminal careers, and population heterogeneity: Specification and estimation of a nonparametric, mixed Poisson model. *Criminology, 31*, 327-362.

Nasow, D. 1985. *Children of the city: At work and play.* Garden City, NY: Anchor Press.

Nelkin, D. and Lindee, S. M. 1995. *The DNA Mystique: The gene as a cultural icon.* New York: Freeman.

Nelson, B. J. 1984. *Making an issue of child abuse.* Chicago: University of Chicago Press.

Nelson, D. A. and Crick, N. R. 1999. Rose-colored glasses: Examining the social information-processing of prosocial young adolescents. *Journal of Early Adolescence, 19*, 17-38.

Nett, E. 1981. Canadian families in social-historical perspective. *Canadian Journal of Sociology, 6*, 239-260.

Nigg, J. T. and Goldsmith, H. H. 1994. Genetics of personality disorders: Perspectives from personality and psychopathology research. *Psychological Bulletin, 115*, 346-380.

Nock, S. L. 1998. *Marriage in men's lives.* New York: Oxford University Press.

Noller, P. 1994. Relationships with parents in adolescence: Process and outcome. In R. Montemayor, G. R. Adams, and T. P. Gullotta (Eds.), *Personal relationships during adolescence* (Advances in Adolescent Development, vol. 6), (pp. 37-77). Thousand Oaks, CA: Sage.

O'Connor, T. G., Deater-Deckard, K., Fulker, D., Rutter, M. L., and Plomin, R. 1998. Genotype-environment correlations in late childhood and early adolescence: Antisocial behavior problems and coercive parenting. *Developmental Psychology, 34,* 970-981.

Ogbu, J. U. 1985. A cultural ecology of competence among inner-city blacks. In M. B. Spencer, G. K. Brooks, and W. R. Allen (Eds.), *Beginnings: The social and affective development of black children* (pp. 45-66). Hillsdale, NJ: Erlbaum.

Oldman, D. 1994. Adult-child relations as class relations. In J. Qvortrup, M. Bardy, G. Sgritta, and H. Wintersberger (Eds.), *Childhood matters: Social theory, practice and politics* (pp. 43-58). Aldershot, UK: Avebury.

Olson, S. L. and Banyard, V. 1993. "Stop the world so I can get off for a while:" Sources of daily stress in the lives of low-income single mothers of young children. *Family Relations, 42,* 50-56.

Pacheco, F. and Eme, R. 1993. An outcome study of the reunion between adoptees and biological parents. *Child Welfare, 72,* 53-64.

Paré, D. A. 1995. Of families and other cultures: The shifting paradigm of family therapy. *Family Process, 34,* 1-19.

Patillo, M. E. 1998. Sweet mothers and gangbusters: Managing crime in a black middle-class neighborhood. *Social Forces, 76,* 747-774.

Patterson, G. R. 1980. Mothers: The unacknowledged victims. *Monographs of the Society for Research in Child Development, 186.*

Patterson, G. R. 1982. *Coercive family processes.* Eugene, OR: Castalia.

Patterson, G. R., Bank, L., and Stoolmiller, M. 1990. The preadolescent's contributions to disrupted family process. In R. Montemayor, G. R. Adams, and T. P. Gullotta (Eds.), *From childhood to adolescence* (pp. 107-133). Newbury Park, CA: Sage.

Patterson, G. R., Reid, J. B., and Dishion, T. J. 1992. *Antisocial boys.* Eugene, OR: Castalia.

Patterson, G. R. and Stouthamer-Loeber, M. 1984. The correlation of family management practices and delinquency. *Child Development, 55,* 1299-1307.

Pearson, J. L., Hunter, A. G., Cook, J. M., Ialongo, N. S., and Kellam, S. G. 1997. Grandmother involvement in child caregiving in an urban community. *The Gerontologist, 37,* 650-657.

Pebley, A. R. and Rudkin, L. L. 1999. Grandparents caring for grandchildren: What do we know? *Journal of Family Issues, 20,* 218-242.

Pelton, L. 1991. Poverty and child protection. *Protecting Children, 7,* 3-5.

Pepler, D. J. and Slaby, R. G. 1994. Theoretical and developmental perspectives on youth and violence. In L. D. Eron et al. (Eds.), *Reason to hope: A psychosocial perspective on violence and youth* (pp. 27-58). Washington, DC: American Psychological Association.

Peters, J. F. 1985. Adolescents as socialization agents to parents. *Adolescence, 20,* 921-933.

Peterson, G. W. and Rollins, B. C. 1987. Parent-child socialization. In M. B. Sussman and S. K. Steinmetz (Eds.), *Handbook of Marriage and the Family.* New York: Plenum Press.

Piercy, P. and Sprenkle, D. 1990. Marriage and family therapy: A decade review. *Journal of Marriage and the Family*, 52, 1116-1126.

Pillemer, K. 1985. The dangers of dependency: New findings on domestic violence against the elderly. *Social Problems*, 33, 147-158.

Pillemer, K. and Suitor, J. J. 1991. "Will I ever escape my child's problems?" Effects of adult children's problems on elderly parents. *Journal of Marriage and the Family*, 53, 585-594.

Plomin, R. 1994. *Genetics and experience. The interplay between nature and nurture*. Thousand Oaks, CA: Sage.

Portes, A. 1995. Children of immigrants: Segmented assimilation and its determinants. In A. Portes (Ed.), *The economic sociology of immigration: Essays on networks, ethnicity, and entrepreneurship* (pp. 248-279). Russell Sage.

Portes, A. and Rumbaut, R. G. 1996. *Immigrant America: A portrait*. Berkeley: University of California Press.

Portes, A. and Zhou, M. 1993. The new second generation: Segmented assimilation and its variants. *Annals of the American Academy of Political and Social Sciences*, 530, 74-96.

Postman, N. 1982. *The disappearance of childhood*. New York: Delacorte.

Pruchno, R. 1999. Raising grandchildren: The experiences of Black and White grandmothers. *Gerontologist*, 39, 209-221.

Pruchno, R., Patrick, J. H., and Burant, C. J. 1997. African American and White mothers of adults with chronic disabilities: Caregiving burden and satisfaction. *Family Relations*, 46, 335-346.

Pulver, A. E. et al. 1990. Schizophrenia: Age at onset, gender, and familial risk. *Acta Psychiatrica Scandinavica*, 82, 344-351.

Purrington, B. T. 1980. *Effects of children on their parents: Parents' perceptions*. PhD Dissertation. Michigan State University.

Pyke, K. 2000. "The normal American family" as an interpretive structure of family life among grown children of Korean and Vietnamese immigrants. *Journal of Marriage and the Family*, 62, 240-255.

Quinton, D., Pickles, A., Maughan, B., and Rutter, M. 1993. Partners, peers, and pathways: Assortative pairing and continuities in conduct disorders. *Development and Psychopathology*, 5, 763-783.

Qvortrup, J. 1995. From useful to useful: The historical continuity of children's constructive participation. *Sociological Studies of Children*, 7, 49-76.

Reiss, D. 1995. Genetic influence on family systems: Implications for development. *Journal of Marriage and the Family*, 57, 543-560.

Richardson, R. A., Abramovitz, R. H., Asp, E. E., and Petersen, A. C. 1986. Parent-child relationships in early adolescence: Effects of family structure. *Journal of Marriage and the Family*, 48, 805-811.

Rodgers, K. B. 1999. Parenting processes related to sexual risk-taking behaviors of adolescent males and females. *Journal of Marriage and the Family*, 61, 99-109.

Ronka, A. and Pulkinen, L. 1995. Accumulation of problems in social functioning in young adulthood: A developmental approach. *Journal of Personality and Social Psychology,* 69, 381-391.

Rosenthal, D. A. and Feldman, S. S. 1990. The influence of perceived family and personal factors in self-reported school performance of Chinese and Western high school students. *Journal of Research on Adolescence,* 1, 135-154.

Roskies, E. 1972. *Abnormality and normality. The mothering of thalidomide children.* Ithaca, NY: Cornell University Press.

Rothman, B. K. 1989. *Recreating motherhood: Ideology and technology in a patriarchal society.* New York: W. W. Norton.

Rowe, D. C. 1994. *The limits of family influence: Genes, experience, and behavior.* New York: Guilford Press.

Rubin, S. and Quinn-Curan, N. 1983. Lost and then found: Parents' journey through the community service maze. In M. Seligman (Ed.), *The family with a handicapped child.* New York: Grune and Stratton.

Rumbaut, R. G. 1996. The crucible within: Ethnic identity, self-esteem, and segmented assimilation among children of immigrants. In A. Portes (Ed.), *The new second generation* (pp. 119-170). New York: Russell Sage.

Rumberger, R. W. and Larson, K. A. 1998. Toward explaining differences in educational achievement among Mexican American language-minority students. *Sociology of Education,* 71, 69-93.

Russell, D. A., Matsey, K. C., Reiss, D., and Hetherington, M. 1995. Debriefing the family: Is research an intervention? *Family Process,* 34, 145-160.

Rutter, M. 1978. Family, area and school influences in the genesis of conduct disorder. In L. A. Hersov et al. (Eds.), *Aggression and anti-social behaviour in childhood and adolescence.* Oxford: Pergamon.

Rutter, M. and Quinton, D. 1987. Parental psychiatric disorder: Effects on children. *Psychological Medicine,* 14, 853-880.

Rutter, M. et al. 1995. Understanding individual differences in environmental-risk exposure. In P. Moen, G. H. Elder Jr., and K. Lüscher (Eds.), *Examining lives in context* (pp. 61-93). Washington, DC: American Psychological Association.

Sachdev, P. 1992. Adoption reunion and after: A study of the search process and experience of adoptees. *Child Welfare,* 71, 53-58.

Saluter, A. F. 1992. Marital status and living arrangements: March 1991. *Current Population Reports, Population Characteristics* (Series P-20, no. 461). Washington, DC: U. S. Government Printing Press.

Sameroff, A. J. and Seifer, R. 1995. Accumulation of environmental risk and child mental health. In H. E. Fitzgerald, B. M. Lester, and B. Zuckerman (Eds.), *Children of poverty* (pp. 223-252). New York: Garland.

Sampson, R. J. 1993. The community context of violent crime. In W. J. Wilson (Ed.), *Sociology and the public agenda* (pp. 259-286). Newbury Park, CA: Sage.

Sampson, R. J. and Wilson, W. J. 1995. Toward a theory of race, crime and urban inequality. In J. Hagan and R. D. Peterson (Eds.), *Crime and inequality* (pp. 37-54). Stanford: Stanford University Press.

Sands, R. G. and Goldberg-Glen, R. S. 2000. Factors associated with stress among grandparents raising their grandchildren. *Family Relations*, 49, 97-105.

Saraceno, C. 1984. The social construction of childhood: Child care and education policies in Italy and the United States. *Social Problems*, 31, 351-363.

Saugstad, L. F. 1989. Social class, marriage, and fertility in schizophrenia. *Schizophrenia Bulletin*, 15, 9-43.

Scarr, S. 1993. Biological and cultural diversity: The legacy of Darwin for development. *Child Development*, 64, 1333-1353.

Scarr, S. 1998. American child care today. *American Psychologist*, 53, 95-108.

Scarr, S. and McCartney, K. 1983. How people make their own environments: A theory of genotype-environment correlations. *Child Development*, 54, 424-435.

Schachar, R. et al. 1987. Change in family function and relationships in children who respond to methylphrenide. *Journal of the American Academy of Child and Adolescent Psychiatry*, 26, 728-732.

Schwartz, B. 2000. Self-determination: The tyranny of freedom. *American Psychologist*, 55, 78-88.

Segal, J. and Yahraes, H. 1978. Bringing up mother. *Psychology Today*, November, 90-96.

Seitz, V., Rosenbaum, L. K., and Apfel, N. H. 1985. Effects of family support intervention: A ten-year follow-up. *Child Development*, 56, 376-391.

Seltzer, J. A. 1994. Consequences of marital dissolution for children. *Annual Review of Sociology*, 20, 235-266.

Serbin, L. A., Cooperman, J. M., Peters, P. L., Lehoux, P. M., Stack, D. M., and Schwartzman, A. E. 1998. Intergenerational transmission of psychosocial risk in women with childhood histories of aggression, withdrawal, or aggression and withdrawal. *Developmental Psychology*, 34, 1246-1262.

Serbin, L. A., Peters, P. L., and Schwartzman, A. E. 1996. Longitudinal study of early childhood injuries and acute illness in the offspring of adolescent mothers who were aggressive, withdrawn, or aggressive-withdrawn in childhood. *Journal of Abnormal Psychology*, 105, 500-507.

Shapiro, A. and Lambert, J. D. 1999. Longitudinal effects of divorce on the quality of the father-child relationship and on fathers' psychological well-being. *Journal of Marriage and the Family*, 61, 397-408.

Sharma, A. R., McGue, M. K., and Benson, P. L. 1998. The psychological adjustment of United States adopted adolescents and their nonadopted siblings. *Child Development*, 69, 791-802.

Sheley, J. F. and Wright, J. D. 1995. *In the line of fire. Youth, guns, and violence in urban America.* Hawthorne, NY: Aldine de Gruyter.

Shiner, R. L. 2000. Linking childhood personality with adaptation: Evidence for continuity and change across time into late adolescence. *Journal of Personality and Social Psychology*, 78, 310-325.

Siegal, M. 1985. *Children, parenthood, and social welfare in the context of developmental psychology.* Oxford: Clarendon Press.

Silverman, A. R. 1993. Outcomes of transracial adoption. *The Future of Children,* 3, 104-118.

Silverstein, M. and Bengtson, V. L. 1991. Do close parent-child relationships reduce the mortality risk of older parents? *Journal of Health and Social Behavior,* 32, 382-395.

Silverstein, M., Parrott, T. M., and Bengtson, V. L. 1995. Factors that predispose middle-aged sons and daughters to provide support to older parents. *Journal of Marriage and the Family,* 57, 465-475.

Silverthorn, P. and Frick, P. J. 1999. Developmental pathways to antisocial behavior: The delayed-onset pathway in girls. *Development and Psychopathology,* 11, 101-126.

Simons, R. L., Johnson, C., Conger, R. D., and Elder, G. H. Jr. 1998. A test of latent trait versus life-course perspectives on the stability of adolescent antisocial behavior. *Criminology,* 36, 217-244.

Simons, R. L., Wu, C., Conger, R. D., and Lorenz, F. O. 1994. Two routes to delinquency: Difference between early and later starters on the impact of parenting and deviant peers. *Criminology,* 32, 247-276.

Simons, R. L., Wu, C., Johnson, C., and Conger, R. D. 1995. A test of various perspectives on the intergenerational transmission of domestic violence. *Criminology,* 33, 141-172.

Singer, J. D., Fuller, B., Keiley, M. K., and Wolf, A. 1998. Early child-care selection: Variation by geographic location, maternal characteristics, and family structure. *Developmental Psychology,* 34, 1129-1144.

Skolnick, A. 1998. Solomon's children: The new biologism, psychological parenthood, attachment theory, and the best interests standard. In M. A. Mason, A. Skolnick, and S. D. Sugarman (Eds.), *All in our families: New policies for a new century.* New York: Oxford University Press.

Small, S. A., Eastman, G., and Cornelius, S. 1988. Adolescent autonomy and parental stress. *Journal of Youth and Adolescence,* 17, 377-391.

Small, S. A. and Eastman, G. 1991. Rearing adolescents in contemporary society: A conceptual framework for understanding the responsibilities and needs of parents. *Family Relations,* 40, 455-462.

Small, S. A. and Kerns, D. 1993. Unwanted sexual activity among peers during early and middle adolescence: Incidence and risk factors. *Journal of Marriage and the Family,* 55, 941-952.

Small, S. A. and Riley, D. 1990. Toward a multidimensional assessment of work spillover into family life. *Journal of Marriage and the Family,* 40, 455-462.

Smock, P. J. 1994. Gender and short-run economic consequences of marital disruption. *Social Forces,* 74, 243-262.

Solomon, J. C. and Marx, J. 1995. "To grandmother's house we go": Health and school adjustment of children raised solely by grandparents. *The Gerontologist,* 35, 386-394.

Sommerville, C. J. 1982. *The rise and fall of childhood.* Beverly Hills, CA: Sage.

Spitze, G. and Logan, J. R. 1991. Sibling structure and intergenerational relations. *Journal of Marriage and the Family,* 53, 871-884.

Spitzer, A., Webster-Stratton, C., and Hollinsworth, T. 1991. Coping with conduct-problem children: Parents gaining knowledge and control. *Journal of Clinical Child Psychology,* 20, 413-427.

Starrels, M. A., Ingersoll-Dayton, B., Dowler, D. W., and Neal, M. B. 1997. The stress of caring for a parent: Effects of the elder's impairment on an employed adult child. *Journal of Marriage and the Family,* 59, 860-872.

Stein, N. 1995. Sexual harassment in school: The public performance of gendered violence. *Harvard Educational Review,* 65, 145-162.

Steinberg, L. and Avenevoli, S. 2000. The role of context in the development of psychopathology: A conceptual framework and some speculative propositions. *Child Development,* 71, 66-74.

Steinberg, L., Darling, N. E., Fletcher, A. C., Brown, B. B., and Dornbusch, S. F. 1995. Authoritative parenting and adolescent adjustment: An ecological journey. In P. Moen, G. H. Elder Jr., and K. Lüscher, (Eds.), *Examining lives in context* (pp. 432-446). Washington, DC: American Psychological Association.

Steinmetz, S. K. 1993. The abused elderly are dependent: Abuse is caused by the perception of stress associated with providing care. In R. J. Gelles and D. Loseke (Eds.), *Current controversies on family violence* (pp. 222-236). Newbury Park, CA: Sage.

Stewart, E., Simons, R. L., and Conger, R. D. 2000. The effects of delinquency and legal sanctions on parenting behaviors. In G. L. Fox and M. L. Benson (Eds.), *Families and crime.* Greenwich, CT: JAI Press.

Stone, L. 1977. *The family, sex, and marriage in England, 1500-1800.* New York: Harper & Row.

Stoneman, Z., Brody, G. H., Churchill, S. L., and Winn, L. L. 1999. Effects of residential instability on Head Start children and their relationships with older siblings: Influences of child emotionality and conflict between family caregivers. *Child Development,* 70, 1246-1262.

Straub, E. 1999. Aggression and self-esteem. APA *Monitor,* 30, January, p. 6.

Strawbridge, W. J., Wallhagen, M. I., Sherma, S. J., and Kaplan, G. A. 1997. New burdens or more of the same? Comparing grandparents, spouse, and adult-child caregivers. *The Gerontologist,* 37, 505-510.

Suarez, L. M. and Baker, B. L. 1997. Child externalizing behavior and parents' stress: The role of social support. *Family Relations,* 47, 373-381.

Suin, R. M. 1993. Practice—It's not what we preached. *The Behavior Therapist,* February, 47-49.

Suitor, J. J. and Pillemer, K. 1991. Family conflict when adult children and elderly parents share a home. In K. Pillemer and K. McCartney (Eds.), *Parent-child relations throughout life* (pp. 179-199). Hillsdale, NJ: Erlbaum.

Sullivan, T. 1992. *Sexual abuse and the rights of children: Reforming Canadian law.* Toronto: University of Toronto.

Tatara, T. 1993. Understanding the nature and scope of domestic elder abuse with the use of state aggregate data: Summaries of the key findings of a national survey of state APS and aging agencies. *Journal of Elder Abuse & Neglect,* 5, 35-57.

Tate, D. C., Reppucci, N. D., and Mulvey, E. P. 1995. Violent juvenile delinquents: Treatment effectiveness and implications for future action. *American Psychologist*, 50, 777-781.

Terkelsen, K. G. 1983. Schizophrenia and the family: II. Adverse effect of family therapy. *Family Process*, 22, 191-200.

Terry, J. 1998. "Momism" and the making of treasonous homosexuals. In M. Ladd-Taylor and L. Umansky (Eds.), *"Bad" mothers: The politics of blame in twentieth-century America* (pp. 169-190). New York: New York University Press.

Teti, D. M., Sakin, J. W., Kucera, K., Corns, K. M., and Eiden, R. D. 1996. And baby makes four: Predictors of attachment security among preschool-age first-borns during the transition to siblinghood. *Child Development*, 67, 579-596.

Thomas, A., and Chess, S. 1980. *The dynamics of psychological development*. New York: Brunner/Mazel.

Thorne, B. 1987. Revisioning women and social change: Where are the children? *Gender and Society*, 1, 85-109.

Thornton, A. and Lin, H.-S. 1994. *Social change and the family in Taiwan*. Chicago: University of Chicago Press.

Trusty, J. 1998. Family influences on educational expectations of late adolescents. *The Journal of Educational Research*, 5, 260-270.

Tyler, N. B. and Kogan, K. L. 1977. Reduction of stress between mothers and their handicapped children. *American Journal of Occupational Therapy*, 31, 151-155.

Tseng, V. and Fuligni, A. J. 2000. Parent-adolescent language use and relationships among immigrant families with East Asian, Filipino, and Latin American backgrounds. *Journal of Marriage and the Family*, 62, 465-476.

Umberson, D. 1989. Relationships with children: Explaining parents' psychological well-being. *Journal of Marriage and the Family*, 51, 999-1012.

Umberson, D., Chen, M. D., House, J. S., Hopkins, K., and Slaten, E. 1996. The effect of social relationships on psychological well-being: Are men and women really so different? *American Sociological Review*, 61, 837-857.

Umberson, D. and Gove, W. E. 1989. Parenthood and psychological well-being. *Journal of Family Issues*, 10, 440-462.

U.S. Department of Justice, 1994. *Domestic violence: Violence between intimates*. Washington, DC: U.S. Department of Justice, Bureau of the Census.

Ventura, S. J., Martin, J. A., Curtin, S. C., and Matthews, T. J. 1999. Births: Final data for 1997. *National Vital Statistics Reports*. Vol. 47, No. 18. Hyattsville, MD: National Center for Health Statistics.

Volling, B. L. and Belsky, J. 1993. Parent, infant, and contextual characteristics related to maternal employment decisions in the first year of infancy. *Family Relations*, 42, 4-12.

Vroegh, K. A. 1997. Transracial adoptees: Developmental status after 17 years. *American Journal of Orthopsychiatry*, 67, 568-575.

Wachs, T. D. 1992. *The nature of nurture*. Newbury Park, CA: Sage.

Walters, J. and Walters, L. H. 1980. Parent-child relationships: A review, 1970-1979. *Journal of Marriage and the Family*, 42, 807-827.

Ward, R. A. and Spitze, G. 1998. Sandwich marriages: The implications of child and parent relations for marital quality in midlife. *Social Forces*, 77, 647-666.

Warren, S. B. 1992. Lower threshold for referral for psychiatric treatment for adopted adolescents. *Journal of the American Academy of Child and Adolescent Psychiatry*, 31, 512-517.

Webster-Stratton, C. and Lindsay, D. W. 1999. Social competence and conduct problems in young children: Issues in assessment. *Journal of Clinical Child Psychology*, 28, 25-43.

Wegar, K. 1992. The sociological significance of ambivalence: An example from adoption research. *Qualitative Sociology*, 15, 87-103.

Wegar, K. 1997. *Adoption, identity, and kinship: The debate over sealed birth records*. New Haven, NJ: Yale University Press.

Weiss, B. and Weisz, J. R. 1995. Relative effectiveness of behavioral versus nonbehavioral child psychotherapy. *Journal of Consulting and Clinical Psychology*, 63, 317-320.

Weissman, M. M., Gammon, G. D., John, K., Merikangas, K. R., Warner, V., Prusoff, B. A., and Sholomskas, D. 1987. Children of depressed parents. *Archives of General Psychiatry*, 44, 847-853.

Weisz, J. R., Donenberg, G. R., Han, S. S., and Weiss, B. 1995. Bridging the gap between laboratory and clinic in child and adolescent psychiatry. *Journal of Consulting and Clinical Psychology*, 63, 688-701.

Weisz, J. R., Weiss, B., Han, S. S., Granger, D. A., and Morton, T. 1995. Effects of psychotherapy with children and adolescents revisited: A meta-analysis of treatment-outcome studies. *Psychological Bulletin*, 117, 450-468.

White, L. and Peterson, D. 1995. The retreat from marriage: Its effect on unmarried children's exchange with parents. *Journal of Marriage and the Family*, 57, 428-434.

Whittaker, T. 1995. Violence, gender, and elder abuse: Toward a feminist analysis and practice. *Journal of Gender Studies*, 4, 35-45.

Widom, C. S. 1990. The intergenerational transmission of violence. In N. A. Weiner and M. E. Wolfgang (Eds.), *Pathways to criminal violence* (pp. 137-201). Newbury Park, CA: Sage.

Wolf, R. and Pillemer, K. 1989. *Helping elderly victims: The reality of elder abuse*. New York: Columbia University Press.

Wright, B. R. E., Caspi, A., Moffitt, T. E., Miech, R. A., and Silva, P. A. 1999. Reconsidering the relationship between SES and delinquency: Causation but not correlation. *Criminology*, 37, 175-194.

Yamaguchi, K. and Ferguson, L. R. 1995. The stopping and spacing of childbirths and their birth-history predictors: Rational-choice theory and event-history analysis. *American Sociological Review*, 60, 272-298.

Ying, Y.-W. 1992. Life satisfaction among San Fransisco Chinese-Americans. *Social Indicators Research*, 26, 1-22.

Zelizer, V. A. R. 1985. *Pricing the priceless child: The changing social value of children*. New York: Basic Books.

Author Index

Gallagher, E. M., 76
Gallagher, S. K., 141
Gamble, W., 23
Ganey, R. F., 165
Ganong, L. H., 65, 126, 174
Gans, H. J., 155
Garbarino, J., 73, 91, 198
Garmezy, N., 84
Garrison, M. E. B., 40
Gecas, V., 33
Gergen, K. J., 126
Gerstel, N., 141
Gillis, J. R., 26
Gladstone, J., 178
Gleeson, J. P., 147
Glendinning, C., 40
Gold, S. J., 154
Goldberg-Glen, R. S., 149
Goldscheider, F. K., 144
Goldsmith, H. H., 83
Goldstein, M. J., 86
Golombok, S., 128
Gonzales, N. A., 111
Goodnow, J. J., 63
Gorman, E. H., 54
Gottesman, I. I., 81, 127
Gove, W. E., 39
Graff, H. J., 26
Grant, L., 53
Greenberg, J. S., 85, 150
Greenberg, M., 46
Greenlay, J. R., 85, 140
Griffin, L. W., 151
Gross, H. E., 175
Grotevant, J., 175
Groze, V., 172
Gruber, E., 27
Grusec, J. E., 63

Hall-McCorquodale, I., 24, 125
Handel, M. H., 81
Hanson, T. L., 21
Harper, L. V., 22
Harrington, R. C., 83
Hawkins, A. J., 25
Hays, S., 28
Heath, D. T., 40
Heffner, E., 203
Heller, T., 85

Henggeler, S. W., 86
Hills, H. I., 126
Hochschild, A. R., 39, 53
Hodges, E. V. E., 113, 115
Hoffer, T., 73, 93, 108, 158, 200, 201
Hofferth, S., 72
Hogan, D. P., 93, 141
Hollinsworth, T., 133
Horowitz, F. D., 43, 187, 192
Horwood, L. J., 71, 92
Hrabowski, F. A., III, 165
Hsieh, K., 85
Huguley, S., 51
Huston, T. L., 56

Ippolito, M. F., 111

Jang, S. J., 92, 97
Jendrek, M. P., 147
Jenkins, E. J., 42
Johnson, M. E., 56
Johnston, C., 75

Kagan, J., 69
Kallman, F. J., 81
Kamo, Y., 143
Karkowski, L. M., 104
Katz, R., 79, 83
Kaufman, G., 54
Kelley, J., 190
Kellogg, S., 27
Kendall, P. C., 130
Kendler, K. S., 71, 82, 104
Kerbow, D., 120
Kerns, D., 116
Kett, J. F., 29
Ketterlinus, R., 96
Kim, U., 154
Kisker, E. E., 146
Kitagawa, E. M., 93
Kochenderfer, B. J., 113
Kogan, K. L., 23
Koller, M. R., 28
Korbin, J. E., 150
Korner, A. F., 23
Kostelny, K., 198

Kotchick, B. A., 21, 46
Kouneski, E. F., 25
Krueger, R. F., 94
Kuczynski, L., 63
Kurdek, L. A., 55

Ladd, G. W., 113, 118
Lamb, M. E., 25. 96
Lambert, J. D., 39
Land, K. C., 91
LaRossa, R., 25
Larson, K. A., 159
Larson, R. W., 38, 192
Laumann, E. O., 116
Lavigueur, S., 78
Lee, G. R., 142
Lee, Y.-J., 144
Lefley, H. P., 125, 150
Lein, L., 61
Lerner, J. V., 53
Lerner, R. M., 18, 23, 31, 44
Letherby, G., 167
Levine, E. S., 174
Levine, J., 69
LeVine, R. A., 26
LeVine, S., 26
Lichtenstein, P., 70
Liem, J. H., 86
Liker, J. K., 23
Lin, H.-S., 26
Lindee, S. M., 169
Lindsay, D. W., 73
Loeber, R., 76, 86
Logan, J. R., 143, 163
Luthar, S. S., 189
Lynskey, M. T., 71, 92
Lytton, H., 34

Maccoby, E. E., 22, 95
Machamer, A. M., 27
MacLeod, C., 74
Magnusson, D., 13, 21
Mahoney, M. M., 174
Majors, R., 162
Malone, M. J., 113
March, K., 171, 177
Martin, J., 22
Marx, J., 148

Masten, A. S., 84
Mathews, A., 74
Maton, K. I., 165
Mayhew, P., 50
Maziade, M., 199
McBride, B. A., 25
McCartney, K., 15
McCrae, R. R., 18
McGee, R., 83
McGue, M. K., 169
McGuffin, P., 79, 83
McKeever, P., 24, 50, 66
McLanahan, S., 21
McLoyd, V. C., 20, 42, 188, 198
McPherson, J. M., 58
Miall, C. E., 170
Miller, K. S., 21, 46
Miller, R. B., 150
Minkler, M., 146, 147
Minton, C. J., 69
Mintz, S., 27
Mirrlees-Black, C., 50
Moffitt, T. E., 91
Montgomery, R. J., 143
Moore, K. A., 116
Mounts, N. S., 111
Mouw, T., 159
Muller, C., 120
Mulvey, E. P., 133
Munch, A., 58
Musgrove, F., 29
Mutran, E., 144

Nagin, D. S., 91
Nasow, D., 26
Nelkin, D., 169
Nelson, B. J., 124
Nelson, D. A., 74
Nett, E., 26
Netzer, J. K., 142
Nigg, J. T., 83
Nock, S. L., 60
Noller, P., 38
Nord, C. W., 116
Norris, D., 54

O'Connell, M., 53
O'Connor, T. G., 71, 187
Ogbu, J. U., 163

Subject Index

Order Your Own Copy of
This Important Book for Your Personal Library!

THE EFFECT OF CHILDREN ON PARENTS
Second Edition

_____ in hardbound at $59.95 (ISBN: 0-7890-0854-8)

_____ in softbound at $24.95 (ISBN: 0-7890-0855-6)

COST OF BOOKS_____

OUTSIDE USA/CANADA/
MEXICO: ADD 20%_____

POSTAGE & HANDLING_____
(US: $4.00 for first book & $1.50
for each additional book)
Outside US: $5.00 for first book
& $2.00 for each additional book)

SUBTOTAL_____

in Canada: add 7% GST_____

STATE TAX_____
(NY, OH & MIN residents, please
add appropriate local sales tax)

FINAL TOTAL_____
(If paying in Canadian funds,
convert using the current
exchange rate, UNESCO
coupons welcome.)

❏ **BILL ME LATER:** ($5 service charge will be added)
(Bill-me option is good on US/Canada/Mexico orders only;
not good to jobbers, wholesalers, or subscription agencies.)

❏ Check here if billing address is different from
shipping address and attach purchase order and
billing address information.

Signature_____

❏ **PAYMENT ENCLOSED: $**_____

❏ **PLEASE CHARGE TO MY CREDIT CARD.**

❏ Visa ❏ MasterCard ❏ AmEx ❏ Discover
❏ Diner's Club ❏ Eurocard ❏ JCB

Account # _____

Exp. Date_____

Signature_____

Prices in US dollars and subject to change without notice.

NAME_____

INSTITUTION_____

ADDRESS_____

CITY_____

STATE/ZIP_____

COUNTRY_____ COUNTY (NY residents only)_____

TEL_____ FAX_____

E-MAIL_____

May we use your e-mail address for confirmations and other types of information? ❏ Yes ❏ No
We appreciate receiving your e-mail address and fax number. Haworth would like to e-mail or fax special
discount offers to you, as a preferred customer. **We will never share, rent, or exchange your e-mail address
or fax number.** We regard such actions as an invasion of your privacy.

Order From Your Local Bookstore or Directly From
The Haworth Press, Inc.
10 Alice Street, Binghamton, New York 13904-1580 • USA
TELEPHONE: 1-800-HAWORTH (1-800-429-6784) / Outside US/Canada: (607) 722-5857
FAX: 1-800-895-0582 / Outside US/Canada: (607) 722-6362
E-mail: getinfo@haworthpressinc.com
PLEASE PHOTOCOPY THIS FORM FOR YOUR PERSONAL USE.
www.HaworthPress.com

BOF00